Mass-Mediated
Culture

Michael R. Real

University of California, San Diego

Mass-Mediated Culture

PRENTICE-HALL, Inc. Englewood Cliffs, N. J. 07632

Library of Congress Cataloging in Publication Data

REAL, Michael R 1940–
   Mass-mediated culture.

   Bibliography: p.
   Includes index.
   1. Mass media—Social aspects—Case studies.
2. Mass media—Moral and religious aspects—Case
studies. 3. Popular culture—Case studies. 1. Title.
HM258.R343   301.2'1   76-30265
ISBN 0-13-559211-9
ISBN 0-13-559203-8 pbk.

301.21

R22m

109201

am 1979

All photographs were taken by Paula and Michael Real and were developed and prepared by Marshall Harrington, except those in chapter 6, which were taken by Phil Steinmetz. The illustration for chapter 5 is by Patrick Marsh. Mickey Mouse cover photo by Charles Woringer.

Printed in the United States of America

10   9   8   7   6   5   4   3   2

Prentice-Hall International, Inc., London
Prentice-Hall of Australia Pty. Limited, Sydney
Prentice-Hall of Canada, Ltd., Toronto
Prentice-Hall of India Private Limited, New Delhi
Prentice-Hall of Japan, Inc., Tokyo
Prentice-Hall of Southeast Asia Pte. Ltd., Singapore
Whitehall Books Limited, Wellington, New Zealand

Contents

Introduction:
Daily Bread
and Burnt Toast

Everyman threatens to kill the opponents as his bet on the playoff game is ground into the turf in Rome . . . Rio . . . Peoria.

The young woman touches her date's arm, looks in his eyes, and says quietly, "You're so sexy you should run for prime minister or star in 'Medical Center.' "

As he emerges from Disney's Flight to the Moon, the young descendent of samurais asks in awe, "Was I really in outer space?"

An elderly Indian, sensing death approaching, gazes at a poster that proclaims "Billy Graham Speaks."

Over these scenes a reporter solemnly intones, "That's the way it is, Tuesday, March. . . ."

These images are characteristic of our daily serving of contemporary culture. People may pray for daily bread, but for many millions in advanced industrial states and, increasingly, throughout the world, cultural sustenance is delivered by the mass media of communication in a form more like burnt toast. The following pages examine the methods and messages of those who "give us this day our daily bread."

Contemporary Mass-Mediated Culture. The studies in this book share a specific focus. They concern **culture** in the form of widespread symbols, rhythms, beliefs, and practices available through **media** in the form of television, radio, records, films, books, periodicals, and other means of communication that transmit in a **mass** manner from a single source to many anonymous receivers. Contemporary expressions of this mass-mediated culture, temporally, are those currently available in the final quarter of the twentieth century and, spatially, are those dominant in the United States, Canada, Western Europe, and Japan. But they are also available in most urban centers and in many Third World countries of Latin America, the Pacific, Africa, and Central Asia; occasionally they are found in Eastern Europe, the Soviet Union, and Eastern Asia.

How much of contemporary mass-mediated culture is nutritious food for the mind, the imagination, the feelings, and the social system? And how much is, for the individual and the collectivity, nothing more than dry, overcooked toast, a charred version of the commercial white bread that James Baldwin calls "blasphemous foam rubber"? In a comparative framework, does the shared symbolic and ritual life of Western, capitalist consumers parallel that of peoples fortified by different cultural diets? On each end of mass-mediated culture, what are the priorities of the mass-consciousness industry that programs it and the quality of the total ecosystem that results from it?

Ethnographic and Critical Case Studies in Cross-Cultural Perspective.
This book constructs answers in the manner of a mosaic. The opening
and closing chapters are holistic overviews emphasizing various intellectual approaches to contemporary mass-mediated culture, the internal
structure of such culture, and alternatives to it. The intervening chapters
are in-depth case studies of specific examples of popular culture made
widely available by mass media. The case studies can be read in any
order according to the subjective preference of the reader. As in a mosaic,
the interconnections between the case studies are complex and multi-
directional; they are not, as in a syllogistic proof, simple, linear, and
sequential.

All of the studies are *ethnographic* in that they attempt to provide
clear, descriptive records of the cases selected. The subjects were chosen
as representative and influential examples of major areas of society: sports,
education, health, politics, and religion. The outside "control" case study
from the Aymara Indians investigates a contrasting example of popular
culture that is not mass-mediated, not Western, not literate, and not
capitalist. The cases go beyond ethnography to *critical analysis* in that
they attempt to unearth the aesthetic and ideological substrata beneath
the misleadingly simple surface of mass-mediated cultural expressions.

These investigations might be classified as *cultural studies* drawing
on critical theory in literature and the arts and as *policy research* utilizing
critical methods and theory from the social sciences. All the case studies
reflect the whole of mass-mediated culture, but each case exemplifies a
specific theme or concept. For example, the Disney study delves into
subjective perceptions; the Graham study into cultural-ideological roots;
the study of media sports into historical development and structural
symbolism; the Welby study into ecological regulatory mechanisms; and
the Aymara and Nixon studies into contrasting examples of political-
economic structures and social-systemic effects.

The *cross-cultural perspective* provides a context and critical frame
for the studies. The cases are contrasted with expressions from different
cultures to achieve greater intelligibility, a sharper sociopolitical focus,
and a quasi-outsider's objectivity in viewing phenomena otherwise too
immediate and pervasive to be scientifically understood. American football and Billy Graham become more intellectually interesting when compared with Tibetan yoga and Chairman Mao.

A Multidimensional Crossroads. Fewer contemporary citizens receive
their culture from the refined hands of Bach, Jefferson, Chinua Achebe,
or Lao-Tsu than from the facile fingers of Isaac Hayes, Beaver Cleaver,
Ann-Margret, and Eric Severeid. Mass-mediated culture is amazingly
popular culture. Most readers of these case studies—and many millions

around the world—are already familiar in various ways with Mickey Mouse, Billy Graham, Richard Nixon, and football. The 1969 moon-walk drew more viewers than any previous event in history, 580 million, until the 1974 World Cup soccer ("Futbol") playoff attracted 600 million viewers. Approximately one billion persons watched the leaders of the United States, the Soviet Union, and thirty-three other nations sign the Helsinki Declaration on August 1, 1975. Yet surprisingly little is known in any serious, sustained, and comprehensive way about contemporary mass-mediated culture, its internal structure and dynamics, its effects on individuals and social institutions, or its subtle but crucial role in enhancing or degrading life on this planet. The reasons for this gap deserve consideration.

Mass-mediated culture sits at a complex and problematic crossroads. It is *immediate* to each individual and *pervasive* throughout the social system. It is capable of receiving serious *intellectual* consideration or the lightest *popular* treatment. It falls within areas of *academic* expertise but is simultaneously of great *public* interest in policy making and per-sonal life. It calls for the *sensibilities* of the humanities and liberal arts and the *techniques* of the social sciences. Its Janus face is intimidating. As a result, many who write or read about popular culture and mass communications are made defensive about their choice of subject matter and carry a confused love-hate feeling about it: They liked the Beatles, but not too much.

Viewed in the perspectives of standard specializations, mass-mediated culture tends to slip through the interstices like a coin falling through the grids of a drain. These case studies draw on literature, art, sociology, psychology, history, philosophy, political science, economics, anthropology, and a variety of subdisciplines. However, a discipline-centered approach here gives way to a problem-centered focus. As the first and last chapters spell out, the key to a holistic grasp of mass-mediated culture is a *multidisciplinary* understanding of such interrelated concepts as *communication, system, structure, institutions,* and *power.*

The Chapters. To varying degrees in each chapter, the research meth-odology, theoretical interpretations, and style of presentation aim at a blend of specialized academic thoroughness and general public relevance.

Chapter 1 is a critical essay designed to set a tone, provide examples and motives, and evaluate approaches to popular culture and mass com-munications.

Chapters 2 through 6 illustrate five fundamental categories of con-temporary mass-mediated culture. *Education*—the excursion into the Disney universe tests criticisms of Disney against the impressions and influence of the 6,500 hours spent in Disneyland by 200 respondents.

Sports—the investigation of the Super Bowl attempts to answer *why* that event is the most lucrative annual spectacle in American media. *Health*— the review of the medical genre of television programming questions not only the innocuously dramatic and positive fictional portrayal of health care but also the absence of healthy messages on mass media. *Politics*—the last Nixon campaign illustrates how media strategies use popular culture and advertising techniques to persuade voters not by informing but by propagandizing. *Religion*—the study of typical Billy Graham telecasts searches out the fundamentals of his specifically American gospel.

Chapter 7 steps outside mass-mediated culture to look in detail at a popular festival celebrated by descendents of the Incas on the shores of Lake Titicaca high in the Andes. Far from utopian, their beleaguered culture nevertheless provides evidence of sophisticated aural exchange and creative, psychoactive rituals. Their current situation raises the question of the fate and contributions of non-Western, nonaligned peoples in the face of expanding American-dominated mass-mediated culture.

The final chapter makes more explicit an argument running through the book: *Mass-mediated culture primarily serves the interests of the relatively small political-economic power elite that sits atop the social pyramid.* It does so by programming mass consciousness through an infrastructural authoritarianism that belies its apparent superstructural egalitarianism. For example, while allegedly "giving the people what they want," commercial television maximizes private corporate profit, restricts choices, fragments consciousness, and masks alienation. The final critique points to alternative possibilities for institutional and personal policy.

Personal acknowledgements are especially necessary for a work on one's own culture. Underneath the stylistic confusion of both "the new journalism" of Tom Wolfe, Hunter S. Thompson, Norman Mailer, Gay Talese, and Joe Estershaus, and "the popular research" of Carlos Castaneda, Imamu Amiri Baraka (formerly Leroi Jones), Eldridge Cleaver, John Lilly, Aldous Huxley, Alan Watts, and others is an admission that most journalists and academics find hard to make. All reporting and research, whatever the supportive technology and personnel, are undertaken by individual persons with limited resources, private opinions, and restricted points of view. This study is no exception.

I wish to acknowledge and thank numerous professional colleagues, my family, and the friends I have made in the rural Midwest; in urban ethnic communities; in medieval Roman Catholic institutions; in alternative communes and communities; in more than two dozen countries scattered around the globe; in traditional humanities and contemporary social science classrooms; and in all my other face-to-face encounters—not to mention the thousands of persons who have entered my life via mass-mediated culture.

Albert Camus once wrote that the grouping we need is one of persons willing to "speak out clearly and pay up personally." Teilhard de Chardin warned that, with the acceleration of historical change, those who make scientific sense about the future are the utopians, not the realists. Heeding both those statements, I offer these pages in hope that heightened critical consciousness of our mass-mediated environment will help to bring about less burnt toast and more daily bread in the collective cultural life that nourishes Muskogee homemakers, Parisian teenagers, New Delhi executives, Watts children, Caracas retirees, and, like it or not, you and me.

Complacency is the enemy of study.
We cannot really learn anything
until we rid ourselves of complacency.
Our attitude towards ourselves should be
'to be insatiable in learning'
and toward others
'to be tireless in teaching.'

—Mao Tse-Tung

1

The Significance of Mass-Mediated Culture

Why expend valuable time and energy studying trivial entertainments?

What cultural levels express rich and poor, black and white, local and international, beneficial and damaging?

Do mass media determine culture?

Why do authorities disagree in judging mass-mediated culture?

How do methods and theories from the social sciences, arts, and humanities explain mass-mediated culture?

How does mass-mediated culture connect with internal personal consciousness and external social structures?

What does any of this have to do with me?

Love, sex, death, politics—how do persons learn to respond to and interpret these fundamental human experiences? Along with other forces and expressions, popular culture transmitted by mass media plays an undeniably significant role in shaping and expressing human belief and behavior. Consider, for example, the feeling and international flavor of this experience:

Suppose you wish to relax in Buenos Aires, Argentina. You may decide to spend an evening in the Marrakesh Discoteque on Maipu Avenue. The Marrakesh attracts several hundred Argentinians each evening to its music, dancing, drinks, and comfort. Below street level in the large, stylish lounge, waiters in classy black suits and bow ties bring drinks from the adjoining bar into a large carpeted area filled with soft chairs and couches. A disc jockey plays records from a glassed-in studio to the left of the elevated dance floor and stage. The sound system dominates. A huge speaker is suspended above each corner of the dancing area; each speaker faces toward the dancers. Other speakers and sound-sensitive lights are set among the couches throughout the lounge.

At midnight couples are dancing slowly to blues from Bill Withers, Roberta Flack, and Curtis Mayfield. By 1 a.m. the beat gradually begins to pick up as the bodies move to Elton John, Stevie Wonder, and Jamaican reggae. At 2 a.m. the house band comes on for its first set. It features standard instrumentation: bass and lead guitars, drums, an organ almost similar to a mellotron, and a singer. The echo mike, singer, and arrangement capture perfectly the sound of the Moody Blues on "Nights in White Satin" and then slide easily into "Good-bye, Yellow Brick Road," followed by numbers from Bruce Springsteen and Janis Ian. The band shifts styles and recreates numbers by various Woodstock

*groups. A newlywed couple in white gown and tails are invited forward
to dance to a special version of the second-place winner in the 1973
All-European Song Competition, "Eres Tu."*

*After a short pause the multicolored spots dim the stage as the
group begins quietly, slowly, dramatically on the Beatles' old number,
"Something." The tension and volume build gradually as they work
through an extended arrangement of the classic "Go to the Mirror, Boy"
("See Me, Hear Me, Touch Me, Feel Me") from the Who's "Tommy."
Finally, the group lets it all hang out in a draining, exhausting Joe
Cocker–style rendition of "I Get By With a Little Help From My Friends."
The singer and group—through sound, light, and movement—have built
up, drawn out, intensified, extended, and finally released a tremendous
emotional charge throughout the audience. They were "on" tonight.
Everybody was with them, right there.*

*The house lights go up slightly, you begin to recover from the
experience, and . . . ah, yes, what country is this? Most of the lyrics were
English, so perhaps the United States or England. But there was one
Spanish song that suggested the Continent. Of course, the strong
rhythms and powerful bluesy emotions recall African, Caribbean, or
Afro-American roots. The clothes of the people present give no hint.
They are standard modern—sweaters, slacks, jeans, a few sports coats,
some mod symbol patches. Even the gestures, the mannerisms, the
dance styles resemble the standard style of every other city you can
remember. Where are you? That's right, it's . . . South America . . . Argentina . . . Buenos Aires. But you are really in the same place you left:
the mass-mediated culture of the European- and American-dominated
global village.*

Why Investigate Mass-Mediated Culture?

Mass-mediated culture offers delights for anyone.

Popular culture available through mass media spills out goodies for
all. Feature films, popular music, video, sports events, political movements, popular religion, science fiction, news weeklies, westerns, detective
fiction—these offer sight, sound, feeling, thinking, and sharing that can
be stimulating, satisfying, and rewarding. The advocate of classical culture can, despite all prejudices, find meaning and significance in a popular
Bergman film, Dylan album, or network documentary. The popular culture aficionado, despite all weaknesses, may find glimmers of genuine
meaning in the game of the week, comic books, talk shows, or fashion
magazines. Hard judgments must be passed against much of mass-mediated culture; nevertheless, as long as *homo sapiens* enjoys laughing, sing-

ing, and feeling, people will find genuine satisfaction in that "willing suspension of disbelief for the moment."

Mass-mediated culture reflects and influences *human life.*

The critic who judges mass-mediated culture too inane to be enjoyed may choose to study the subject for the same reason investigators study disease and crime. As a virtually omnipresent symbolic form, mass-mediated culture expresses and determines human descriptions of life and definitions of reality. Research and analysis, much of it cited in these pages, establish that mass-mediated culture has the power (a) to shape behavior and beliefs; (b) to determine aesthetic taste in cultural and artistic matters; (c) to maintain or modify the arrangement of society; and, through all of these, (d) to play a part in ordering or disordering personal, group, and international life.

Mass-mediated culture spreads specific values and ideology internationally.

As early as the 1950s, art critic Clement Greenberg complained that the mass cultural products of Western industrialism were becoming "the first universal culture ever beheld."[1] Studies of the international flow of television programs, movies, printed materials, and other mass-mediated cultural expressions find that flow largely unidirectional—from small centers in the United States and Europe to countries all over the world. Kaarle Nordenstreng estimates the flow of cultural products from industrialized nations to Third World countries at one hundred times the returning trickle.[2] The foregoing example of rock music in Argentina illustrates the result, and chapter 7 on non-Western popular culture elaborates on the details and consequences of this international spread of mass-mediated culture.

Mass-mediated culture raises far-reaching policy questions.

Consumers, producers, corporations, and governments face the responsibility of developing understanding of and responses to the cultural expressions that surround them. Among the numerous areas of public and private concern are

- the evolution and function of popular expressions of culture
- the interaction of mass media, popular culture, and society
- the dominant genres and themes in popular culture

- the differences between inherited Western and non-Western value systems
- the ideological conflicts between capitalists and Marxists
- the priorities in the human and environmental ecosystem
- the possibilities of genuinely humanistic culture

All these areas intrude in an extended analysis of mass-mediated culture. As William F. Lynch concluded in his study of *The Image Industries,*[3] artists, academics, media managers, and public officials, as well as the public at large, share a responsibility for encouraging the best, discouraging the worst, and providing for self-determination in cultural matters.

Mass-mediated culture challenges education and research.

Numerous studies reveal that today the average American child, youth, or adult spends more time with television than with formal schooling.[4] Yet the schools, biased toward print and elite culture, have been uncertain how to respond to this threat to their hegemony over the socialization of youth. Mass communications and popular culture have constituted not a *discipline* characterized by unique theories and methodologies but rather an eclectic *field* characterized by related objects of study. Traditional disciplines such as literature, sociology, and economics have contributed to an understanding of mass-mediated culture, but its full breadth and complexity escape any one discipline.

In recent years research and teaching in popular culture and media have mushroomed. Courses on topics in popular culture are widely available in college and university departments of literature, art, sociology, and American studies. Academic departments, journals, and professional organizations in the field of popular culture have emerged at the same time that communications analysis has focused increased attention on the cultural role, products, and effects of media. Those in the traditional disciplines of history, anthropology, psychology, and music, as well as those in the fields of speech, journalism, environmental ecology, urban planning, foreign service, and many others, have conducted research, offered courses, and in general turned increasing attention to dimensions of mass-mediated culture. Recognizing that the typical student graduates from high school having spent 10,800 hours in the classroom but 15,000 hours watching television,[5] secondary schools over the past generation have generated study in media as well as language, in popular expression as well as classical art. Still, the majority of explanation and analysis of mass-mediated culture comes from the popular media themselves. Academic progress has been achieved, but it has merely touched the tip of the iceberg of mass-mediated culture.

Mass-mediated culture is us.

To investigate mass-mediated culture is merely to apply the ancient directive of Socrates: Know thyself. What does it mean to admit that Johnny Carson and Merv Griffin may influence us more directly than do Geoffrey Chaucer and John Milton? These pages are attempts to bring attention to bear on, to describe, where possible to explain, where necessary to criticize, and through all of this to contribute, however meagerly, to the improvement of a major dimension of our human existence, a dimension that can wash over senses, minds, and feelings as a drowning flood or refresh us as a cleansing tide—that combination of popular expression and contemporary communications called mass-mediated culture.

Taste Levels and Conveyors of Culture

What sort of vocabulary is most helpful in understanding the rock music of an Argentine discoteque in its aesthetic value, its semiotic significance (symbolism and sign value), and its cultural and ideological role? A necessary starting point is the standard terminology for distinguishing various levels of the popular arts and taste cultures, as well as the standard designations of the various mass media. The precise parameters and subleties of these categories have inspired unresolved debates. Here initially we will simply indicate briefly the common meanings of the terms and the foci of mass-mediated culture. Music provides handy examples for each term.

A Definition of Terms

Elite Art. Frequently referred to as classical art or high culture, elite art includes the music of Mozart quartets, Bach fugues, Verdi operas, Stravinsky ballets, and all that makes music appreciation classes, FM classical stations, and the art of the upper class so readily identifiable. Matthew Arnold, in *Literature and Dogma,* spoke of this level of culture as that which is "the best that has been said and thought in the world." More specifically, Russell Nye defines elite art as that "produced by known artists within a consciously aesthetic context and by an accepted set of rules, its attainment (or failure) judged by reference to a normative body of recognized classics." He describes it as subjective, exclusive, particular, individualistic, technically and thematically complex and its aim as "the discovery of new ways of recording and interpreting experience."[6]

Folk Art. At the opposite extreme from elite art is the unsophisticated, localized, grassroots, folk tradition in art, which includes traditional blues music, rural and frontier songs, gospel music, drinking songs, country ballads, ethnic dances, and many other forms, such as those that have sometimes been rescued from obscurity by Folkways and other specialized recording labels. Folk art is not constructed around the complex aesthetics of elite classics; rather, as Oscar Handlin notes, it deals directly with the concrete world intensely familiar to its audience and is marked by a close relationship between performer and audience.[7] Joseph Arpad clarifies folk art by contrasting the characteristics of folklore with those of literature:[8]

Folklore	Literature
Oral	Written
Performance	Text
Face-to-Face Communication	Indirect Communication
Ephemeral	Permanent
Communal (event)	Individual (event)
Re-Creation	Creation
Variation	Revision
Tradition	Innovation
Unconscious Structure	Conscious Design
Collective Representations	Selective Representations
Public (ownership)	Private (ownership)
Diffusion	Distribution
Memory (recollection)	Re-Reading (recollection)

More picturesquely, folk art resembles "the people's own institution, their private little garden walled off from the great formal park of their masters' High Culture."[9]

Popular Art. In the last two centuries a category of popular expression has emerged between elite and folk art. It includes the music of Billie Holiday, Leonard Cohen, John Prine, Buffy Sainte-Marie, and others, many of whom have a foot in the folk and blues tradition but have stepped with the other foot onto commercial stages and into popular media. Charlie Chaplin exemplified how popular art brought together the familiarity of recognized conventions and the creative originality of art. Popular art maintains genuine contact between audience and performer, but in this form the audience-as-community depends heavily on the personal style of the individual performer to articulate common experiences. John Denver's live concerts, comprised of his performance of music and lyrics he has composed, are generally popular art, while his television specials, built around professionally written skits and monologues, guest appearances, and bits of music fall into the next category, mass culture and art.

Mass Art. Abhorrent to classical critics but a haven for entrepreneurs and empiricists, mass art (if those two terms can be placed in juxtaposition) draws on the three categories above and peddles a completely commercialized hybrid derived from each. Its music includes the "Hit Parade" of Snooky Lanson, Giselle McKenzie, Russell Arms, and Dorothy Collins; the sounds of "American Bandstand" and "Soul Train"; the top 40 playlists of AM radio; the Hollywood and Detroit LP industries; the theatrics of glitter rock; the Country Western bonanzas of Merle Haggard, Johnny Cash, and Nashville; the perennials of Lawrence Welk and Barbra Streisand; popular cuts of switched-on Bach and Wagner's greatest hits; and most of the remainder of the *$4 billion a year* mass music industry.[10]

Mass art and culture are "cultural products manufactured solely for a mass market," in the words of Harold Wilensky. Because mass culture aims to please the average taste of an undifferentiated audience, it is characterized by *standardization* of product and *mass behavior*.[11] Raymond Williams observes that elite, folk, and popular culture are generally developed *by* a people, whereas mass culture "has been developed *for* a people by an internal or external social group, and embedded in them by a range of processes from repressive imposition to commercial saturation."[12]

Other Terms. Various labels have come and gone in popular culture analysis, and a few have reappeared in revised forms. In the 1950s, much was made of the culture of the rich as "high-brow culture," of the poor as "low-brow culture," and of those in between as "middle-brow culture." Herbert Gans has resurrected and expanded these distinctions by economic class by breaking *taste cultures* down into (a) High Culture, defined as creator-oriented "serious" art; (b) Upper-Middle Culture, the less abstract preferences of "professionals, executives, managers, and their wives"; (c) Lower-Middle Culture, embraced by lower status professions and white-collar workers who like situation comedies, popular drama, and variety shows; (d) Low Culture, the choice of skilled and semiskilled workers who prefer action, melodrama, and a predictable status quo; and (e) Quasi-Folk Low Culture, preferred by those who are poor and many of whom are nonwhite and rural or of rural origins. Gans goes on to classify separately the specialized taste cultures of (a) youth, (b) blacks, along with Puerto Rican, Chicano, Asian-American, and other non-European, nonwhite equivalents, and (c) ethnic European-descent cultures.[13]

Other terms have enjoyed at least temporary utilization in cultural analysis: *Avant-garde* identifies cultural innovation especially against the grain in elite art; *kitsch* refers to the trash in mass culture; *counter-culture* was Theodore Roszak's label for the rebellious aesthetic-ideological movement that developed from the turmoil of the 1960s; *populist culture* was Kingsley Widmer's redaction of a similar concept; and *consciousness III* was Charles Reich's label for that new sensibility.

Interrelatedness of Areas. The standard vocabulary is useful—especially distinctions among elite, folk, popular, and mass—but limited. Ray Browne points out that "all areas draw from one another." Mass draws the most from others with little alteration. Elite draws from folk and popular. Popular draws from the other three but imposes creative changes in the process. As illustrated in Figure 1–1, for picturing all this Browne suggests a metaphorical lens through which culture is expressed and received:[14]

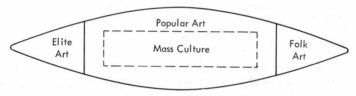

FIGURE 1–1   The Cultural Lens

George Lewis has extended the metaphor to incorporate economic class, specialized taste cultures, and diffusion patterns but in so doing has been forced to combine mass and popular culture and move elite and folk culture off the ends of the lens. Figure 1–2 is Lewis's attempt to summarize taste levels of culture and their interaction.[15]

Culture. Anthropologists generally define culture as the systematic way of construing reality that a people acquires as a consequence of living in a group. That definition applies even when modifiers like popular, folk, or mass-mediated precede the term *culture* specifying its scope in a given context. Chapter 8 further clarifies this meaning of culture.

Rise of Media Carriers of Culture

Mass Communication. Briefly put, *communication* is interaction through messages, or, in slightly more detail, communication consists of the process by which messages are transmitted from a source through a medium to a receiver resulting in feedback. Etymologically its Greek and

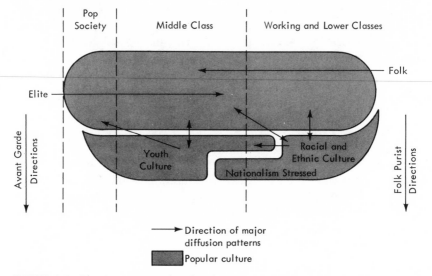

FIGURE 1–2 The Interaction of Cultural Taste Levels (From George H. Lewis, ed., *Side-Saddle on the Golden Calf.* Pacific Palisades, Calif.: Goodyear Publishing Company, 1972.)

Latin roots mean "to make one with" (*comm-uni-care*). *Mass communication* is communication that emanates from a single individual or organizational source through electronic or mechanical coding and multiplication of the message to a relatively large, heterogeneous, and anonymous audience with only limited and indirect means of feedback.[16] In terms of this definition, the experience of rock music in a Buenos Aires discoteque is more face-to-face interpersonal communication than mass communication. But since the original music came to both performers and audience initially via mass communication, the experience illustrates one of the more subtle manifestations of mass-mediated culture. In fact, live attendance at an event such as a Billy Graham crusade or Disneyland remains mass communication since it fits all the aspects of the definition including electronic sound and other relay systems.

The term *media,* the plural of *medium,* is often used interchangeably with mass communication. Marshall McLuhan defines media more broadly as extensions of the human organism outside itself. Thus, industrial media, or what Marx and others call the means of production, such as the wheel and the machine, extend the human capacity to produce and exchange material goods. More specifically, *communication media* extend the human capacity to share and process information in the form of data, images, ideas, and even feelings.[17]

As McLuhan and others have emphasized, changes in dominant communication forms are causal sources of major historical change. The successive development of speech, picture writing, the phonetic alphabet, printing presses, and electronic communication affected virtually every dimension of human social and personal life, changing human ecology and creating new forms of cultural expression. Indications of the consequences of media developments recur throughout these pages and are pursued more fully in the final chapter.

Evolution of Communication Media. Important dates in the development of human communication are worth noting, especially because of the accelerating pace of innovations in the nineteenth and twentieth centuries.[18]

4,000,000–400,000	B.C.	Human speech
3,300		Writing—Sumer
1,500		Writing—China
?		Writing—Mayan Mexico
800		Phonetic alphabet—Phoenicia
450	A.D.	Block printing—Asia
1456		Moveable type (printing press)—Gutenberg Bible
1621		Newspaper—Amsterdam
1731		Magazine—London
1839		Photography—Daguerre
1844		Telegraph—Morse
1876		Telephone—Bell
1877		Phonograph—Edison
1886		Linotype—Merganthaler
1891		Motion pictures—Lumiere/Edison
1895		Wireless telegraphy (radio)—Marconi
1906		Radio (voice transmission)—Fessendon
1920		Radio broadcasting—KDKA Pittsburgh
1923		Television—transmitted New York to Philadelphia
1927		Sound motion pictures
1928		Regular television broadcast—WGY Schenectady
1935		FM radio—Armstrong
1941		Commercial television standardized
1946		Electronic computer—University of Pennsylvania
1948		Television expands—during year the number of sets increase from 100,000 to 1 million.
1952		Federal Communications Commission permits many new TV stations
1954		Regular color telecasts
1957		Global satellite ("Sputnik")
1950s		Transistor, maser, laser
1960s		Holography, cable television, portable video
1990		Artificial intelligence

2000	Electronic global library
2010	Telesensory devices
2020	Logical languages and robots
2030	Regular contact with extraterrestrials
2050	Memory playback
2080	Machine intelligence exceeds human's
3000	World brain
4000	Universal consciousness

As a consequence of the evolution and implementation of media, the United States entered the final third of the twentieth century as virually a single integrated communications system, a "wired nation." Television was the most pervasive cultural influence. More than 95 percent of American homes had television sets—more than had bath tubs— and the average home played the set more than six hours per day. By the 1970s media units in the United States numbered:[19]

934	television stations (85 million receiver sets)
7,500	radio stations (300 million receiver sets)
3,450	cable television systems
1,749	daily newspapers
9,000	weekly newspapers
8,000	magazines
900	book publishers (making $2.5 billion per year)
1,500	film-making organizations
13,000	indoor film theaters
4,500	outdoor film theaters

At that time the expenditures of the industries communicating culture in the United States were (in billions of dollars):

75.3	education
8.0	postal service
19.8	telephone
.6	telegraph
27.8	research and development
25.0	printing and publishing
5.6	paper mills (excluding paper for the construction industry)
7.4	office and computing machinery
13.0	communication equipment
4.3	photographic equipment and supplies
25.6	advertising (all kinds)

The total expenditures of the communications and culture segment of American industry was more than $200 billion, or about 15 percent of the gross national product.

The figures on this immense "consciousness industry" are only those of the United States. Globally, the figures would have to be multiplied many times over. "Bonanza" was transmitted weekly by NBC to 350 million viewers in sixty countries. The Apollo 11 moon landing in 1969 was viewed by an estimated 528 million persons from more than 238,000 miles away. More than one billion viewers can be reached simultaneously by contemporary television broadcasting.

A sense of the consciousness industry, which produces and disseminates cultural symbols globally on an awesome scale, must complement a sense of popular arts and taste cultures in assessing mass-mediated culture. The *significance* of mass-mediated culture, the topic of this introductory chapter, stems from both the size and spread of the *media* and the content and style of the *message* as these two cultural components exist in the last third of the twentieth century in an identifiable international system. As Edward R. Murrow said of television in 1958, "This instrument can teach, it can illuminate, yes, and it can even inspire. But it can do so only to the extent that humans are determined to use it to those ends. Otherwise it is merely lights and wires in a box."

The Phrase "Mass-Mediated Culture"

A cursory look at the growth and spread of contemporary media hints at the inadequacy of relying too heavily on distinctions among taste cultures and cultural levels in approaching contemporary culture. The phrase *mass-mediated culture* signifies the attempt to move beyond the limits of the standard vocabulary and to transcend the distance between social analysis of communications media and humanistic analysis of popular arts.

Both consumers and producers of contemporary culture fail to respect even the distinction between high and popular culture. Russell Nye questions the presumed dichotomy between levels of culture when he asks: "Do the culturally elite never search for entertainment, and the so-called 'masses' never seek insight? Is culture *only* a matter of class, income, and education?"[20] John Cawelti noted that creative artists and performers in the 1960s—Andy Warhol, Leonard Cohen, Roy Lichtenstein, Claes Oldenburg, the Beatles—dealt with media, messages, and audiences on both popular and elite cultural levels. Having grown up with mass culture, these artists ignored many traditional distinctions in order to accept, understand, cope with, and express "a new aesthetic," as Cawelti called it. These were "signs of a major transformation in our culture which is rapidly throwing into question not only the brow theory of culture, but many of our traditional assumptions about the nature and function of the arts."[21]

The increasing disseminaiton of culture through mass instruments of communication blurs the traditional distinctions between elite, folk, and popular art. A person preoccupied with elite art may pursue it by reading poems and plays that are *mass* printed and distributed, and by listening to classical music on recordings that are *mass* pressed and marketed. On the other end of the spectrum, a West Virginia mountaineer may satisfy his liking for folk music through the local outlet of the *mass* medium radio. In both cases the traditional concepts of personalism, immediacy, spontaneity, creator-orientation, and similar qualities, which are said to distinguish elite and folk art from mass culture, disappear in the process of reproduction and distribution. At what point do recordings of acknowledged classics, marketed in a glossy album featuring Leonard Bernstein conducting, leave the world of elite art? Do albums of Pink Floyd and Vivaldi provide cultural experiences on *absolutely* different levels? Are not a Palestrina mass and a Moody Blues concert more closely related as *live celebrations* than live celebrations of any kind are related to the individual auditing of a recorded work?

In order to step back and gain a sense of the whole that is at once simpler and more inclusive, we use the concept of *mass-mediated culture* here to refer to expressions of culture as they are received from contemporary mass media, whether they arise from elite, folk, popular, or mass origins.

This redefinition of focus assumes that all culture when transmitted by mass media becomes in effect popular culture. Popular culture *not* transmitted by mass media exists but has decreased in importance both aesthetically and socially. Details and implications of focusing on mass-mediated culture should become clearer in succeeding sections of this chapter, which deal with (a) conflicting critical evaluations of mass and popular culture; (b) methodologies for investigating the subject; and (c) concepts drawn from general systems theory to identify the overall role and significance of mass-mediated culture.

Conflicting Judgments

By 1973 The Godfather *had made more money than any previous motion picture, only to be surpassed two years later by* Jaws. *The Godfather's rental income from distributors in the United States and Canada —substantially less than its full box office income—passed $85 million in the film's second year in circulation. This placed the 1972 Paramount film ahead of the 1965 Twentieth Century Fox production* Sound of Music *($83 million), the 1939 Metro-Goldwyn-Mayer production* Gone with the Wind *($77.9 million), and the other films that at that time had* *rental incomes totalling more than $40 million:* Love Story, The Graduate, Doctor Zhivago, Airport, The Ten Commandments, Ben Hur, Mary Poppins, *and* The Poseidon Adventure.[22]

In addition to its North American earnings, The Godfather, *like most of the other top ten money-makers, was highly successful in the foreign market where, according to* Variety, *rental incomes sometimes equal, or slightly surpass, the domestic payoff. Also, Paramount sold the television rights for one showing in November, 1974, to NBC for $10 million, an amount that NBC did not make up in direct advertising sales for the telecast but that represented an investment for prestige and for overall network ratings and sales. By 1975* The Godfather *had earned $260 million. At the same time, Mario Puzo's novel, the basis for the plot of the movie, was a bestseller in many countries in many languages. The film* Godfather II *further cashed in on* The Godfather's *success. Among its other fringe benefits,* The Godfather *revived the career of its star Marlon Brando, created new stars Al Pacino and James Caan, and catapulted its director Francis Ford Coppola into the first rank of film directors. Within thirty days of the immensely successful release of* The Godfather, *the stock of ABC-Paramount's parent conglomerate, Gulf and Western, went up in value more than $90 million.[23]*

One culturally important effect of all this was that Gulf and Western, ABC-Paramount, Coppola, producer Ruddy, Brando, and others involved commanded for some four hours the undivided attention of several hundred million persons scattered over much of the globe. They entertained, influenced, and made money on a scale impossible or even unimaginable a hundred years before. What do critics and analysts make of all this?

Six Critical Positions

Efforts at grouping critical positions into meaningful clusters are at once frustrating and necessary. They are frustrating because it is impossible in a reasonable space to do justice to the number and variety of critical positions, each developed with its own nuances. But reviewing and grouping positions is necessary to ensure that observations, conclusions, and case studies, such as those in the remaining chapters of this book, will build on and clarify what has gone before. The grouping of positions also indicates something of the significance and nature of the area of study by identifying the large number, variety, and adamancy of positions. Finally, the content of the groupings establishes major intellectual, theoretical, and methodological questions in the field of mass culture. While "mass-mediated culture" is more specific than the all-encompassing "mass culture," the terms are taken here as operationally and functionally equivalent concepts.

Various schemas have been developed to categorize critical evaluations of mass culture. Harold Rosenberg, in 1957, utilized political labels, distinguishing *radicals* and *arch-conservatives*, (both of whom are repelled by machine civilization and its mass culture) and placing *liberals* in the middle. In 1964 Stuart Hall and Paddy Whannel proposed categories for (a) the *Providers* turning out mass culture, (b) the *Traditionalists* condemning it in favor of elitist classical culture, (c) the *Progressives* offering more limited criticism within an optimistic evolutionary perspective, and (d) the *Radicals* arguing that mass culture exploits twentieth-century minds in the same way that industry exploited nineteenth-century laborers. Russell Nye, in 1970, grouped writers more generically, as (a) *elitist* (this terms includes the Marxists), and (b) *optimist*, depending on their basic rejection or acceptance of mass culture; he also spoke of (c) *revisionists*, who approach communications and culture without the elitist-optimist categories. In 1974 Horace Newcomb divided positions into (a) *visionaries*, who imagine what is utopianly possible, (b) *social scientists*, who measure and debate the effects, (c) *culture critics*, who apply aesthetic standards, and (d) *popular arts analysts*, who examine formulas and genres in terms of positive cultural characteristics.[24]

Most evaluative positions on mass culture can be grouped into one of six categories. The categories constitute distinct points on a continuum ranging from positive *acceptance* of mass culture as good on one end, to absolute *rejection* of mass culture and all it reflects and stands for on the other end. The positions can roughly be labelled

1. Liberal Apologists
2. Empirical, Descriptive, or Historical "Objectivists"
3. Progressive Elitists
4. Traditional Elitists
5. Cultural Separatist Radicals
6. Marxist Structural Radicals

Liberal Apologists. Liberal apologists defend mass culture against its critics. The apologists accept and defend *The Godfather* and the rest of the output of mass culture as freely and democratically chosen by people, as not seriously more brutal than the popular cultures of other times and places, as widely varied and on occasion richly imaginative, and as generally tending in a positive historical direction toward providing better culture for more people.

Empirical, Descriptive, or Historical "Objectivists." Large numbers of studies by social scientists and features by journalists provide information about popular culture in purportedly objective and value-free presentations. Such studies may convey a wealth of unconscious biases and directly reinforce the status quo they avoid evaluating, but they claim "objectivity" and are at least helpful data banks.

Despite their differences in style and depth, the writings of Tom Wolfe representing the "new journalism," those of Marshall McLuhan developing theories of media and culture, and those of Susan Sontag identifying new dimensions of aesthetics form a middle ground between the first two categories. Like the objectivists they attempt only to describe, rather than to judge, mass culture, but like the apologists they move inside the popular aesthetic and, therefore, are generally assumed to endorse popular and mass culture.

Progressive Elitists. A number of critics judge mass culture against the high standards of elite art but refuse to harken back to the ideals and social structure of neoclassical aristocracies for a solution. They find mass culture seriously wanting for depth of feeling, variety of viewpoints, subtlety and complexity of subjects. They propose to improve it by education and regulation without rejecting the economic and political systems that stand behind mass culture.

A more critical liberalism marks many of the major academic units concerned with mass culture. The work of the academicians is generally objective and data-based but includes rather than avoids value judgments about the content and overall system of mass culture. Writing as neither traditionalists nor revolutionaries, they nevertheless emphasize the great need for reform and improvement in mass communications and popular culture.

Traditional Elitists. Much of the most serious aesthetic analysis of mass culture has been provided by articulate proponents of classical, elite culture. They deplore modern industrial culture and would sacrifice egalitarian democratic practices in popular culture in order to elevate the general level of individual culture. William Gass spoke for many of these critics when he said, "The products of popular culture, by and large, have no more esthetic quality than a brick in the street."[25]

Elitists, both progressive and traditional, tended to find some good points in *The Godfather* but were put off by its explicit violence, the continued glamorizing of gangsters, and the absence of subtlety and complexity characteristic of recognized elite art.

Cultural-Separatist Radicals. An important tradition of mass culture criticism, which appears in virtually none of the standard summaries, comes from black American authors. They share a unique vantage point as ones who know the dominant system from the inside but who have consistently been ostracized to the point where they also view the system as outsiders. They tend to share the serious criticisms of the progressive and traditional elitists against the low cultural level of mass culture. But they look neither to Western culture's past nor to its evolving future for improvements. Rather, they step outside the Western tradition—and often into an Afro-American cultural and nationalist position—to find sources of hope for themselves and for human culture.

Similar critical traditions have become evident in recent years from Chicanos, Puerto Ricans, Native Americans, other ethnic groups, and feminists. A parallel approach emerged for a time in the late 1960s among white youth led by such mass culture figures as Abby Hoffman and Jerry Rubin. Those cultural revolutionaries who became specifically ideological and Marxist should be placed in the next category.

Marxist Structural Radicals. Sharing in the above criticisms of mass culture but tracing their causes to the exploitative commercial political economy of capitalism, a small but vigorous group of politically radical critics offer the most total rejection of mass culture. To them art and culture are servants of politics, economics, and ideology. They propose socialist realist art to instruct and inspire the masses. In capitalist countries, they emphasize how mass culture anesthetizes and controls the masses in order to protect and preserve the advantages of the power elite who control the economy, shape the politics, and own the media in advanced industrial states. With varying degrees of Marxist orthodoxy, they argue that the institutional structures and the people who control them account for the imperialistic exploitation of the less powerful in the advanced countries and throughout the Third World.

Radicals were inclined to view *The Godfather* as Brando intended it, a picture of how America and multinational corporations are run. But they objected that even the more explicitly political *Godfather II* fell short by not criticizing more explicitly and inclusively the white capitalist elite and the exploitative system and ideology that keep "godfathers" in charge. They charged that the film also failed to show tactics of resistance and liberation or desirable alternative social arrangements.

The Positions Summarized

No one individual can be placed absolutely in one specific category. For example, Raymond Williams has written persuasively from virtually all six positions. As a socialist he has argued the radical institutional analysis, as a literary humanist he effectively presents the elitist criticisms, and as an objective observer he has defended a certain serious legitimacy in popular culture and the need for detachment from cultural bias in studying it. Similarly, *The TV Establishment,* edited by Gaye Tuchman, reflects the objective methods of social science, having a solid base in empirical data and social theory, but at the same time it critically evaluates television from an institutional perspective.[26]

Despite the oversimplifications, describing six positions in the above fashion does suggest a progression from category to category. It is possible cumulatively to synthesize a consistent general position; one that takes into account the positive aspects of the defenses offered by liberal apologists and the information generated by historical and descriptive empiricists but also recognizes the criticisms offered by elitists of both progressive and traditional bents, and that draws its overall explanatory framework from a radical analysis of white, Western, capitalist political and economic institutions. (This is, very generally, the critical position of this book.)

The points of similarity and contrast among critics may be compared by compressing the six positions into three basic categories. (See Table 1–1.) The populist "liberal" category represents the tolerant and moderately progressive position of the defenders of mass culture. The "elitist" critique is the traditionalist position of the aristocratic classicist. The

TABLE 1–1.   Critical Positions on Mass Culture

	"LIBERAL"	"ELITIST"	"RADICAL"
Judgment of mass culture	okay	bad	bad
Orientation historically	present	past	future
Lowest tolerable level of art	high, folk, pop	high	folk, high
Who should judge art	majority	cultured elite	political elite
Criterion for judging	numbers	aesthetics	social totality
Attitude toward media	dependent on popular taste	independent variable	dependent on economics
Cause of mass cult deficiencies	human nature	media panderers	profit-power priorities
Positions they oppose	the elitists	the uncritical	the partial critics
Literary style	description	criticism	prescription
Their goal for mass culture	continuance	elevation	total reorientation

activist "radical" category reflects those who trace the criticisms to what they see as the roots ("radical" comes from the Latin *radix* meaning "root") of the system.

The Pros and Cons of Mass Culture

While critics themselves cannot be reduced to two camps, aspects of their evaluations of mass culture can be separated into (a) charges against mass culture, and (b) defenses of mass culture. Statements in this "great debate" on mass culture may oversimplify and distort issues, but they deserve at least a simplified summary here.

Offered by both elitists and radicals, the criminal indictment against mass culture includes several important charges.

The present organization of mass culture is inherently imbalanced, monopolistic, and exploitative.

Gaye Tuchman's description of the television establishment illustrates this charge.[27]

1. Ownership and regulation of television is dominated by the economic interests of huge telecommunications conglomerates such as RCA, NBC, and Gulf and Western.
2. Networks and stations form an interlocking, one-way distribution system that aims not at serving the genuine needs and interests of their audience but at selling advertising and maximizing corporate profits.
3. Political influence, personal associations, and professional organizations reinforce this closed, monopolistic system more than they modify it.
4. The net effect is to maintain an ideological hegemony and legitimize the status quo.

The effect of mass culture on individuals corrupts and distorts the entire range of human perceptions, expressions, and sensibilities.

Dwight MacDonald, Hall and Whannel, Jacques Ellul, and many others provide the following catalog of disastrous personal results of mass-mediated culture:

1. An obsession with *quantity* replaces any concern with *quality* as producers and distributors compete to reach the same undifferentiated majority, and formulaic mass reproductions turned out by hacks replace creativity and originality.
2. *Mediocrity* is flattered by the thesis that no issue is too complex

to solve simply by counting heads, and people are treated not as *active* participants in social decision making but as *passive* consumers pursuing false escapes from reality.

3. The faddishness and pervasiveness of mass culture destroys folk art, dehydrates popular art, and threatens fine art.

4. The loss of individuality in the conforming mass is compensated by a cult of personality infatuated with the manipulated images of stars and idols without substance.

5. Manipulation of the imagination restricts perceptions of reality to standardized and trivialized stereotypes at the same time that it reduces the ability to fantasize and to distinguish fantasy from reality.

6. Psychological damage includes psychic dissociations within thinking and feeling, crystallization of simplistic tendencies, and conditioned reflexes to stimuli and the need for stimuli.

7. Over time, the steady diet provided by the manipulators of mass media creates public addiction to useless fare similar to the psychological dependency associated with many kinds of drugs, including cigarettes and coffee.

The effects of mass culture on collectivities *destroys meaningful group life and choice.*

1. Television, comic books, films, and other mass media—including many readily available to the very young—teach crime, violence, and exploitative sexual practices.

2. Mass culture concentrates and protects power in a few hands and creates totalitarian conditions and practices, while it fosters the illusion of egalitarian, democratic tolerance.

3. Mass culture has become a most effective weapon of cultural aggression and imperialism against powerless majorities within advanced countries and against entire populations of underdeveloped countries.

4. Mass culture fosters racism and ethnocentrism by stereotyping minorities, borrowing from their creative works, and excluding them from any benefits.

5. Mass culture constitutes a vast spectacle that diverts attention from the concrete conditions of material life and immerses everyone in a propaganda system that dictates behavior and is total, enduring, continuous, and organized.

The Defense. Numerous researchers and commentators on mass culture choose to emphasize its assets rather than its liabilities.

1. Most charges against mass culture *mistake the effect* (the low level of mass culture) *for the causes* (the low taste of persons or repressive political-economic systems).

2. Mass culture merely *gives the people what they want.* By turning the dial, buying the ticket or product, the people, not the "manipulators," determine their mass culture.

3. Only the *"fallacy of verisimilitude"* demands literal correspondence of mass culture to everyday life. Like the novel, television and the rest of mass culture can construct hypothetical reality as an autonomous form of expression.

4. Mass culture *increases potential access to cultural riches* more than has any other factor in history. For example, more people view one performance of Shakespeare on television than saw all the plays of Shakespeare in the Globe theater.

5. Critics *should not generalize* from the peculiarly monolithic organization of the latest mass medium, television, to all media such as radio and movies, which are obviously more fragmented than television, or to print, which is a genuinely diverse mass medium.

6. Mass culture is almost the sole preserve of *genuine, simple, basic human virtues and feelings* such as friendship, heroism, and the family. Love, for example, has stood against the onslaughts of commercialism and depersonalization through its preservation in popular music more than through its defenses in sermons and technical tracts.

7. The variety of mass culture has opened the way to *new concerns,* such as protest songs, and *new experiences,* such as the kinesthetic, communal alternatives sought by counter-cultures.

8. *Technological innovations* in mass culture create new cultural possibilities, such as the aural, inclusive, mythic, in-depth global villages that are made possible by electronic media supplementing visual, restrictive print media.

9. *Mass culture is here to stay,* and it is more realistic to tame than slay the monster. Even if the charges of the critics are true, they offer little choice to the individual other than withdrawal from society and little choice to the system other than revolution. Why not develop critical understanding, awareness, and appreciation within the context of mass culture rather than in a mythic past or future?

10. All judgments of mass culture are *relative* to the personal predi-

lections and ultimate ideology of the one judging. They can be made absolute only in reference to a larger system, and then the debate is over not mass culture, but the larger system.

The last defense is similar to the first. Both point to the need for expanding the theoretical perspectives and assumptions of the debate. More broadly based theory relates mass-mediated culture to systems, ecology, and the structuring of human institutions and consciousness.

Systems, Ecology, and Mass-Mediated Culture

The Relativity of Critical Judgments

Most positions in the debate on mass culture draw the standards for their judgments from outside the world of mass culture itself. An elitist critic may judge mass culture according to the standards of high art and the tastes of a leisure class. A liberal observer may assess mass culture by its multiple uses and gratifications for individuals and the social whole. A radical critic may condemn mass culture for serving the interests of a political and economic elite. Each is concerned with something more than just mass culture in and by itself. Usually that "something more" has to do with quality of life in individual experience and taste and/or in social systems and culture.

James Baldwin's criticism of American and Western mass culture illustrates this "principle of relativity" in the mass culture debate. He is concerned with the whole of the culture and not just its mass art. For example, the following statement by Baldwin reflects a broad perspective on the place and role of mass culture:

> Perhaps life is not the black, unutterably beautiful, mysterious and lonely thing the creative artist tends to think of it as being; but it is certainly not the sunlit playpen in which so many Americans lose first their identities and then their minds.
>
> I feel very strongly, though, that this amorphous people are in desperate search for something which will help them reestablish their connection with themselves and with one another. This can only begin to happen as the truth begins to be told. We are in the middle of an immense metamorphosis here, a metamorphosis which will, it is devoutly to be hoped, rob us of our myths and give us our history, which will destroy our attitudes and give us back our personalities. The *mass culture,* in the meantime, can only reflect our chaos: and perhaps we had better remember that this chaos contains life—and a great transforming energy.[28]

Racism in American culture and media reveals a great deal to a black writer like Baldwin. At least three general expressions of racism come through in mass media and popular culture: *stereotyping, borrowing,* and *excluding.* Many studies document how racial minorities, especially blacks, have been grotesquely stereotyped in popular media. For example, films such as "Birth of a Nation," "Wooing and Wedding of a Coon," "Green Pastures," the Tarzan series, and Shirley Temple movies, as well as many others throughout the history of Hollywood, have depicted blacks, in the words of Donald Bogle, as *Toms, Coons, Mulattoes, Mammies, and Bucks.*[29] Leroi Jones describes the constant borrowing from Afro-American musical innovations in blues, jazz, swing, bebop, modern jazz, hard (or funky) bop, rhythm and blues, and rock. Cleaver describes the Beatles as borrowing their early "yeah, yeah, yeah" from Ray Charles and envisioned white people as "getting back" their bodies through the twist of Chubby Checker.[30] The uglier flip side of the borrowing has been the *excluding* of ethnic minorities, especially ethnics of color, from receiving full benefits from their contributions to popular media and mass culture. White musicians make big-selling albums using black innovations, and white promoters make big profits off black performers.

Baldwin's concern is with *why* blacks have been dealt with in this manner by mass culture and Western society in general. He sees the basis in the history of racist and reactionary exploitation, epitomized by slavery, and in an inability to face and correct that tradition. He once remarked: "Until America realizes what it has done to the American Indian, to Mexican-Americans, and to black Americans, it will not realize what it has done to itself."[31] More recently and more sweepingly he has written: "All of the Western nations have been caught in a lie, the lie of their pretended humanism."[32]

Baldwin sees that in an effort to cover up atrocities and maintain their pride, America and the West are living behind the mask of a complex set of myths—myths that are reflected in the mass culture. Stereotyping and discrimination arise from the desire for a scapegoat and an unwillingness to face reality as it is. "The black man has functioned in the white man's world as a fixed star," and anything but the stereotype threatens white Americans with "the loss of their identity."[33] During the course of a televised interview, Baldwin faced the camera directly and warned:

> What white people have to do is try to find out in their own hearts why it was necessary to have a nigger in the first place. Because I'm not a nigger, I am a man, but if you think I'm a nigger, it means you need it. . . . If I'm not the nigger here and if you invented him—you, the white people, invented him—then you've got to find out why. And the future of the country depends on that. Whether or not it's able to ask that question.[34]

Themes of history, identity, and honesty recur throughout Baldwin's cultural critique:

I think that the past is all that makes the present coherent, and further, that the past will remain horrible for exactly as long as we refuse to assess it honestly. . . .[35]

It is a terrible, an inexorable, law that one cannot deny the humanity of another without diminishing one's own: in the face of one's victim, one sees oneself. Walk through the streets of Harlem and see what we, this nation, have become.[36]

In 1963, *The Fire Next Time* warned of the dangerous exploitation and falsehoods that mask America and that were to burst into flames in the urban conflicts of the later 1960s. Baldwin contrasted the realism of black feeling for the blues with white fears of "sensuality," of "being present in all that one does from making love to breaking bread." He added that replacing bread with "blasphemous and tasteless foam rubber" was a revealing sign. Baldwin stated his thesis bluntly:

This is the crime of which I accuse my country and my countrymen, and for which neither I nor time nor history will ever forgive them, that they have destroyed and are destroying hundreds of thousands of lives and do not know it and do not want to know it. . . . But it is not permissible that the authors of devastation should also be innocent. It is the innocence which constitutes the crime.[37]

The result of failing to face history and reality is a false innocence and protective conformity that bring to mind situation comedies, film and television censorship, Walt Disney, Billy Graham, and many other aspects of popular American culture. Baldwin speaks of it as one both *inside* that "sunlit playpen," as a creator of, commentator on, and celebrity of mass-mediated culture, and as one *outside* its mainstream, a black and a bisexual. Aware of the suppressed undercurrents, he compares relationships in this culture to an imagined conversation with a friend who has murdered his mother and stored her body in the closet of the room in which they converse.[38]

Hope, for Baldwin, comes from outside the white, capitalist, "macho" power circles. In the final dénouement of *Another Country*, Ida, a black woman from Harlem, stands hugging a weeping Vivaldo, the white central character, "stroking the innocence out of him. . . ."[39] Almost a decade later in the epilogue to *No Name in the Street*, Baldwin summarized his vision of white America, Western culture, and history:

An old order is dying, and a new one, kicking in the belly of its mother, time, announces that it is ready to be born. This birth will not be easy, and many of us are doomed to discover that we are exceedingly clumsy midwives. . . . There will be bloody holding actions all over the world, for years to come: but the Western party is over, and the white man's sun has set. Period.[40]

Baldwin's critique assumes that culture is a "system," an integrated whole, of which media, popular arts, race relations, and other components are *interrelated* parts. Evaluative critiques further assume that the cultural system and its component parts constitute an "ecology" that directs the nature and quality of life in that culture. These assumptions are developed more precisely in the next few pages with the aid of general systems theory. Such a "systemic" approach places popular art and media, not in isolation, but in the context of the society in which they live and breathe and have their being.

Why are Baldwin's conclusions so different from those of an expert on high and popular culture like Herbert Gans? Gans accepts Western society and its cultures and is not persuaded by critiques of mass culture. He disputes charges that mass culture has negative effects on creativity, high culture, audiences, and society. He cites research that supports his position and finds contrary arguments "biased."[41] Unlike Baldwin, Gans has no fundamental underlying objection to Western society and America. What Baldwin and Gans illustrate is a general trend that surfaces in certain mass and popular culture debates: the observer (for example, a liberal apologist) who likes the present sociocultural system of the United States and the West will tend to favor mass culture; the critic (for example, an elitist or radical) who dislikes that system will be inclined to reject mass culture.

Broadening the Debate. The Latin adage "de gustibus non est disputandum" is a healthy reminder that questions defined solely in terms of taste are virtually unanswerable by argument. However, shifting the focus of the debate from literary taste and sociological data to a more anthropological sense of culture as a system opens the possibility of considering specific expressions of culture, such as mass-mediated popular culture, as integral and significant *subsets* of a cultural-ecological *system*. By stepping back a giant stride and assuming a larger ecological perspective, we can place judgments for and against mass-mediated culture in their proper context and can make the criteria of evaluation more explicit.

Consider advertising as a subsystem (genre, formula, or theme) within the system of mass-mediated culture and the larger supersystem of multinational capitalism.

The manifest function of advertising within the system is to provide information to consumers about specific products and services. The less obvious latent function is to create the consumer and expand the consumer economy by replacing information with persuasion. Advertising persuasion combines with built-in obsolescence and style changes to maximize sales, income, and employment for the immediate benefit of the multinational capitalist system.[42]

As a result, advertising in the past hundred years has become a major and effective subsystem. Ten percent of production and distribution costs are minimally assigned to advertising for many product categories. By conservative accounting, in the United States advertising cost more than $23 billion in 1972, a typical year. Of that amount, $4.1 billion bought local and national television time for advertising, $1.5 billion purchased radio time, and $8.4 billion was spent on newspaper and magazine space.[43] *Advertising is obviously effective since pragmatic businesses do not spend such amounts on vague chances.*[44] *In fact, advertising is generally a more persuasive proof of the effectiveness of media in modifying human behavior than are the numerous ambiguous research studies on the effect of media. For example, the Surgeon General's five volumes of research findings confirm what advertising makes obvious: that media influence individual and group attitudes and behavior.*[45]

As a subsystem interlocking with other subsystems and systems, advertising performs numerous functions in addition to selling goods and services. Like the Super Bowl, its role can be described as mythic. Advertising pictures a world of fables in which Cinderella is transformed into a glamorous woman by the magic of cosmetics rather than the fairy godmother's wand; and a beast becomes a handsome suitor through the miracles of toothpastes, mouthwashes, deodorants, blow driers, and fashion. Like Disneyland, advertising enacts a morality play of virtuous actions, acquisitions, and beliefs. Like the televised picture of health in Marcus Welby, advertising reflects and reinforces imbalances in the distribution of power and priorities in the larger social system. Like Nixon's 1972 CRP campaign and Billy Graham crusades, advertising is a conscious, coordinated, multi-media, progressively phased campaign to cause specific human decisions. And, in Third World settings like the Peruvian Andes, advertising converts other cultural systems to a consumer economy. The final chapter of this book will raise the question of advertising's negative alienating effects on personal identity and cultural values.

In these and other ways, advertising is thoroughly integrated into a system and has multiple relations with other parts of the system. Isolating advertising or considering it from only one perspective does not do the subject justice. The same is true of other parts of mass-mediated culture and of the whole.

Between Institutions and Consciousness

Mass-mediated culture, such as advertising, provides the link between (a) the material and institutional infrastructures of a culture, and (b) the symbolic structures and internal consciousness of that same culture. Roughly speaking, the three subsystems—material and institutional infrastructures, mass-mediated and interpersonal communication, and internal symbolic structures—are structurally similar to each other (isomorphic) and to the cultural system as a whole. These concepts and relations require some explanation.

System. Weather cannot be understood, predicted, or planned for without the perception of isolated facts of temperature, humidity, atmospheric pressure, and similar data in patterns within a total weather system. In a similar manner, mass-mediated culture cannot be understood or dealt with as a whole without the perception of advertising, crime fiction, westerns, and the rest in patterns within a cultural whole. A sense of the whole enables studies of mass communication and popular culture to achieve a scientifically significant level of generalizability.

Structure. All systems and subsystems are structured into specific patterns and relationships. Cultural and social systems and subsystems are structured wholes. Edward Shils argues that societies, by definition, have a *central zone* of symbols, values, and beliefs that govern that society, and that membership consists of relations with the central zone.[46] The thesis is similar to Malinowski's "principle of totality" in cultures. Raymond Williams notes that the artist draws from the dominant structure of the totality of a specific culture and time: "In principle, it seems clear that the dramatic conventions of any given period are fundamentally related to the 'structure of feeling' in that period."[47]

From such a perspective we can outline contemporary mass-mediated culture through its representative structural expressions in sports, education, politics, medicine, religion, and other areas. The structure of that cultural whole can then be contrasted with other cultures. As in structural linguistics, both universal and culturally specific principles should emerge.

The structures of a cultural system can be pictured as existing on three levels, as in Figure 1–3.

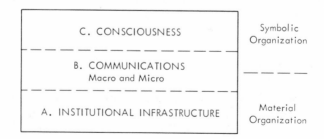

FIGURE 1–3   The Structures of a Cultural System

Institutional Infrastructure. A political and economic structure— ideologically labelled capitalism, communism, democracy, or something similar—forms the institutional foundation of a given society, explaining why, beneath the bewildering variety of popular expressions of a culture, there is an underlying unity that distinguishes it from other cultures. The institutional infrastructure directly influences the organization of resources like raw materials and labor, decision making and concentrations of power, and systemic orientations toward dominant values and priorities. For example, the nature and structure of commercial advertising stem from the nature and structure of advanced capitalism.

Consciousness. Human consciousness concerns the internal awareness within the individual human organism. William James described consciousness as "a theatre of simultaneous possibilities" where the reinforcing and inhibiting agency of attention compares, selects, and represses those possibilities.[48] Robert Ornstein describes two modes of consciousness corresponding to the two hemispheres of the brain—one verbal, rational, and sequential; the other intuitive, holistic, and creative. He notes that in the West the latter is "a mode we often devalue, culturally, personally, and even physiologically."[49] Advertising utilizes both modes effectively —the informational and the mythic—as a socializing agent structuring assumptions, feelings, attitudes, and beliefs in the internal consciousness of contemporary individuals. Advertising creates consumers by structuring their conscious and unconscious responses along lines required by the structure of advanced multinational capitalism.

Communications. Communications, or interaction through messages, is the crucial link between the institutional infrastructure and internal consciousness. Communications, in both mass-mediated and interpersonal forms, conveys "structures" as well as content from institutions to consciousness and from consciousness to institutions. Advertising, as a genre of communication, transmits messages from commercial producers to consumers for the purpose of influencing internal decision making concerning product selection. As a system, advertising cumulatively conveys an integrated value structure determining individual and group living. Communication takes place in the opposite direction, from consumer to producer, by the purchase of products and services. Also, consumer interests and needs for information, humor, sexual enticement, security against death, familiar but not tiresome phrases and melodies, a "meaningful" environment, and so on, communicate from consumers to producers determining which advertisements are most effective and, sometimes, which goods and services should be produced. Any interaction or experience structurally reflects culture-specific institutions, communications, and consciousness.

In this three-part diagram presented in Figure 1–3, *communications*, through mass media and popular culture as well as interpersonal channels, structures *institutions* and *consciousness*. Because these structural relations underlie all the case studies to follow, they warrant elaboration at this point.

Ecosystems and Mass-Mediated Culture

Communications on both micro (interpersonal) and macro (mass-mediated) levels are shaped into a series of intelligible categories called "symbolic forms" or "cultural screens." The amount of raw data available to the human senses at any given time is impossibly beyond the human capacity to absorb and process consciously. The senses form the first level of a "data reduction system" selecting out patterns and details most useful for the human organism and its survival. Knowledge is then screened through and grouped into organized systems of symbolic forms which Ernst Cassirer categorized as language, science, history, myth, religion, and art.[50] This process is illustrated in Figure 1–4.

Advertising illustrates this data-reducing and choice-restricting function of symbolic forms. A Ford commercial not only persuades consumers to purchase a specific model, it also defines automobiles as desirable objects in general. More broadly still, it implies that humans are organisms that survive and flourish by purchasing and using consumer commodities. In fact, commercial advertising taken as a system can, with the help of other cultural forces, reduce human existence to a depersonalized scramble to own and consume as many arbitrarily defined status objects as possible.[51]

Humans can be defined as sophisticated symbol-making and symbol-using animals. The ability to develop and utilize complex symbolic sys-

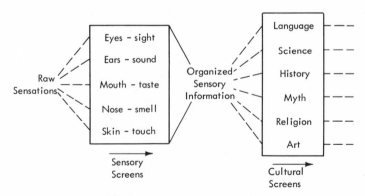

FIGURE 1–4   Data Reduction Process

tems uniquely enables humans to represent and regulate their relations with the environment and their experience of existence. The resulting symbol systems are *relative* in that they are arbitrary in themselves but specific for given purposes. The scientist and the poet may describe a hawk very differently, but each description is "true" insofar as it works for the purposes of its user. Entire sets of cultural symbols may vary considerably with specific variations arising from peculiar needs of a cultural system. For example, agrarian or hunt-and-gather cultures possess elaborate vocabularies for vegetation and the natural environment, while industrial and technological cultures specialize in mechanical, mathematical, and electronic symbols. Benjamin Lee Whorf has even argued that (industrialized) English is static and noun-dominated, while (agrarian) Hopi is a dynamic verb-dominated linguistic system.[52]

Advertising, like the remainder of mass communication and popular culture, can be taken as a "language" or a symbolic system of arbitrary, relative, culture-specific, effective instruments for the representation and regulation of existence.

Within general systems theory, a *system* is broadly defined as "any entity, conceptual or physical, which consists of interdependent parts."[53] An *ecosystem* is a living system interacting with an environment; that is, an ecosystem includes the relationships within a living system and between that system and its environment. *Ecology* studies the relations between a system and its environment. Within the ecosystems of human groups, the subsystem on the material level of biological and institutional structures can be logically (although not really) distinguished from the subsystem on the symbolic level of consciousness and cognitive structures. *Mass-mediated culture* is an increasingly important component of the latter subsystem. Studying the *ecology of mass-mediated culture* thus means looking at mass-mediated culture in terms of the relationship between (a) the human ecosystem of which mass-mediated culture is a part and (b) the global environment.

Figure 1–5 summarizes these highly compressed statements, which form a theoretical explanation of the cultural role of mass communication, popular culture, and the case studies in this book.

In the diagram, the outer *(A)* dimension represents the material subsystem and the inner *(C)* dimension represents the symbolic subsystem, in one total human ecosystem. The material and symbolic subsystems are mediated by *(B)* communication, and in a given ecosystem are isomorphic, or similarly structured. The manner in which a given society *symbolically* represents itself, for example in popular culture and media, is part and parcel of the manner in which that society *materially* organizes itself. They are dialectically related so that, if one changes, the other must change; if one remains unchanged, the other cannot change. Distortions

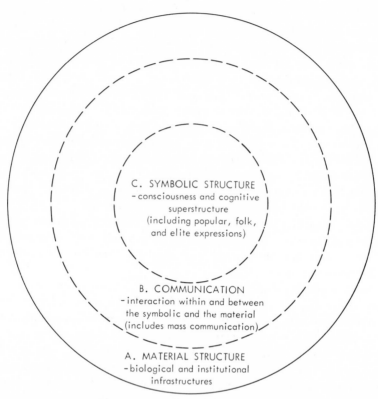

C. SYMBOLIC STRUCTURE
– consciousness and cognitive
superstructure
(including popular, folk,
and elite expressions)

B. COMMUNICATION
– interaction within and between
the symbolic and the material
(includes mass communication)

A. MATERIAL STRUCTURE
– biological and institutional
infrastructures

FIGURE 1–5   Diagram of a Human Ecosystem

in the structural distribution of income, property, energy, food, and other items in the material subsystem are both cause and effect of distortions in the symbolic subsystem. For example, in keeping with James Baldwin's analysis, if black Americans receive disproportionately little material wealth, symbolic representations will also demean the symbolic significance of blacks. Further, to improve the total condition of black Americans, neither symbolic improvement alone in quantity (more Stepin Fetchits) or quality (a Sidney Poitier) nor material improvement alone (better paying jobs but with continued stereotyping and prejudice) is as effective as improvement in *both* symbolic and material treatment and conditions.

The importance of these relationships for the subject at hand is that popular culture transmitted by mass media expresses a major portion of the symbolic subsystem in contemporary society and therefore has ecological importance as both cause and effect of balances and imbalances, justice and injustices, sensitivity and brutality, in contemporary society as a whole. In short, mass-mediated culture is anything but *irrelevant* as the common term "entertainment" unfortunately implies. Moreover, mass media and popular or folk cultures are significant and worthy of serious study not only in themselves but also in their *symbolic associations* as revealing expressions of a cultural system.

Even a brief, tentative summary of a systems-and-symbols approach to cultural expression serves various purposes. First, it indicates why conflicting judgments of mass culture tend to be *relative* to broader, more inclusive criteria than is immediately evident. Second, this approach explains the *symmetry* between mass-mediated culture and the total political-economic system in a given society, a symmetry that reciprocally structures both, as will be explained more fully in the final chapter. Third, it justifies *cross-cultural* comparisons of cultural expressions as significant and revealing. Fourth, it indicates the importance of *policy* decisions concerning maintainance or change in mass-mediated culture as it reflects and regulates a total human ecosystem.

In summary, rock music in Buenos Aires, *The Godfather*, and commercial advertising take on theoretical significance and become intelligible to the extent that they are consciously understood as specific symbolic interpretations of existence, as structured reflections and regulators of material conditions, and as semiotic manifestations of a cultural whole.

Cultural Exegesis

Although most do not recognize his name, Norman Lear has influenced the lives of many millions of Americans more directly than have Dante, Shakespeare, Freud, and Picasso combined. Research indicates, for example, that Lear may be responsible for a worker feeling free to refer to a fellow employee as a "chink" or to a family on the next block as "the coloreds." In other cases, Lear may have made a student feel that redneck bigotry and white racism are stupid and laughable. For better or for worse, Lear has provided the subjects for millions of conversations in living rooms, supermarkets, gas stations, dormitories, bars, restaurants, nightclubs, and locker rooms.

Norman Lear developed and coproduced, along with Bud Yorkin, "All in the Family," for five years the television program ranked first in the Nielsen ratings. Lear developed the program in the late 1960s from a popular BBC series, "Till Death Us Do Part." ABC originally rejected his pilot programs of "Those Were the Days," but two years later CBS bought the program under the new title "All in the Family," and from January, 1971, Archie Bunker, Dingbat, Meathead, Gloria, and America's most clichéd prejudices, stereotypes, and frustrations became standard fare for up to 50 million Americans each week.

*Innovations like "I Love Lucy," "Laugh-In," and "All in the Family,"
when they succeed, have a snowball effect. A year after the socially
conscious and controversial "All in the Family" was first aired, "Sanford
and Son" appeared with black comedian Redd Foxx playing the lead
in an adaptation of a BBC cockney satire "Steptoe and Son." Lear also
developed "Maude," "Good Times," "The Jeffersons," "One Day at a
Time," and "Mary Hartman, Mary Hartman," making his influence on
American culture indisputable. Similar claims of cultural influence could
be made for such slightly known figures as Bernie Taupin, songwriter
for the omnipresent Elton John; Liz Bolten, former head of NBC-TV's
daytime programming with its endless serials and game shows; Carlos
Castaneda, bestselling interpreter of Native American animism and
sorcery; and Berry Gordy, chief executive of flashy Motown records and
productions.*

*What kind of "influence," what manner of "culture" is this? How
can these be meaningfully interpreted? What analytic procedures are
most productive for the study of mass communication and popular
culture?*

Methodologies

Important studies and explanatory theories typically overflow the
boundaries of disciplines. Literary analysis, for example, may be formal-
istic, psychological, sociological, archetypal, mythic, structuralist, or of
another school, each type of analysis reflecting theories that bridge several
disciplines. The study of popular culture draws from a variety of academic specializations. A survey by John Cawelti found that courses on
popular culture are of three main types: *Mass media survey courses* are
offered by (a) communications and journalism departments with an emphasis on professional aspects; (b) sociology departments with more focus
on empirical material and social theory; or (c) departments in the humanities with a stress on evaluating cultural and aesthetic content. *Popular
arts courses* feature either surveys of the popular arts in America or studies of a particular form such as the western or science fiction. Courses in
nonelite cultures and arts concern such traditions as that of Afro-American culture.[54] Popular culture research reflects similar blends and separations. The "anomalous" character of popular culture, as Joseph Arpad
has aptly characterized it, elicits multidisciplinary approaches generally
emphasizing aesthetic, functionalist, or structuralist methodology.

Aesthetic. The approach to mass-mediated culture as popular art
emphasizes literary, dramatic, and artistic conventions and concerns. As
an example, "All in the Family" bears an interesting resemblance to
Commedia Dell'arte, a form of Italian low comedy that dates from early
times and was especially popular around the sixteenth century. *Commedia*

developed simple scenarios exploiting stock character types: a miserly father, his henchman, a harlequin narrator, and two lovers. The action was performed outside before a live audience, with little or no change of scenery. The plot developed around conflict situations and misunderstandings presented through rapid-fire dialogue replete with puns and *double entendre.* The length was only 20 to 30 minutes, and the audience was a broad cross section of the population.[55] Like *Commedia Dell'arte,* "All in the Family" and a great deal of television comedy exploit types through the four basic characters, are filmed before a live audience without retakes, last about 24 minutes, mirror the common confusions of the audience, and employ a variety of comic conventions.

Other aesthetic approaches may focus on a particular work, author, genre, formula, theme, or medium. Stylistic, semiotic, thematic, or content analyses provide insight into popular westerns, detective fiction, comics, musicals, and advertising.

Functional. The study of mass communication has emphasized functionalist research on influence and diffusion, motives and judgments, dissonance, uses and gratifications, and audience effects of various sorts.

Attitudinal functional research on "All in the Family" has yielded controversial results. Producer Lear, star Carroll O'Connor, and *New York Times* television critic John J. O'Connor have argued that the program *is* effective as a satire on bigotry and emphasize that Archie's narrow-minded prejudices cause him to "lose" in the end of nearly every episode. But research confirms the "selective perception" at work among viewers, confirming the classical scholastic principle *"Quidquid recipitur recipitur secundum modum recipientis."** Stuart Surlin's research in Georgia coincides with the joint American-Canadian study conducted by Neil Vidmar and Milton Rokeach. The latter found that 62 percent of their sample of viewers admired Archie more than any other character in the show and only 10 percent believed him the character most made fun of. They concluded that "high prejudiced persons were likely to watch 'All in the Family' more often than low prejudiced persons, to identify more often with Archie Bunker, and to see him winning in the end. . . . [suggesting] the program is more likely reinforcing prejudice than combating it." Others disputed that conclusion.[56] But while liberals took delight in the blasts at Archie's bigotry, evidence indicated that larger numbers of viewers seemed to use the program to rationalize their own prejudices and repopularize old racial and ethnic slurs.

The largest volume of media research correlates messages and audiences to serve the interests of the media industries. These include Nielsen ratings for television; ARB ratings for radio; Standard Rate and Data Service circulation figures for periodicals; media data reported in *Variety,*

---

*Whatever is received is received according to the manner of the one receiving it.

Broadcasting, or *Billboard;* research findings locked away in advertising agencies and corporations; poll data from Gallup, Roper, Yankelevitch, and others; and a variety of other standard sources. Social psychology has identified many functions of popular media, among them status-conferral, enforcement of social norms, and a narcotizing effect, as summarized by Lazarsfeld and Merton years ago.[57] James Carey and Albert Kreiling have summarized the role of the broad "uses and gratifications" approach to popular culture and suggested an alternative methodology. They suggest moving from predefined sociological needs and uses to conceiving popular culture as shared expressive cultural processes that provide meaning, value, and reassurance for everyday life.[58] Researchers and critics in Australia and England echo that suggestion.[59]

Structural. Too complex to summarize easily, structuralism focuses on constituent units, relations among units and bundles of units, and systems and universals expressed by the relations.[60]

A structural analysis of "All in the Family" might begin with the relations and communications patterns within the Bunker family, especially Archie's dominance. The structure of Archie's beliefs and bigotry parallel the common human preference for the familiar and the self-serving. The structure of the racially, generationally, sexually, and economically stratified social order surrounding the Bunkers recapitulates Archie's internal structure and the Bunker household's interaction structures. Beyond the internal structures within the program, the structure of CBS and its parent conglomerate, RCA, permits but controls the innovations and controversies of "All in the Family" for the purpose of maximizing number of viewers, advertising revenue, and profits. The program did this by releasing certain social tensions, skirting others, and providing a structure for the collective expression of dominant cultural values.

Structural analysis aids in identifying ideology, mythic and ritual elements, values, and the organization of consciousness in expressions of popular culture. George Gerbner identifies three areas of analysis, all of which involve structure: (a) analysis of institutional processes, which includes how, in the mass media, decisions are made, message systems are composed, and other institutions are involved; (b) analysis of bodies of messages in terms of how they can be observed as dynamic systems with symbolic functions that have social consequences; and (c) cultivation analysis, which asks what common assumptions, points of view, images, and associations the message systems tend to cultivate in the public and what the implications are for policy.[61] Gerbner's "cultural indicators" approach is somewhat similar to, but more complex than, the methodology adopted in the case studies in this book.

Cultural Exegesis and Case Studies

The approach taken in the studies in this book draws from all three methodologies. As Roy Harvey Pearce argues, study of mass and popular culture works from three perspectives at once: historical, sociological, and formal.[62] The blend of methods varies from chapter to chapter but a concern for structure and system predominates. Formal terminology and tedious methodological discussions have been avoided in order to allow primary data to come through clearly, as Ray Browne has emphasized with the *Journal of Popular Culture*.[63]

More specifically, in light of the theoretical and methodological picture drawn in this chapter, certain specific procedures were used in selecting and approaching topics for the case studies. As a preparation for the case studies, this chapter follows the standard organizational design for research: (a) statement of the problem, (b) definition of terms, (c) search of the literature, (d) hypotheses and theoretical implications, and (e) methodology. The six case studies of Chapters 2 through 7 (f) identify and analyze the empirical evidence. The final chapter (g) reviews the entire "experiment," (h) draws conclusions, and (i) identifies certain theoretical and practical implications.

Criteria for Selection of Topics. The subjects of analysis in the case studies were chosen according to a specific set of requirements. They are *focused* on a specific event or person as a *dominant* and widespread cultural expression that *continues* over a period of years, represents a major *institutional* area or subsystem of society, and is significant as an expression of a total cultural *system*.

Each of the case studies fits all these criteria. For example, the focus on the structure of the Disney universe drew limits around the possible data for analysis and yet dealt with the nature of a major socializing force for youth throughout the world—hence, the label "education." The Super Bowl is the most lucrative annual spectacle on United States media; it is, therefore, a dominant as well as continuing expression of culture, uniquely revealing of American structures and values. The continuing success of fictionalized portrayals of medicine, exemplified by "Marcus Welby," points to a structural similarity between health care in the genre of medical fiction, in this case televised medical fiction, and health care in the "real world" of the larger cultural system. The Nixon CRP (Committee to Reelect the President) effort typifies dominant political campaigns and commercial advertising in placing persuasion and results above all else in orchestrating a sophisticated media campaign. Billy Graham has been a continuing success for decades throughout the English-speaking world and represents a popular religious consciousness appropriate to contemporary capitalist democracies. The popular Aymara religious celebration, while presented as a contrast to mass-mediated culture, is also a focused, dominant, continuing, typical expression of a major institutional area of a cultural system considered as a whole.

The criteria for selection of topics ensure that each case study is somehow typical of a culture and that findings can be generalized to other cases and issues.

Procedural Steps. The instrumentation and experimental procedures applied to the topics are widely varied but can be summarized as ethnographic, exegetical, typological, cross-cultural, critical, and policy oriented.

Each case study implicitly follows these procedures. The study of Billy Graham explicitly defines *ethnography* and *exegesis*. The former identifies an experience in exact detail together with historical and other necessary factual background; the latter identifies the precise meaning of the experience both intensively in itself and extensively in its association. When well executed, the two define what an individual case *typifies* about a culture. The *cross-cultural* comparisons are most evident in the Aymara study, which compares and contrasts characteristic structures of a non-mass-mediated culture with the culture represented in the other case studies. *Critical procedures* seek precise understanding of subtle associations, implications, and potential problem areas. They seek both positive appreciation and negative sensitizing to potential exploitation and unconscious excesses. As Ernst Cassirer warned about myths in general, uncomprehending infatuation can lead to dangerous excesses unless balanced by healthy intellectual, aesthetic, and ethical forces.[64] Therefore, a final procedure in these studies points beyond understanding only and suggests appropriate and constructive responses. All of this, it should be remembered, proceeds in the manner of a probe rather than a proof; these are exploratory field studies rather than definitive laboratory experiments.

The criteria and procedures of this method of "cultural exegesis of case studies" structure the movement from particulars to universals, from specific inductive empirical reality to general deductive scientific laws and intellectual comprehension. In this, they follow classical intellectual and epistemological principles as ancient as Aristotle's *Organon*.

Scope, Perspective, and Limitations

In these pages, *mass-mediated culture* refers to expressions of culture as they are transmitted by mass media, whether they arise from elite, folk, popular, or mass commercial origins. This definition allows for the inclusion of media content from recreational, educational, political, religious, and economic institutionalized sources, as well as from the more narrowly identifiable popular arts. The studies focus on the newer media, especially electronic media, as well as the more easily studied printed expressions of culture. Emphasis is directed away from myriad restricted topics of purely personal, archaic, or elitist interest in order to fasten attention on how mass-mediated culture expresses dominant and typical cultural myths, rituals, values, beliefs, customs, concepts, images, symbols, fears, hopes, and dreams for large areas of the world.

A useful perspective for viewing mass-mediated culture requires coupling imagination with reason. In this task, science fiction fantasy may be helpful.

For example, imagine approaching mass-mediated culture as a foreign anthropologist fresh from the New Guinea hills and Trobriand Islands. As a curious outsider, you try to understand "Nacirema" culture with its developed market economy and reliance on charmboxes on the bathroom wall or in the corner of the living room.[65] Or, imagine viewing these subjects as an archeologist a millenium hence who has uncovered a cache of buried artifacts from a bygone era, the late twentieth century. In A.D. 2980 you attempt to piece together what life was like a thousand years earlier from the evidence of a videotape of prime-time television, recordings of popular music, mass magazines, and similar remnants of a twentieth-century popular counterpart to the Library of Hammurabi or the Tomb of Tutankhamen. Or, imagine you approach earth in a UFO from another planet. You have only this book in your hands as evidence of what human life is like and you must verify, expand, and modify its findings. Instructions for any of these three imagined investigations from outside might be contained in a "Mission Impossible" tape that never self-destructed: "Your task, Jim, should you choose to accept it, is to determine how and why these objects and events held such power."

Two notes of caution are in order concerning this book. First, mass-mediated culture is too real and diverse to be pinned down and dissected completely, even when it is laid out, Prufrock-style, "like a patient etherized upon a table." Its complex, living diversity remains, as do all primary experiences, elusively beyond the power of words, methodologies, or theories.

The second caution has to do with the fact that this book brings us together, by definition, within mass-mediated culture. This book is the product of the first thoroughly "mass" medium, printing. As such, it can actively be used by the reader to clarify experience or it can be passively received as propaganda. In the thirteenth century Thomas Aquinas admonished that learning was an activity by the docent, not a gift from an instructor. Since his time, the multiplication of media has amplified the need for that reminder. A book, like the rest of mass-mediated culture, is ultimately liberating only to the extent that it shifts control from the writer to the reader. If mass-mediated culture is to be tackled, then information must be gathered, feelings stimulated, insights sparked, questions asked, tastes sensitized, perspective achieved, and consciousness developed—but all with the humbling awareness that we are like fish trying to analyze water and with the liberating realization that each of us bears the burden and shares the glory of shaping our own lives, both personally and collectively.

Notes

1. "Avant-Garde and Kitsch," in Bernard Rosenberg and David Manning White; eds., *Mass Culture: The Popular Arts in America* (New York: Free Press, 1957), p. 103.

2. "Mass Media and Developing Nations," *The Democratic Journalist,* no. 1 (1975), pp. 6–7.

3. *The Image Industries* (New York: Sheed & Ward, 1959).

4. See, for example, Nicholas Johnson, *How To Talk Back to Your Television Set* (New York: Bantam, 1970).

5. Ibid.

6. *The Unembarrassed Muse: The Popular Arts in America* (New York: Dial Press, 1970), p. 3.

7. "Mass and Popular Culture," in Norman Jacob, ed., *Culture for the Millions* (New York: Van Nostrand, 1961).

8. "Between Folklore and Literature: Popular Culture as Anomaly," *Journal of Popular Culture* 9, no. 2 (Fall 1975), p. 404.

9. Dwight MacDonald, "A Theory of Mass Culture," in Rosenberg and White, eds., *Mass Culture.*

10. Approximately half the $4 billion amount comes from sales of recorded music. Sidney Shemel and M. William Krasiovsky, *This Business of Music,* Paul Ackerman, ed. (New York: Billboard Publications, 1971), xvii–xxv.

11. "Mass Society and Mass Culture: Interdependence or Independence?" *American Sociological Review* 29 (April 1964), p. 175; also reprinted in Gayle Tuchman, ed., *The TV Establishment: Programming for Power and Profit* (Englewood Cliffs, N.J.: Prentice-Hall, 1974).

12. Raymond Williams, "On High and Popular Culture," *The New Republic* (November 23, 1974), p. 15.

13. *Popular Culture and High Culture: An Analysis and Evaluation of Taste* (New York: Basic Books, 1974). David Thornburn accused Gans in this book of a condescending "liberal tolerance hard to distinguish from mere insult." See David Thornburn, "Art and the Masses," *Commentary,* May, 1975.

14. "Popular Culture: Notes Toward a Definition," in *Popular Culture and Curriculum,* Ray B. Browne and Ronald J. Ambrosetti, eds. (Bowling Green, Ohio: Bowling Green University Popular Press, 1970), pp. 5–6.

15. Lewis's diagram is from George H. Lewis, ed., *Side-Saddle on the Golden Calf: Social Structure and Popular Culture in America* (Pacific Palisades, Calif.: Goodyear, 1972), p. 20.

16. This definition expands on that of Charles R. Wright in *Mass Communication: A Sociological Perspective* (New York: Random House, 1959). See also Melvin L. LeFleur, *Theories of Mass Communication*, 2nd ed. (New York: David McKay, 1970).

17. See especially Marshall McLuhan, *Understanding Media: The Extensions of Man* (New York: McGraw-Hill, 1964).

18. These dates are from various sources. A similar list appears in Wilbur Schramm, ed., *Mass Communications* (Urbana: University of Illinois Press, 1960), pp. 5–7. Extrapolations into the future are based on Arthur C. Clarke's *Profiles of the Future,* supplemented with McLuhan and Teilhard de Chardin.

19. The two lists of figures are abridged and adapted from pp. 136–7 and 144–5 in Wilbur Schramm, *Men, Messages, and Media* (New York: Harper & Row, 1973). Copyright © by Wilbur Schramm. By permission of Harper & Row, Publishers, Inc.

20. "Notes on Popular Culture," *Journal of Popular Culture* 4, no. 4 (Winter 1971).

21. "Beatles, Batman, and the New Aesthetic," *Midway* (Autumn 1968), pp. 49–70.

22. "Updated All-Time Film Champs," *Variety,* January 9, 1974, p. 23.

23. Gene Shalit, "Today," NBC-TV, November 1974.

24. Bernard Rosenberg, "Mass Culture in America," in White and Rosenberg, eds., *Mass Culture,* p. 4; Stuart Hall and Paddy Whannel, *The Popular Arts* (New York: Pantheon Books, 1965), pp. 370–84; Russell Nye, *The Unembarrassed Muse,* pp. 417–20; Horace Newcomb, *TV: The Most Popular Art* (Garden City, N. Y.: Anchor Books, 1974), pp. 1–24.

25. William H. Gass, "Even if by all the Oxen in the World," in *Frontiers of American Culture,* Ray B. Browne and others, eds. (Lafayett, Indiana: Purdue University Press, 1968).

26. Gaye Tuchman, ed., *The TV Establishment: Programming for Power and Profit* (Englewood Cliffs, N.J.: Prentice-Hall, 1974).

27. Ibid., pp. 1–39.

28. Italics added. Quoted from *Daedalus.*

29. Donald Bogle, *Toms, Coons, Mulattoes, Mammies, and Bucks* (New York: Viking Press, 1973). Similar points are documented in Peter Noble, *The Negro in Films* (London: Knapp, Drewett and Sons, 1936), now reissued by the New York Times–Arno Press, and in Edward Mapp, *Blacks in American Films: Today and Yesterday* (Metuchen, N.J.: Scarecrow Press, 1972). The most effective compilation of this information, including numerous film clips, is in "Black History: Lost, Stolen, or Strayed?" narrated by Bill Cosby in the CBS-TV series "Of Black America," 1968.

30. Eldridge Cleaver, *Soul on Ice* (New York: Dell, 1968).

31. Lecture, Chicago, Illinois, July, 1962.

32. *No Name in the Street* (New York: Dell, 1962); p. 85. Copyright © James Baldwin.

33. *The Fire Next Time* (New York: Dial Press, 1963), p. 23. Copyright © James Baldwin.

34. Quoted in *The Negro Protest,* p. 14.

35. *Notes of a Native Son* (New York: Dial Press, 1958), pp. 6–7. Copyright © James Baldwin.

36. *Nobody Knows My Name* (New York: Dial Press, 1960), p. 66. Copyright © James Baldwin.

37. *The Fire Next Time,* p. 19.

38. *Nobody Knows My Name,* p. 124.

39. *Another Country* (New York: Dial Press, 1964), p. 362. Copyright © James Baldwin.

40. *No Name in the Street*, pp. 196–97.

41. Gans, *Popular Culture and High Culture*.

42. See, for example, Paul Baran and Paul Sweezy, "The Sales Effort" in *Monopoly Capital* (New York: Monthly Review Press, 1966).

43. Schramm, *Men, Messages, and Media*, p. 137.

44. Johnson, *How To Talk Back*, p. 21.

45. Surgeon General's Scientific Advisory Committee on Television and Social Behavior, *Television and Growing Up: The Impact of Televised Violence* (Washington: U. S. Government Printing Office, 1972).

46. Edward Shils, "Centre and Periphery," in *The Logic of Personal Knowledge: Essays Presented to Michael Polanyi*, Paul Ignotos and others, eds. (London: Routledge and Kegan Paul, 1961).

47. Raymond Williams, *Preface to Film*, quoted in Hall and Whannel, *The Popular Arts*, p. 45.

48. William James, *The Principles of Psychology* (New York: Dover, 1950), vol. I, pp. 288–89.

49. *The Psychology of Consciousness* (San Francisco: W. H. Freeman, 1972), p. x.

50. Ernst Cassirer, *An Essay on Man* (New Haven: Yale University Press, 1944).

51. The pathetic effect is described in Richard Altschuler and Nicholas M. Regush, *Open Reality* (New York: Putnam's, 1974), especially in the introductory section "John: A Parable."

52. *Language, Thought, and Reality: Selected Writings of Benjamin Lee Whorf*, John B. Carroll, ed. (Boston: The Technology Press of Massachusetts Institute of Technology, 1957).

53. R. L. Ackoff, "Systems, Organizations, and Interdisciplinary Research," in *Systems Thinking*, F. E. Emery, ed. (Baltimore: Penguin Books, 1969), p. 332.

54. John G. Cawelti, "Popular Culture Programs," in *Popular Culture and Curriculum*, Ray B. Browne and Ronald J. Ambrosetti, eds. (Bowling Green, Ohio: Bowling Green University Popular Press, 1970), pp. 23–46.

55. This description of *Commedia Dell'arte* is based on C. Hugh Holman, *A Handbook to Literature*, 3rd ed. (Indianapolis: Odyssey Press, 1975) and other data gathered by Frank Condon and Susan Jane Lewis.

56. Neal Vidmar and Milton Rokeach, "Archie Bunker's Bigotry: A Study in Selective Perception and Exposure," *Journal of Communication* 24, no. 1 (Winter 1974), pp. 36–47. For other positions see, for example, those cited in Leonard Gross, "Do the Bigots Miss the Message?" *TV Guide*, November 8, 1975, pp. 14–18.

57. Paul F. Lazarsfeld and Robert K. Merton, "Mass Communication, Popular Taste, and Organized Social Action," in Rosenberg and White, eds., *Mass Culture*, pp. 457–73.

58. James W. Carey and Albert L. Kreiling, "Popular Culture and Uses and Gratifications: Notes Toward an Accommodation," in *The Uses of Mass Communications: Current Perspectives on Gratifications Research*, Jay G. Blumler and Elihu Katz, eds. (Beverly Hills: Sage Publications, 1974), pp. 225–48.

59. See the articles by Patricia Edgar, Mick Counihan, and Graham Murdock in *The Australian and New Zealand Journal of Sociology* 9, no. 2 (June 1975).

60. This very brief summary draws especially from Claude Lévi-Strauss, *Structural Anthropology*, trans. Claire Jacobson and Brooke Grundfest Schoepf (New York: Basic Books, 1963), and from Hayden White, "Structuralism and Popular Culture," *Journal of Popular Culture* 7, no. 4 (Spring 1974), pp. 759–75.

61. George Gerbner, "Communication and Social Environment," *Scientific American* 227, no. 3 (September 1972), pp. 152–60.

62. Roy Harvey Pearce, *Historicism Once More* (Princeton, N.J.: Princeton University Press, 1969), especially Chapter 3, "Mass Culture/Popular Culture: Notes for a Humanist's Primer."

63. See, for example, Ray B. Browne, "Can Opener," introduction to a special section on theories and methodologies in popular culture, *Journal of Popular Culture* 9, no. 2 (Fall 1975), pp. 353–54.

64. See Ernst Cassirer, *The Myth of the State* (New Haven: Yale University Press, 1946), p. 298.

65. See Horace Miner, "Body Ritual Among the Nacirema," *American Anthropologist* 58 (June 1956), pp. 503–7. Nacirema, of course, is the name of a well-known culture spelled backwards.

Education

Donald Duck, directing streetcar passengers in Hiroshima, Japan, hints at the international influence of mass-mediated culture. Those awaiting the Mark Twain Steamboat at Disneyland are experiencing a structured universe of symbols, values, ideology, and meaning.

2

The Disney Universe: Morality Play

What threads connect Mouseketeers, Donald Duck, Mary Poppins, the Lovebug, jungle cats, Fantasia, and magic kingdoms?

What are the international influence and historical evolution of the Disney empire?

How do the Disney amusement parks capture the essence of the Disney message and media?

What do the various offerings in the parks represent, and which are most popular?

What kind of utopian multimedia morality play does Disney offer?

How does an audience experience values and ideology in the Disney "universe of semantic meaning"?

Why do critics disagree about Walt Disney Productions, Inc., which was proposed to head the United States Bicentennial?

How does "entertainment" compare with schools, homes, and churches as a socializing force in the construction of reality?

The visitors walk from the entrance up cheery, commercial Main Street, U.S.A. They approach the base of the snow-capped Matterhorn. To the right, they see a shiny future of science, technology, and space travel. To the left are adventures among tropical jungles and islands. Further ahead, to the left, they glimpse the mythic past of the American frontier, bordered by a land of bears and a quaint New Orleans square replete with pirates and a haunted mansion. The visitors sense that on the far side of the mountain, between the American past and the shiny future, waits a fantasy of fairies and witches, princes and princesses, talking animals, and a world-famous mouse.

In what exotic place are these visitors? They stand in the heart of a special universe, the "happiest place on earth" begat by Walter Elias Disney.

Disney's Utopian Influence

The existential experience of being in the Disney universe has touched the life of virtually every American and of hundreds of millions of others throughout the world through films, television, comics, parks, records, and nearly every other medium. This chapter investigates the phenomenological structure of Disney meanings by reporting the results of a detailed questionnaire administered to 200 people who have spent a total of approximately 6,500 hours in the epitome of the Disney universe, the Disneyland amusement park in Anaheim, California. Their responses indicate how Disneyland is perceived by those attending, how individual attractions and the park as a whole are evaluated, and what the overall meaning and influence of the experience might be. In addition, the data test two major hypotheses concerning Walt Disney Productions, Inc., as a whole.

Disney attracts participants into mass-mediated utopian typifications.

Disney media products attract audiences with original and often highly imaginative animations and other creative expressions. They create an inclusive environment that involves participants by offering a mixture of media, a development of universally known themes and settings, and an imaginative recounting of familiar immediate human experiences. For example, Disneyland was consciously designed as a total environment made of dramatic productions complete with plot, scenery, and characters. The visitor passes through a Disney experience just as a viewer is carried through scenes in a film by a camera.[1] However, the Disney visitor participates actively by selecting and entering into a unique combination of plots to create an individual experience. Disneyland reverses Goffman's dramaturgic analysis in which individuals in everyday life, like actors, manage impressions and give off cues to those surrounding them.[2] In Disneyland, the surroundings manage impressions and give off cues to those within. Disneyland as a medium thus involves and influences visitors by combining the flexibility and freedom of a stroll through the park with the structure and security of preprogrammed narrative plots.

Disney media products typify fundamental assumptions of the dominant culture but in a *utopian,* idealized form. In this regard they parallel what Dante's work represented in the classical medieval world. *The Divine Comedy* summarized the spirit and worldview of thirteenth century Europe in a single literary classic by creatively synthesizing the ideals of Albert the Great, Thomas Aquinas, and other scholastic theologians as well as popular literary, dramatic, and moral ideals of the time. Disney products are mass, not elite, and they come through many media and themes rather than in a unified written corpus. Nevertheless, Disney's work typifies twentieth-century America's self-image and worldview much as Dante's work typified medieval Catholicism. Both idealize fundamental characteristics into utopian worlds of absolutes.

This "typification hypothesis" borrows from Leo Lowenthal's thesis that popular culture *reflects* political-economic structures, Paul Lazarsfeld and Robert Merton's thesis that popular culture and mass media *channel* vague tendencies in specific directions, and C. Wright Mills's thesis that media *cause* behavior and belief.[3] Mills argued that available methods of social research cannot measure the subtle and pervasive effects of mass media because "the media not only give us information; they guide our very experiences." The "pictures in our head," as Walter Lippmann called them, gained from media tend to replace our own fragmentary experience as our standards of reality. Does Disney provide any evidence of the following charges made by Mills in *The Power Elite*?

> The media tell people in the mass who they are—they give *identity*.
> The media tell people what they want to be—they give *aspirations*.
> They tell people how to get that way—they give *technique*.
> They tell people how to feel they are that way even when they are not—they give *escape*.[4]

Disney instructs through morality plays that structure personal values and ideology.

This hypothesis suggests that Disney productions be taken seriously (a) as *educators*, a label that Disney was willing to accept for his role in instructing youth and adults, and (b) as *moralists*, a powerful role in the "value-free" atmosphere of contemporary secular society. Moral education carries with it, of course, an *ideology* and worldview.

As this chapter illustrates, many Disney productions closely resemble the traditional *morality play*. Medieval mystery plays, which were based on scriptural themes and liturgical actions, gave birth to the morality play as "a dramatized allegory in which the abstract virtues and vices (like Mercy, Conscience, Perseverance, and Shame) appear in a personified form, the good and the bad usually being engaged in a struggle for the soul of man."[5] *Snow White, Pollyanna,* and other Disney productions become contemporary examples of *Everyman* by placing goodness and evil in an allegorical conflict that illustrates how virtues such as innocence, beauty, kindness, and patriotism triumph over vices and finally result in happiness. Walt Disney's overriding goal was "happiness," the core of ethical systems since Aristotle.

Critics and fans of Disney, many of whom are cited in this chapter, agree that Disney is a significant cultural influence. Disney has been praised as the twentieth century's greatest educator and condemned for distorting history, geography, economics, the social structure, and the future. Disneyland has been acclaimed as a model of the "global village" and criticized for presenting other peoples and countries as caricatures warped by ethnocentric American bias. Does a detailed collective trip through the Disney universe provide evidence for or against these judgments?

As we mentioned earlier, to develop empirical data with which to test the two hypotheses and various theories, a 41-item questionnaire was administered to over 200 persons, primarily students, and 192 usable questionnaires were returned. All but 7 respondents had attended Disneyland at least once. Of the respondents, 114 were male and 78 female. Thirty were black, Chicano, Asian, Native American (American Indian), or from other non-Caucasian groups. The ages ranged from fifteen to forty-two and averaged slightly over twenty-one years. The majority lived less than a hundred miles from Disneyland. Most important, respondents had visited the Disneyland amusement park an average of 4.87 times and had spent an average of 6.97 hours there each time. Forty-five had been there 10 or more times; several more than 50 times; and one on each of his 23 birthdays. This sample, therefore, does not represent the general public but might be characterized as "expert," in the sense that it represents young Americans who have easy access to the California capital of the Disney empire.

In addition, more than half the 192 respondents reported that they had been "exposed to" these other Disney productions: feature animated films (161); nature films (148); short animated films (141); weekly television shows (139); cartoon strips (132); comic books (121); daily television shows (120); live action films (117); souvenirs (106); mixed live and animated films (106); and records (91). Only 15 respondents had been to Walt Disney World in Florida and only 4 of those liked it well, but the majority had otherwise been exposed to every major category of Disney production. At least half of those exposed to a category liked it well except in three cases. Comic books, daily television shows, and records were well liked by one-third of those exposed to them. The majority of respondents "liked well" the feature animated films (125 of 161), Disneyland (100 of 142), and short animated features (90 of 141). The sample, therefore, represented not only "experts" on Disneyland, but persons very familiar with the full range of Disney representations, many of which are no more common in California than throughout the United States and various other countries.

The Experience of Disneyland

This chapter on Disneyland takes the park as a summary of the Disney universe of media experiences by moving through (a) a collective, in-depth trip through the park; (b) analogs and lessons of the Disney experience; (c) historical and economic background; (d) ideological implications; and (e) overall structural and semiotic meaning in Disney. Ethnographic descriptions attempt to convey a feeling for the delights of Disney as well as the conscious perceptions of visitors and more subtle meanings.

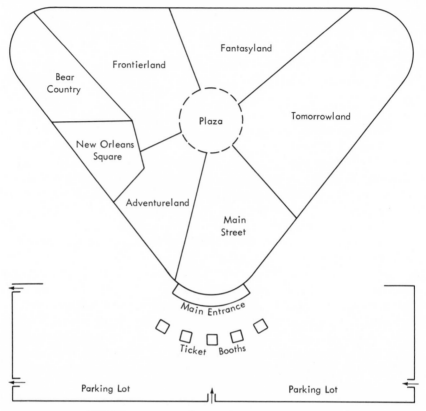

FIGURE 2–1   Map of Disneyland Amusement Park

Disneyland occupies 73.4 acres in Anaheim, California, an Orange County suburb of Los Angeles. It differs from amusement parks like Coney Island because of Walt's insistence on cleanliness, details of sight and sound, an emphasis on fun over "thrills," and story "themes" for attractions and areas in the park. It was constructed in one year at a cost of $17 million and opened on July 17, 1955 with 22 attractions. Twenty years later it offered 54 attractions, 30 food facilities, 50 shops, and services ranging from banking to pet care, and had given birth to an expanded East Coast park, Walt Disney World, near Orlando, Florida. Disneyland attracts about 10 million people a year, employs 3,500 (expanding to 6,500 in the summer months), and has nearly $200 million invested in it, with several major expansions in progress.[6] The map of the park shows six thematic "lands."

A plaque over the entrance to Disneyland reads: "Here you leave today and enter the world of yesterday, tomorrow, and fantasy." Park brochures quote Walt as saying, "I don't want the public to see the real world they live in while they're in the park. I want them to feel they are in another world." Disney explained the focus to Lloyd Shearer on a preview tour of Disneyland in 1955:

> What I'm trying to sell here in Anaheim is what everyone wants, happiness. You can call it corn or cotton candy or escape, or anything you want. But to me I'm selling happiness.
> Now, what's most conducive to happiness? Simply a pleasant experience in the company of happy, smiling, friendly people.... If this park ever becomes successful, and everyone tells me it's gonna fall flat on its face, it won't be because we keep it clean and don't sell gum or because we provide great fun and games—it will be because our personnel sincerely sells happiness. Hell! That's what we all want, isn't it? A little bit of happiness![7]

Providing an experience of "happiness" requires a careful screening out of undesirable elements and the staging of special activities expressing archetypal ideals. The Garden of Eden in the book of Genesis, Plato's Republic, Augustine's City of God, and the island Utopia of Thomas More were pictured as idealized, circumscribed visions of a perfect society. Monastic leaders like St. Benedict and community leaders like William Penn attempted to flesh out their ideals by creating living utopias. Disneyland similarly constitutes a world apart. It has clearcut physical boundaries, and it has established social boundaries as well by screening potential employees and visitors.

Disneyland is separated from the endless sprawl and freeway that make up greater Los Angeles by three physical boundaries: a parking lot with more acreage (107.3) than the park, a row of ticket booths, and the Santa Fe–Disneyland railroad which circumscribes the park. Strict standards restrict entry to the quasi-sacred interior of the park.

Hiring of park personnel is selective, and all employees are trained at the University of Disneyland, whose director specifies, "Our image is kind of square. We like outgoing, cleancut, enthusiastic people. And that's the kind who apply."[8] The vice-president in charge of both Disneyland and Walt Disney World adds, "When we hire a girl, we point out that we're not hiring her for a job, but casting her for a role in our show. And we give her a costume and a philosophy to prove it."[9] The "University" provides at least two days of talks, films, and walking through Disneyland. For years the park fought against long hair or facial hair on males or eye make-up on females, maintaining stricter grooming standards than the United States military. One employee observed that Jesus Christ, Louis Pasteur, Alfred Einstein, Sigmund Freud, and even Walt Disney with his mustache could not have worked at Disneyland.[10] Salaries are minimal; Disneyland summer salaries were raised in 1974 from

$1.70 to $2.20 per hour.[11] Despite these restrictions, when Walt Disney World opened in 1971, 35,000 persons applied for its 9,000 jobs.

Visitors to Disneyland, or "guests" as employees are taught to call them, are also screened. As they approach the ticket booths, a pleasant recorded voice welcomes them and explains the various ticket packages. Money is the first *sine qua non* for attendance. Of the questionnaire respondents, 85 usually purchased the least expensive ticket package ($6.00 for adults), 60 the most expensive ($7.00 for adults), and 24 admission only ($4.50, but since discontinued); another 24 attended as part of a group arrangement. Many attended with their immediate family (88) or with friends (59), and their groups averaged from 5 to 6 persons. Margaret King reports that adults outnumber children four to one in the park, and informal counts confirm that interesting proportion.[12] The ticket booths screen out the very poor and replace everyday currency with A, B, C, D, and E tickets, which circumvent irritating money changing inside and are special tokens allowing participation in the utopian dramas.

Visitors who pass the economic test must still meet the standards of Disneyland's appearance code. A dozen security officers unobtrusively scan the 2,000 persons who enter each hour, looking for glassy-eyed evidence of drugs, liquor smells, or large bags or backpacks, which are prohibited. But most rejections occur for wearing clothes the Disney ethic judges too skimpy or too controversial. Halter tops and bare midriffs were forbidden until 1973. Hot pants and microminis are allowed only if "not too much of the buttocks is hanging out," as a Disney official explains. Brassieres are preferred and the obviously braless are often rejected. According to Edwin Black, Disneyland and Walt Disney World prohibit *any* controversial or political messages on patches, buttons, or T-shirts, such as references to drugs, the Latin word *cannabis*, protests like "Make Love Not War," and certain political endorsements like "Don't blame me, I voted for McGovern."[13] The strictest standards are maintained at the high school graduation parties for which Disneyland remains open all night. The screening at the entrance preserves the "sacredness" of Disneyland just as similar appearance codes enforced by the Swiss guard in costumes designed by Michaelangelo ensure the sacredness of St. Peter's Basilica in the Vatican.

The initiate who passes the ritual requirements for entry then proceeds into a special universe centered on happiness. Here the sparkle and tinkle of delights help the initiate relax, eliminate any critical resistance, and receive the pleasures and lessons of the magic kingdom. In its representations of the frontier past and hypothetical future, of childhood fantasies and remote peoples and places, Disneyland becomes a trip deep inside the American psyche. Its popular images and assumptions are as typical and revealing of a particular culture as are the myths and legends of Arthurian knights, Bantu warriors, Hindi avatars, Cuban liberators, or Greek gods.

Questionnaire respondents ranked the lands of Disneyland on a 7-point scale from positive (7) to negative (1):

TABLE 2–1. Disneyland Preference Scale

	FEMALES	MALES	COMBINED
New Orleans Square	5.24	5.35	5.30
Tomorrowland	5.00	5.31	5.15
Fantasyland	5.08	4.59	4.83
Main Street	4.61	4.27	4.44
Adventureland	3.82	4.50	4.15
Frontierland	3.89	4.28	4.11
Bear Country	3.20	3.50	3.35

Variations according to sex were slight but interesting. Both sexes most preferred New Orleans Square. But for second place males chose the mechanical technology of Tomorrowland while females chose Fantasyland. Among males, commercialized Main Street ranked sixth and Fantasyland third. Females ranked Tomorrowland third and Main Street fourth. Next came Frontierland and Adventureland with males preferring Adventureland and females Frontierland. Both sexes ranked Bear Country last.

These rankings and the semiological significance of each area become more meaningful as we inquire in depth into the character of each area and identify both the surface representations and the more subtle perceptions of respondents.

Main Street, U.S.A.

Main Street, U.S.A., ushers the visitor/actor onto the stage, provides a reference point leading from fantasy to reality, opens onto and integrates other areas of the park, and constitutes a theme area of its own. This unavoidable first role also directly identifies the utopia with a particular country (the United States), a particular time (the turn of the century), a particular setting (a small Midwestern town), and a particular population (the middle class). Immigrants, cities, ethnic minorities, and factory or mine workers—past or present—are bypassed in the park brochure's quotes from Walt Disney:

> Many of us fondly remember our "small home town" and its friendly way
> of life at the turn of the century. To me, this era represents an important

part of our nation's heritage. On Main Street we have endeavored to re-capture those by-gone years. . . .

When you visit the arcades, the ice cream parlor, the market house and cinema where silent films play, we hope you will visualize, as I often do, your own home town Main Street, or the one your parents and grand-parents have told you about. Main Street is everyone's home town—the heartline of America.[14]

Main Street is an antique shop in reverse: the buildings are old-fashioned, the products modern. Paid attractions include brightly painted horse-drawn street cars, horseless carriages, an omnibus, fire engine, and terminals for the Santa Fe and Disneyland railroad. A recent Gulf Oil Corporation contribution offers a free museum and film of the Walt Disney story. For 25 cents the Main Street Cinema surrounds patrons with six silent classics playing simultaneously, including the first "story" film, Edwin S. Porter's 12-minute *The Great Train Robbery* from 1903, Disney's first Mickey Mouse film, and the first sound animated short, *Steamboat Willie* from 1928. Twenty-seven shops, stores, and food outlets border Main Street's sidewalks, featuring such quintessential American corporations as Coca-Cola, Carnation, Sunkist, Hallmark, Hills Brothers, Elgin, and Bank of America.

Typical of Disney's movie-set design sensitivity is the scale of the buildings on Main Street. Disney once said,

> It's not apparent at a casual glance that this street is only a scale model. We had every brick and shingle and gas lamp made seven-eighths true size. This costs more, but made the street a toy, and the imagination can play more freely with a toy. Besides, people like to think their world is somehow more grown up than Papa's was.[15]

According to Christopher Finch, the seven-eighths scale buildings in Walt Disney World in Florida "become even smaller in scale as they rise, creating an illusion of greater height by creating a distorted perspective."[16]

Responses to Main Street on the questionnaire were mixed. It was ranked fourth by females and sixth by males. Asked for "one word that represents your impressions of the area," respondents split in two direc-tions. Positive responses emphasized its quaint and neat qualities and included the following terms: first boom of excitement; colorful; amus-ing; fun; interesting; model-like; old; nostalgic; different; potpourri; musical; and fantastic. Negative responses showed a sense that Main Street was fundamentally a shopping center through which every Disney-land patron was forced to pass twice, and it was rated as trifling; plastic; crowded; tacky; and junk. Several terms from respondents referred nega-tively to the commercialism of Main Street: money; commercial; sales; spend; gyp joint; exploitative; rip-off.

Many respondents were conscious that behind the marching brass bands and costumed Disney characters on Main Street the purpose was realistic: to consume present day goods with real money. Louis Marin observes that the evocation of history serves to reconcile an idealized past with a real present, which legitimizes mundane commercialism for consumers suspicious of mass manipulation.[17] In addition, respondents remarked on the identified correspondence between Disneyland and the United States, which is made explicit in the plaque in the town square on Main Street. The plaque reads

TO ALL WHO COME TO THIS HAPPY PLACE:
WELCOME.
DISNEYLAND IS YOUR LAND. HERE AGE
RELIVES FOND MEMORIES OF THE PAST . . .
AND HERE YOUTH MAY SAVOR THE CHALLENGE
AND PROMISE OF THE FUTURE.
DISNEYLAND IS DEDICATED
TO THE IDEALS, THE DREAMS, AND THE HARD
FACTS THAT HAVE CREATED AMERICA . . .
WITH THE HOPE THAT IT WILL BE A SOURCE OF
JOY AND INSPIRATION TO ALL THE WORLD.
JULY 17, 1955.

Main Street makes it clear to the initiate that Disneyland is not pure, arbitrary fiction created whimsically in the spirit of Tolkein, or science fiction or entertainment unrelated to any real world. Rather, Main Street ushers the visitor into an indistinguishable mixture of fantasy and reality, enticingly blurring the edges of each. It performs three communications functions, as Marin has pointed out. First, it performs the *phatic* function of providing a primitive conduit that enables the participant to engage in communication. Second, it performs a *referential* function, referring the visitor from reality to fantasy, from a world of seemingly unambiguous definitions to a sphere in which reality becomes a phantasm and fantasies become real. Third, Main Street performs an *integrative* function, dividing Disneyland into the past on the left side and the future on the right side and interrelating the two.[18] While visitors to the park do not consciously consider such functions, the sample considered here was aware of the confusingly mixed result: a clever, quaint, delightful facade covering a subtly commercial, circumscribed experience.

Tomorrowland

Main Street brings the visitor to the foot of the Matterhorn; the area to the left is cluttered, but the right opens out to flowered lanes and the shiny sweep of Tomorrowland. Perhaps because of this, the majority of respondents, 90 of the 153 who identified their route, turned right toward Tomorrowland first, rather than left as suggested in the Disneyland guide.

Crowded Tomorrowland pictures the future in terms of space—outer space and inner space as envisioned by "America's foremost men of science and industry," according to Disney.[19] Ten ticketed attractions include smooth, noiseless people movers, rockets to the moon, submarines, and a trip into the inner space of the body: cells, molecules, atoms, and particles.

Male respondents ranked Tomorrowland second only to New Orleans Square, while females ranked it third. Positive one-word responses included several "spacey" and "imaginative" associations. Other positive terms were: modern; technology; progressive; imaginative; educational; decent; reassuring; all right; semi-informative; creative; unique; striking; fantastic; one of the best; love it; and yea. Those who chose negative terms for Tomorrowland emphasized an oddly outdated and plastic quality in Tomorrowland's concept of the future. Respondents called Tomorrowland: tinny; junk; simple; stupid; dumb; boring; loud; no feeling; old hat; for the old; commercial; and terrifying. One respondent labelled it simply "capitalist future."

Disneyland's representation of the future is pleasantly laid out, but its symbolic union of American past and universal future, its glorification of technology, and its cautious attachment to projections from current science and industry may help explain the reservations many voiced about its vision.

The United States and the American past are associated with Tomorrowland through the location at its entrance of the free, attractive, and well-known Bell presentation of the 360-degree film "America, the Beautiful." (Monsanto sponsors the same attraction in the Florida park.) After a smiling woman in the waiting room welcomes visitors on behalf of "the one million men and women of the Bell System," several hundred at a time are ushered into a large circular room divided by rails to lean on. Visitors then are free to stand, turn, and gasp as they are surrounded by a nine-section wrap-around movie projection that carries them, with lush musical accompaniment, through several dozen scenes from across the United States: mountains, plains, national parks, colonial villages, cowboys and cattle, skyscrapers, the Golden Gate, Gettysburg, the military academies, Jefferson and Lincoln monuments, the White House and Capitol, and closing shots of the Statue of Liberty in a violet dusk backed by a chorus ringing out "from sea to shining sea."

Another major free attraction dominated Tomorrowland until it was replaced in 1974: the GE Carousel of Progress. Extolling electronic and technological gadgetry, the exhibit featured stationary stages representing periods from 1880 to the near future—each populated with an *audioanimatronic* (mechanically moving and talking) father-narrator; a mother; a yipping, ear-wiggling family dog; and occasionally grandparents and teenagers. The seated audience was slid en masse around the five or six stage sections of the circular center to the accompaniment of a catchy tune about a "big, bright beautiful tomorrow."

In 1974 the Carousel of Progress was replaced by an audioanimatronic "America Sings," which slides audiences around animated performances of traditional Southern, Western, Gay Nineties, and Ragtime-Blues-Jazz-Rock oldies.The new attraction requires a paid ticket and ignores Tomorrowland's theme of the future in a tour of the American musical past reminiscent of Lawrence Welk.

Tomorrowland's future identifies with conventional industrial and scientific progress through its glorification of the machine. Nature, which can be found in artificial forms in other parts of the park, is absent from Tomorrowland. Electronic devices, mechanical conveniences, and industrial utensils provide movement, food, music, and words. Marin charges that the spectator, immobilized and passive, being passed around the circular stage, symbolizes "the passive satisfaction of endlessly increasing needs."[20] Tomorrowland does not deal with questions of specifically human welfare or of variations in social organization and ideals—nor was it ever intended to do so. In its effort to provide happiness, Tomorrowland suggests the future dreaded by Huxley and Orwell and the cool, efficient, multilevel city under Osaka, Japan, or the empty landscape of Kurt Vonnegut's *Breakfast of Champions*. The surface, of course, is bright and pleasant. When the Kids of the Kingdom rock group rises up with the Tomorrowland stage to sing endless choruses of "Joy to the World" from "Jeremiah Was a Bullfrog," whether they are real or audioanimatronic is a question the visitor is conditioned to care about no longer.

It is ironic that in a park built on imagination, as Peter Blake phrased it in *Architectural Forum*, "Tomorrowland may be the only disappointing piece of the giant cake." As he pointed out, "the *real* Tomorrowland is the vast infrastructure that no paying customer ever sees." The serious futuristics are in the huge basement that contains all the utilities and equipment; in the RCA communications network that monitors for mechanical and physical malfunctions throughout the park; in the jet-engined power plant; in the efficient, low-polluting mass transportation; and in the innumerable innovations in design throughout Disneyland and Walt Disney World.[21] Disney's original plans for the real domed city EPCOT (Experimental Prototype Community of Tomorow) as part of the Florida development are far more exciting than Tomorrowland with its evasion of housing, schools, employment, politics, and other probable problems of the future.

The symbolism of the first two areas of the park has nationalistic implications. Main Street canonizes the American past in the form of a small, middle-class Midwestern town. Tomorrowland baptizes the American future by glorifying mechanical science and consumer technology. Disneyland tends to capitalize on reflexes already familiar to its visitors without challenging or expanding them and provides the visitor with little motivation for critical self-awareness.

Fantasyland

Adjacent to Tomorrowland is a land ranked second by females and third by males. It is vintage Disney: Fantasyland. The park's pictorial souvenir quotes Disney as saying,

> When we were planning Fantasyland, we culled the lyrics of the song, "When You Wish Upon a Star." The words of that melody from our picture "Pinocchio," inspired us to create a land where dreams "come true." . . .
>
> Here in the "happiest kingdom of them all" you can journey with Snow White through the dark forest to the diamond mine of the Seven Dwarfs; flee the clutches of Mr. Smee and Captain Hook with Peter Pan; and race with Mr. Toad on his wild auto ride through the streets of Old London town.
>
> Dumbo, the elephant with the aerodynamic ears, will take you on a flight high above Fantasyland, while the haughty Caterpillar of Alice in Wonderland carries you down the Rabbit Hole into Upside Down Room and Tulgey Wood. In colorful Dutch canal boats or the Casey Jr. Circus Train, you'll journey through Storybook Land to see the homes of the Three Little Pigs, Pinocchio's Village, and Cinderella's Castle.[22]

Fantasyland is filled with images, characters, animals, and stories illustrated and made famous in animated films by Disney Productions. Images are here brought into three dimensions by transformation into wood, stone, plaster, plastic, and paint and by persons costumed as characters. It is a Jungian land of archetypes and myths, recalling some of Disney's greatest triumphs. Francis Clarke Sayers charges Disney with "debasement of the traditional literature of childhood" and criticizes "his treatment of folklore without regard for its anthropological, spiritual, or psychological truths."[23] But Richard Schickel separates out the early animations of Disney as his best creations, including the feature length animations:

> The best of them unpretentiously, perhaps unconsciously touched the great mythic themes: they were tales of loss and of quests, and even their most comic moments were haunted by weird and frightening figments of untrammeled imaginations. They were dream works, not in the press agent's sense of the word, but in Jung's. Snow White's flight through a forest

that seemed to come alive and clutch at her; the vision of the creation of the world in *Fantasia;* Pinocchio's search for his father, taking him through the grotesque amusement park on the island of lost boys and into the belly of a whale—these sequences strummed psychic chords that live-action comedies like *The Barefoot Executive* (1971) do not aspire to touch.[24]

Schickel is not satisfied with Disneyland, objecting that its "rides and electronic puppet shows are plasticized, sanitized pseudo experiences, pedestrian reductions of fantasies and adventures. They boggle the mind without stimulating it."[25] Louis Marin criticizes Fantasyland for its "phantasms of death, super-power, violence, destruction, annihilation" which present "reality in a regressive and hallucinatory form."[26]

Optimism and happy endings abound in Fantasyland, and William McReynolds finds life as a "glad game" at the heart of Disney's appeal. The plots of *Snow White, Sleeping Beauty, Dumbo, 101 Dalmations, Pollyanna,* and others cater to American optimism "by emphasizing the smiling aspects of life and insuring that goodness would eventually triumph."[27] McReynolds traces Disney's optimism to Dale Carnegie, Norman Vincent Peale, and politicians as divergent as Andrew Jackson, Dwight Eisenhower, and Hubert Humphrey. The figures of Snow White, Dumbo, the third Little Pig, Sleeping Beauty, and Pollyanna are goodness personified, while the Wicked Queen, the Big Bad Wolf, Malificient (the Fairy of Darkness), and the villainess Cruella De Vil represent unredeemable evil. Annihilation of the evil figures resolves the conflict. It is a simple child*ish* rather than child*like* world: divide into obvious good and evil, denounce and destroy the evil, watch goodness triumph "with a smile and a song."

Not all of Fantasyland fits that mold. The Small World attraction is a boat ride through banks of singing, swaying dolls. The park brochure says "Our musical fantasy features the songs and dances of youngsters from more than 100 nations, each singing in his own native language. For the grand finale, all children in the world join in to sing, 'It's a small world after all.' " As usual, there is no intellectual content, but in accordance with Coleridge's notion of the "willing suspension of disbelief for the moment," visitors can be utterly charmed. They wait in line in a rackety, busy environment, step down into a small boat that glides quietly on its track into a calm interior tunnel, and hear greetings and instructions piped in from girls in several languages. Quietly, children's voices sing the simple tune of "It's a Small World" with only the language and musical style of accompaniment, not the melody, changing as the visitors pass by each nationality of dolls. Many peoples and cultures are represented in caricature—except middle-class America. The music culminates in a bright, tinkling panoply of sound just before the visitors reemerge into the glaring, noisy external world with the Small World's last message subtly reminding everyone that Bank of America, too, extends throughout the world.

The cartoons playing in the Fantasyland Theatre are among the most historically and aesthetically interesting attractions in the park. Mickey Mouse and Donald Duck classics from the 1930s are shown in their full-color, flowing animation and with their gutsy, barnyard humor. *The Band Concert* (1935), which Gilbert Seldes called "Disney's greatest single work,"[28] can be viewed there, as can such delights as Mickey playing Alice in *Through the Mirror* (1938) or Donald, Mickey, and Goofy at their best in *Mickey's Trailer* (1936). Both the film of Walt Disney's life and the semiofficial book on his art are subtitled "From Mickey Mouse to the Magic Kingdom." If the parks are considered Walt Disney's most impressive medium, the Mickey Mouse cartoons have remained his most clever. Mickey, as the Disney trademark, has aged well, from his early Academy awards through his 1955 to 1959 stint as star of a daily television show featuring Annette, Cubby, Spin, Marty, and many mouseketeers, to his revival in *The Mouse Factory* and other features in the 1970s.

Survey respondents tended to be positive in their comments on Fantasyland. Few were bothered by its simplicity or the sometimes violent absoluteness of the resolutions of its plots. They enjoyed rather than worried about its lack of verisimilitude. The negative terms labelled Fantasyland unarousing; bland; monotonous; unimaginative; outdated; stupid; rank; escape; tinsel; and "drunk." Positive responses emphasized its childish fantasy assets: far out; bitching; best; favorite; exciting; alive; get high; spacey; ingenious; dream-like; another world; creative; for the young; and classic. William F. Lynch has argued that cultures have a perfect right to fantasy, but they must know what is fantasy and what is reality.[29] The honesty of Fantasyland is that there is no attempt to blur the difference. Ethnocentrism abounds in the exclusively WASP characterization in fairy tales, as Sayers puts it, "in which every prince looks like a badly drawn portrait of Cary Grant, every princess a sex symbol."[30] Nevertheless, Fantasyland recalls some of the early greatness of Disney. For older Disney fans, it makes even more regrettable the arrested development that kept his creativity safely popular and commercial and prevented his maturing as a genuine artist.

Frontierland

To the left side of the entrance and Main Street lie the less popular Frontierland and Adventureland, along with the unsuccessful Bear Country, and New Orleans Square, the most popular area in the park.

As the actors move on from the scripts of Fantasyland, they are likely to proceed to the mythic American past represented by Frontierland. The frontier has served as a backdrop for many of Disney's successes, from his first *Steamboat Willie* cartoon to the Davy Crockett fads.

Respondents altogether ranked Frontierland lowest of the six lands, although females ranked it slightly higher than Adventureland and males slightly preferred it over Main Street. Frontierland is perhaps less suited to our sample than it would be to a sample of older visitors, who might enjoy a placid ride aboard the Mark Twain steamboat, or of younger visitors, who could play on Tom Sawyer's Island. The island, according to employees, is the only attraction in the park designed completely by Disney himself. It offers a play fort, log cabins, and mules to ride—all for free. Disney once said, "I put in all the things I wanted to do as a kid—and couldn't, including getting into something free."[31] The island is free, of course, only to those who have already paid admission to the park.

Visitor responses to Frontierland included positive terms like quaint; nostalgic; rustic; intriguing; idealistic; fun with kids; relaxing; sing and relax; superb; and zowie. Several mentioned its physical and athletic qualities. Neutral associations included western; Indians; shooting galleries; souvenirs; flashback to early Disney effects; and something to do. Negative terms emphasized that the area was corny; stereotyped; a drag; had too many guns; and, according to many, dull. Other negative words that appeared only once each from respondents included slow; boring; plain; dud; mechanical; crowded; and unappealing. One respondent called Frontierland biased, and several said the Indians portrayed in it were "the least appropriate elements in the entire park."

As Marin emphasizes, Frontierland is built around scenes of conquest—conquest of the American frontier, of the American Indian who lived there, and of nature itself. It conveys the familiar drama, immortalized in textbooks and movies, of brave white men hewing out a living from the wilderness and bringing progress and civilization to a new land. Dick Gregory pinpoints a blind spot in such histories by suggesting that, when one wishes to seize another's property in a socially acceptable way, one does not steal, but "discovers" it.[32] Studies of popular westerns by John Cawelti[33] and Will Wright[34] suggest that the myth of the American West is more dependent on popular art formulas and current social conditions than on actual history. More specifically, Joseph Arpad's study of Davy Crockett has established how far removed the Disney–Fess Parker version of the man was from the actual historical figure, an egotistical hustler who loved ticker-tape parades and would never consider wearing a buckskin outfit in proper company.[35]

The myths of the Old West glorify barbaric treatment of American Indians and Mexican-Americans, just as myths of the Old South, such as New Orleans Square, whitewash the treatment of black slaves. The ethnocentrism of the frontiersman is maintained in Frontierland, continuing the mandate from Genesis to "subdue the earth," exploiting people and resources. Mechanically reconstructed animals and plants in the Nature's Wonderland part of Frontierland stand out as an antithesis to the sensitivity to nature maintained in real life by Native Americans. Disney is pictured in the official park brochures standing in Frontierland attired in full Indian headdress before Indian drums, but there is little evidence in Frontierland that he or the park ever seriously contemplated the Native American experience of the "opening of the frontier." Disneyland prefers popular middle-class stereotypes to firsthand evidence such as this description by Chief Luther Standing Bear of the Oglala Sioux:

> We did not think of the great open plains, the beautiful rolling hills, and winding streams with tangled growth, as "wild." Only to the white man was nature a "wilderness" and only to him was the land "infested" with "wild" animals and "savage" people. To us it was tame. Earth was bountiful and we were surrounded with the blessings of the Great Mystery. Not until the hairy man from the east came and with brutal frenzy heaped injustices upon us and the families we loved was it "wild" for us. When the very animals of the forest began fleeing from his approach, then it was that for us the "Wild West" began.[36]

Bear Country

An offshoot of Frontierland is Bear Country, ranked least popular among Disneyland's attractions. In fact, 51 respondents also designated Bear Country as the "least appropriate" attraction in the park, more than twice the number of objections to any other single attraction. Bear Country opened in 1973 and is the clearest example of the decline in quality control since Disney's death.

Bear Country reconstructs the feeling of the Northwest featuring a large lodge with restaurants and a floor show nestled among trees and a stream. The show, called the Country Bear Jamboree, recalls folksy mountain hospitality displayed by large stuffed bears singing and playing audioanimatronically.

Several respondents called Bear Country cute and nice, while others managed to avoid condemning it by calling it decent, mild, or marginal. Negatives came more easily, reemphasizing Bear Country's bottom ranking. Seven called it stupid, several blah, while others wrote wasted; boring; silly; absurd; plastic; hoaky; dumb; hickish; terrible; bad/sad; ugh; yuck; and zilcho. In many ways, Bear Country lacks the Disney touch. Traditional variety and balance in characters are absent. No small charming Jiminy Cricket, Timothy Mouse, or Tinker Belle offsets the slow, dull bulk of the mechanical bears. The usual park genius for participation and movement is forfeited in this floor-show motif, leaving the audience sitting passively in a large auditorium.

While in his later years Disney allowed many live-action formula films of minimal quality to be distributed, he constantly tinkered to improve details of his beloved park—where he kept an apartment on Main Street—and possessed a sharp eye for quality control in the projects he cared about. For example, he was not satisfied in *20,000 Leagues Under the Sea* with the scene of the battle between a giant squid and the submarine Nautilus, although it had been shot at tremendous expense. Walt insisted they change the backdrop from a pink sky to a simulated storm, prepare a new squid, and reshoot the entire sequence.[37]

Disney's own explanation of his role in the company came with his response to a boy to whom he had admitted that not only did he not draw Mickey Mouse but that he could not, nor could he possibly think up all the jokes and ideas. (Disney could not even imitate the flowing, world-famous "Walt Disney's" signature developed by studio artists.) He finally explained to the boy, "Sometimes I think of myself as a little bee. I go from one area of the studio to another and gather pollen and sort of stimulate everybody."[38] In fact, he was the Disney corporation's perfectionist, a quality control expert, as Schickel describes him. The mechanical routine and superficiality of Bear Country illustrate what his loss has meant to Disney enterprises.

Adventureland

As the actors proceed from their roles in the Old West of Frontierland to the exotic locales of Adventureland, they are much less likely to reflect on the bias and distortion of these scenes of the past and remote areas than to delight in the experience of feeling part of other times and places. Adventureland contains four main attractions: the Enchanted Tiki Room, a shooting gallery, the jungle river cruise, and a Swiss Family Robinson treehouse—and eight shops and stands.

Female respondents ranked Adventureland next to last, and males ranked it fourth. The usual contrasts of boring and dull as opposed to fun and exciting appeared. Other associations were: worthwhile; neat; big rides; dig it; silly but exciting; jungle-cruise; exotic; treehouse. Several obviously confused Adventureland and Frontierland, placing Tom Sawyer's Island here. Negative terms covered a range: fake; phony; plastic; asphalt; puzzling; disappointing; touristy; unreal; so-so; semi-boring; racist; and Ziegler. The last two terms deserve expansion.

In their book on breaking the Watergate conspiracy, Robert Woodward and Carl Bernstein interrupt a description of presidential press secretary Ron Ziegler's denials of White House involvement, in order to recall Ziegler's earlier work:

> Some of the reporters recalled that Ziegler's talent for communication had first been tested as a Disneyland barker during summer vacations from college, taking tourists on the Jungle Ride. "Welcome aboard, folks. My name is Ron. I'm your skipper and guide down the River of Adventure. . . . Note the alligators. Please keep your hands inside the boat. They're always looking for a hand out. Look back at the dock; it may be the last time you ever see it. Note the natives on the bank; they're always trying to get a head.
>
> Now Ziegler was running the President's Jungle Ride.[39]

In fact, Richard Nixon, and another Republican president, Dwight Eisenhower, are prominent in the Gulf displays and film on Main Street, U.S.A., in "The Walt Disney Story." (Walt Disney's ties with conservative Republican politics became more noticeable late in his life, culminating in his support for Barry Goldwater in 1964, the year before Disney died.)

One black, male respondent charged that "Adventureland Africans are a racist stereotype." On the Jungle Cruise, besides the spear-waving natives along the shore, is the "humorous trapped safari," which consists of four red-capped porters, all blacks, who cling bug-eyed to a tree with their white client above them as a menacing rhinoceros stands below. Why such racist images are popular and why Americans (and others) react so uncritically to them are described in detail in Richard A. Maynard's study, "How Dark Is a Dark Continent?—Myths about Tropical Africa Created by Motion Pictures." From *Trader Horn* and *Tarzan, the Ape Man* through *Stanley and Livingston, King Solomon's Mines, Something of Value,* and *The Nun's Story* to *The Naked Prey* and *Dark of the Sun,* Hollywood films set in Africa give the impression "that Africa spawned a savage people, a lower form of life. How could the American descendants of such people be expected to turn out much better?"[40]

Maynard does not mention Disney, but Edmund Carpenter does.

> The success of Disney's TV series on people and places was based on this formula. Twenty cultures were chosen, scattered among tundra, desert and jungle, but even though the people dressed in different clothes and ate different foods, they were all alike, members of a single culture. That culture was *our* culture—more accurately, our cliched image of ourselves: the Hallmark Greeting Card view.
>
> . . . . What if they aren't like us?

Carpenter adds a warning that raises serious questions about Disneyland's freedom with history and geography:

It's easy to enslave souls within media. One begins by depriving a man of his true identity, which he controls, then substituting a false identity, which the conqueror controls.[41]

Frontierland and Adventureland, in and by themselves, do not destroy authentic identities and implant false identities. But in conjunction with similar distortions and falsifications in textbooks, travelogues, and throughout mass meda, unchecked by contrary accurate and objective pictures of the American past or the Third World, Disneyland does enable false myths to survive. Indeed, it undoubtedly strengthens them. The visitors' reality-testing mechanisms are suspended in the park. Even the sense organs do not work because nothing is what it appears to be and nature is replaced by mechanical reproductions. The elephant rocking and spouting playfully under the waterfall on the Jungle Cruise is a machine, just as President Lincoln on Main Street is a machine that stands and talks. Marin is suspicious of this falsificatoin of the natural in Frontierland and Adventureland. He writes

On the left of the map, we see the culture supplied by the Americans in nineteenth century America, or by adult, civilized, male, white people at the same time in exotic and remote countries. Now, all the living beings we meet in this part are only the reproduction of real living beings . . . this world is only the appearance taken on by the machine in the utopian play. In other words, what is signified in the left part of the map is this assumption: the Machine is truth, the actuality of the living. Mechanism and a mechanical conception of the world, which are basic tenets of the utopian mode of thinking from the sixteenth century until today, are at work in Disneyland, no longer as a form of knowledge but as a disguised apparatus which can be taken for its contrary: natural life.[42]

Not all critics would agree that racism and imperialism are evident in the ethnocentricity of Adventureland and Frontierland, and questionnaire responses certainly do not prove the charge. Still, four black respondents noted the absence of black history from Disneyland, and many respondents requested fairer representations of ethnic minorities and other cultures. Many Asians, Chicanos, and Afro-Americans visit the park; their history and culture are not represented even though Disney products are spread throughout the world. Mickey Mouse may be the most universally recognized symbol in the world, comparable to the Coke bottle. Disneyland and Walt Disney World attract thousands of foreign visitors. The parks and other Disney media could offer highly imaginative myths, legends, and natural wonders drawn from all over the world rather than focusing heavily on American and European tales evident in Frontierland and other areas of the park.

Marshall McLuhan notes that "whatever pleases teaches more effectively."[43] In the "Walt Disney Story" showing on Main Street, Walt explains that the True-Life Adventure series of films, which began with *Seal Island* in 1949 and included more than a dozen two-reel and feature-length films between 1950 and 1960, were motivated by a desire to educate, but to educate by entertaining. Adventureland is the park's equivalent to innovative films such as *The Living Desert* and *The African Lion*. But Adventureland's mechanical and narrow representations of remote lands raises the fear as much as the hope that the area may teach as well as entertain.

New Orleans Square

The actor has one major role left to play in Disneyland—that of a visitor to an old New Orleans complete with pirates and a haunted mansion. This area was ranked number one by respondents. On a 7-point scale, males rated it 5.35 and females 5.24, to give New Orleans Square an overall rating of 5.30. The only other area to rate above 5 was Tomorrowland, at 5.15. However, 17 male respondents listed New Orleans Square as an inappropriate part of the park, a negative response surpassed only by the reaction of the 51 people who said the same of Bear Country. New Orleans Square apparently has high impact. It is unique in the midst of eclectic and generically titled areas like Fantasyland, Tomorrowland, Adventureland, and Frontierland; it refers to a specific city.

The reproductions are exquisite in detail and features like jazz combos liven the area, but Pirates of the Caribbean and the Haunted Mansion are the big attractions in New Orleans Square. One-word associations of respondents seemed to apply to the area in general. A few negative or neutral terms were offered: empty; satirized; rip-off; technical; elderly; too unreal; honky-tonk; and gingerbread. A few positive terms referred to the periodicity of the area, with five respondents mentioning nostalgia and others mentioning quaint; historic; and reminiscent. The style of New Orleans Square evoked: classic; elegant; realistic; and artistic. The experience was described as: busy; participating; enjoyable; fun to do; fantastic; relaxing; super-neat; a flash; and there were several of the inevitable "far outs." Other characteristics elicited were: cool (in degrees); food; jazz; and not-scary haunted house.

Pirates of the Caribbean was by far the most popular attraction in the park; 52 named it "most favorite," well ahead of the second-place Matterhorn ride. Pirates of the Caribbean takes the visitor on an undersea boat ride to a seaport being looted and burned by buccaneers. Marin suggests moral and economic interpretations of the symbolism in this attraction, focusing on the opening sequence in which skulls and skeletons lie on heaps of gold, silver, diamonds and pearls.

The narrative unfolds its moments in reverse chronological order; the first scene in the tour-narrative is the last scene in the "real" story. And this inversion has an ethical meaning: crime does not pay. The morality of the fable is presented before the reading of the story in order to constrain the understanding of the fable by a pre-existing moral code. So the potential force of the narrative, its unpredictability, is neutralized by the moral code which makes up all of the representations.... Main Street, USA, signifies to the visitor that life is an endless exchange and a constant consumption and, reciprocally, that the feudal accumulation of riches, the Spanish hoarding of treasure, the Old World conception of gold and money, are not only morally criminal, but are economic signs and symptoms of death. The treasure buried in the ground is a dead thing, a corpse. The commodity produced and sold is a living good, because it can be consumed.[44]

While Marin's is a possible interpretation of Pirates of the Caribbean, an interpretation from Ariel Dorfman and Armand Mattelart's study of Disney comic books seems more likely. The condemnation of the pirate treasure is ambiguous and the distinction between accumulating wealth and constantly consuming seems secondary to the emphasis on wealth and consumption in general.

Dorfman and Mattelart analyzed the plots and symbolism of 103 issues of Disney comic books in South America. They found that over 75 percent of the plots were built around a search for treasure in the form of gold, jewels, pearls, crowns, precious idols, and the like. For example, Donald Duck and his nephews were commissioned by Uncle Scrooge to locate a long-lost treasure in Inca-Blinca Land where they encountered the Beagle Boys (or a local equivalent) and, after a struggle, won the treasure for Uncle Scrooge and themselves. Dorfman and Mattelart observed that the treasure was then removed from the local "savages" who had failed to appreciate its worth, converted into money, and placed in Uncle Scrooge's bins full of dollars and coins. The researchers concluded that the overriding goal was monetarization: *"Disneylandización es una dinerización."*[45] While the Pirates of the Caribbean seem rather like Scrooge, they also recall the cowboy virtues of Frontierland: the competitive, individualistic scramble for wealth and power through the use of ingenuity and force.

A second popular attraction in New Orleans Square is the more recently constructed Haunted Mansion. The experience is constructed and controlled as in a motion picture, moving the audience through a plot by a structured sequence of visual devices. The place of the camera is taken by the visitor as he/she is carried by a cart running on rails.

In the Haunted Mansion the techniques are varied and the evil threats are obviously superficial. There is less reliance on the cumbersome audioanimatronic figures and more on clever special effects such as glass and mirror constructions that make wispy ghosts float around an otherwise empty ballroom, a hologram of a witch's head, humorous spirits made to appear to ride in the cart with the visitor, and various coffins, skeletons, vultures, and cemeteries. The creaky sounds, eerie voices, and visual effects provide antiseptic horrors that in no way threaten the visitor. They are not disorienting in the way the scary scenes in *Snow White* and other early Disney features were. Pauline Kael accused Disney of immorality in making terror so real for children. She says she did not want her children to see the scene in *Dumbo* where Dumbo is torn from his mother during a terrible storm with circus tents flapping and collapsing and elephants shrieking wildly. It is the most immediately threatening experience a child can imagine.[46] The Haunted Mansion is innocuous compared to that scene, the fire scene in *Bambi,* or the Island of Lost Boys in *Pinocchio.*

Some evidence indicates that the overall effect of the left side of Disneyland and its picture of the American past and geographically distant places blends into an indistinct whole in the impressions of the visitor. The borderlines between Frontierland, Adventureland, and New Orleans Square are recalled imprecisely. For example, several respondents placed Mark Twain in New Orleans Square and Tom Sawyer in Adventureland, whereas both appear in Frontierland. The representations of the American past mix with and reinforce those of Main Street. In Walt Disney World, the nationalism and patriotism are more explicit with the addition of Liberty Square, a reproduction of a colonial town.

Mr. Lincoln

On leaving or entering Disneyland, the visitor inevitably enters the Main Street theater featuring "Great Moments with Mr. Lincoln." Walt Disney World's expanded version surounds Mr. Lincoln with the other computerized, vinyl-clad presidents from Washington to the incumbent. First created as the Illinois pavilion for the 1964 New York World's Fair, the Lincoln exhibit combined Walt Disney's ideal folk hero and his ideal of animation in the round, "the grand combination of all the arts." The audioanimatronic technique had first been attempted with mechanical dancing Buddy Ebsen dolls as early as 1945 in the Disney studios. Finally, with the transitorized miniaturization and magnetic tape controls developed by NASA, in 1964 the facial and bodily movements of a figure controlled by pneumatic and hydraulic valves could be synchronized with dialogue, music, light, and sound, combining up to 438 cues per second. As Richard Schickel remarked, "Thus was the sixteenth president, martyr, hero and summary of the virtues of democratic man turned into a living doll."[47] Finch noted that, unless the energy locked up in the figure can be precisely controlled, "the figure can become quite violent."[48] One survey respondent recalled seeing Mr. Lincoln jerk out of control in mid-performance and almost threaten the disgruntled audience with his violent twitchings.

Disneyland's Lincoln has provoked conflicting judgments. Finch labels "extraordinary" the impact of the gestures, facial expressions, eye movements and shifting of weight, all culminating in a soaring "Battle Hymn of the Republic."[49] Leo Litwak remarks that Lincoln's speech is surprisingly uncontroversial.

> [It] needn't offend any political persuasion whether Robert Welch's or Jefferson Davis'. Lincoln has been redeemed for all America as a nonpartisan President whose rhetoric is reminiscent of General Douglas MacArthur's. . . . There is no evidence in his speech of the slavery issue, or the Civil War. This is the Lincoln we can all accept without reservation.[50]

Schickel is blunt:

> Disney, caught in the grip of his technical mania and protected by his awesome innocence about aesthetic and philosophical matters, had brought forth a monster of wretched taste which, for all the phony reverence and pomposity surrounding its presentation, leaves one in a state of troubled tension. Are we really supposed to revere this ridiculous contraption, this weird agglomeration of wires and plastic, transferring to it, in the process, whatever genuine emotions we may have toward Lincoln in particular, toward mankind in general.[51]

But the Lincoln exhibit remains popular and evoked only a few cynical remarks from questionnaire respondents.

The Effects of Disneyland

And so the actors leave Disneyland, exiting from their many roles, and go off stage, generally exhausted, delighted, and incapable of, as well as disinclined toward, analyzing the meaning and effect of the jumbled experience. Consciously, visitors can mumble "It was fun." Only later can they begin to filter out the subliminal or conscious lessons of the park. The questionnaire asked a number of questions designed to outline these effects. "How have your feelings toward Disneyland changed over time?" "What other experiences in your life have been similar to attending Disneyland?" "What personal virtues do Disney presentations approve and what vices do they disapprove?" "Does Disney represent a social ideology?" "Has Disney influenced you very much?" In general, the responses of the 192 subjects tended to bear out the utopian morality play interpretation; that is, that the Disney universe teaches values while it entertains.

Despite critical comments, the overwhelming reaction to the park was positive, especially during early years. Asked to rank on a 7-point scale their overall feelings toward Disneyland at different ages and to estimate their parents' feelings, the sample's responses are shown in Table 2–2. Only 10 respondents took a clearly militant stand and said they would *not* take their chlidren to Disneyland.

TABLE 2–2. Reactions to Disneyland

	FEMALE	MALE	COMBINED
Age 0–14	6.16	6.13	6.15
Age 14–20	5.58	5.04	5.25
Presently	4.57	4.38	4.45
Parents	4.91	4.74	4.79

Effects on the Individual

The analogs of Disneyland, as identified by respondents, are revealing of the nature of the Disney universe of meaning. The questionnaire asked, "What other experiences in your life have seemed most like the experience of attending Disneyland?" Some responses were predictable, others surprising, and a few (notably comparisons to drugs) presumably embarrassing to usual Disney standards.

Other amusements were the most common answer. Specific amusement parks were mentioned by 28 respondents. Each of the following were mentioned at least three times: Knott's Berry Farm, Six Flags Over Texas, Magic Mountain, and the World's Fair. Other parks mentioned were Sea World in San Diego; Marineland in Los Angeles; Riverview in Chicago; West Point Park in Pennsylvania; Harper's Ferry in Virginia; and Balboa Park in San Diego. More general amusement places and events mentioned were national parks; fairs; zoos; a carnival; a parade; western towns; historical landmarks; and picnics.

Specific activities similar to attending Disneyland also included reading fairy tales; reading *Readers Digest*; watching television; viewing *Sound of Music*; attending a football game; and, according to four respondents, attending a rock concert. Respondents also referred to specific places as similar to Disneyland: Las Vegas; San Diego; Fashion Valley

Shopping Center; the University of California; and, in the words of one, "school (really!)." Others mentioned travel, specifying Europe, India, and Nepal; driving; being always on the go; and flying an F-4 Phantom. Some comparisons were ethereal or sentimental. Eight compared Disneyland to dreaming; one mentioned Christmas, another puberty; one said marriage, and another specified having a girl friend.

Inevitably in Southern California, comparison was made with altered states of consciousness stimulated not from outside as in Disney experiences but from inside by drugs. Roughly 10 percent of the sample (19 respondents in all) mentioned the effect of drugs as the experience most similar to Disneyland. Six simply said "drugs." Two mentioned keg parties with LSD. Ten named LSD itself. One mentioned psylopsybin, or magic mushrooms. In her comments, one respondent described riding in the Monsanto trip through inner space and noting that "the place reeked of pot."

Disneyland's association with drugs is curious. In the 1960s, when acid and other hallucinogens became fads, certain Disney movies were received with renewed popularity on campuses and among the youthful counter-culture. *Life* ran a feature in 1969 on the inventive aspects of *Fantasia* under the heading "Disney's Secret Freak-Out." Undocumented rumors allege both that Disney was an early experimenter in hallucinogens back in the 1930s and that *Alice in Wonderland* was withheld from normal recirculation for a time in the late 1960s or early 1970s because of its association with drug-induced hallucinatory experiences.

Undoubtedly, the Jefferson Airplane's popular "White Rabbit," which Art Linkletter condemned across the nation for its "one pill makes you larger, and one pill makes you small" lyrics, evoked Disney images in the minds of listeners. Disneyland officially, however, has always been opposed even to the clothing and hair styles associated with so-called drug cultures. The tension of attraction and rejection erupted in the Yippie invasion and seizure of Tom Sawyer Island where they raised a revolutionary flag in August of 1970.

Despite the park's adamant opposition to drugs and dissent, including arresting and prosecuting for possession of marijuana, respondents in 1975 still mentioned getting stoned or tripping to go to Disneyland. (In fact, the author himself has seen an Englishman on a bench near the submarine ride openly rolling and smoking a substance carried in a tobacco package but smelling unmistakeably like marijuana.) One respondent remarked, "I enjoy Disneyland more now because I always get stoned." Disneyland insists that its high should be strictly natural, but the experience is too "trippy" ever to evade completely the association with what John Prine sings of as an "illegal smile." One twenty-one-year-old white male who has visited Disneyland over forty times responded, "Disneyland is like an LSD experience without taking the drug."

More generally, respondents did not compare Disneyland to their home town, their youth, or the Midwest, despite the obvious references in various Disneyland attractions. Instead, they compared the park to specific planned experiences. They emphasized commercial entertainment but mixed in euphoric feelings and secure peak experiences. They seemed concerned with the sensation more than the symbolism, with the medium more than the message of the park. Almost without exception, the comparisons reveal Disneyland as an experience entered into for its own sake. Eschewing parallels engaged in for secondary or deferred rewards, respondents seemed to enjoy the park directly as an end in itself.

Does Disney Influence? When directly confronted with Disney's influence on them, respondents replied ambiguously. Responses to the question, "Do you think Disney products have influenced you very much?" are given in Table 2-3.

TABLE 2-3. The Influence of Disney Products

	FEMALES	MALES	COMBINED
Yes	40	53	93
No	24	47	71

However, some who denied it had influenced them qualified their response. They seemed to take the "very much" as an absolute. For example, one respondent, who had visited the park eight times for an average of eight hours each time, had been exposed to every category of Disney product, and had liked very much the products in ten of those thirteen categories, claimed no influence. Another who had visited Disneyland more than twenty times for an average of six hours per visit claimed the same. A twenty-year-old Asian male expressed the reaction of many: "The frightening thing is that I do not know the extent of the influence."

Those who explained what kind of influence Disney had had on them were generally grateful. Respondents mentioned that Disney had given American children a feeling for nature and wildlife, especially children confined to the "asphalt jungles," as one put it. Disney, they said, had stimulated their imaginations, taught them how to make believe, and even encouraged them to talk to animals. Disney provided leisure and security. Several mentioned that Disney characters had been their "teachers," and seven felt Disney had taught them middle-class virtues. One striking response came from a twenty-three-year-old black female: "Yes. I grew up on Disney films. That's all I was allowed to see. I wanted to have adventures and have money and be spoiled like these lucky white kids were. Hayley Mills was my idol. Pollyanna was my dream." Another respondent summarized: "Disney products were a very important socializing force on my early childhood."

Disney Virtues and Vices. If Disneyland functions in any sense as a morality play, audiences should easily identify virtues and vices in Disney presentations. Responses supported that hypothesis.

The question was: "What personal virtues do you think are especially approved in Disney presentations?" The first column in Table 2–4 lists virtues mentioned most frequently, the second column lists virtues associated with Americanism (since these seemed to form a distinct category), the third column presents virtues mentioned only by females, and the fourth column lists those virtues mentioned only by males.

A similar distribution, shown in Table 2–5, can be made of answers to the question, "What personal vices do you think are especially disapproved in Disney presentations?"

The contrasts between the two tables indicate how clear and unam-

TABLE 2–4. Virtues Approved by Disney

MULTIPLE MENTION	AMERICANISM	FEMALE	MALE	
kindness	America	order	reverence	acceptance
honesty	All American	nobility	courage	no conflict
truth	apple pie	black vs. white	godliness	tolerance
happiness	mom & apple pie	motherly	helpfulness	complacency
smile	patriotism	good samaritan	recreation	benevolence
friendliness	(six mentions)	fortitude	cuteness	escapism
innocence		virginity	progressivism	curiosity
sweetness		accuracy	punctuality	Boy Scouts
generosity		compassion	precision	compete
sharing		beauty	resourcefulness	
creativity			winning	
thriftiness			spend money	
money			consumption	
industriousness			imperialism	
obedience			naiveté	
cleanliness				

TABLE 2–5   Vices Disapproved by Disney

MULTIPLE MENTION	FEMALE	MALE
sex	hippies	controversy
violence	individuality	bohemianism
greed	deviation from norm	urbanism
dope	idleness	serious anger
long hair	slovenliness	adulthood
crime	rudeness	hate
stealing	unkindness	meanness
smoking	dishonesty	cussing
laziness	hoarding money	poverty
lying	cheating	ambition
un-American activities	selfishness	intelligence
left politics	cruelty to animals	left wing
	debauchery	

biguous are Disney lessons on virtues and vices. Certain virtues, such as kindness, were mentioned a dozen times, and one so-called vice, sex, was mentioned sixteen times. But there was no crossing over. No one mistook for a virtue what someone else thought was presented as a vice, and vice-versa. Whether respondents thought Disney influenced them or not, they knew what Disney presentations approved or disapproved.

Disney's Perceived Relation to the Social System

In order to test whether respondents also thought Disney presentations approved and disapproved specific political and economic structures, the questionnaire asked, "Do you think Disney presents a particular social ideology?" To that, 144 answered yes and 19 no, with the males responding negatively more frequently than the females. Respondents' explanations of their answers suggest further dimensions of the internal landscape that Disney shaped in audiences.

A number of such explanations specified concepts not associated with any one particular social system. For example, many respondents mentioned fun, leisure, perfection, and entertainment. A number of responses referred to childhood imagination: fantasy; fantasizes life; make believe; stimulates childhood dreams; we are all children occasionally; and imagination is okay. Various respondents, even ones who disagreed with Disney's ideology, mentioned that Disney nevertheless enabled them "to grow up with an imagination." Another simply said gratefully, "I never knew a Disneyless world." Other positive phrases mentioned in regard to social ideology portrayed such universal ideals as a happy world; good triumphs; peace; harmony; security; samaritanism; and the family.

More system-specific references mentioned formal ideologies. For example, four respondents mentioned democracy and eleven capitalism as Disney's ideology. Others, especially those in high school, mentioned aspects of Americanism: all-American; God and country; American dream theme; nationalism; and mom's apple pie. At least four categories of response referred to race: separatism; white-washed ideology; stereotyping; and white middle class. Other negative comments on ideological implications included intellectual anaesthesia; disregard of reality; means of escape; and anthropomorphic unrealistic way of life.

A few participant observations on the ideology questions warrant quoting. A twenty-year-old white female complained, "All the characters get married, have kids, the men work . . . middle-class stereotypes even in cartoons." Another called Disney's universe "a world constructed without regard for certain realities—sex, unequal wealth, intellect." Three black female respondents from different schools remarked in turn: "white, middle-class America," "white, middle-class America—the American Dream," and "All-American-Anglo-Saxon-Democracy—Equality and Justice for All." A twenty-three-year-old white female respondent expanded on the answer by writing

> Disney has accurately and professionally done an excellent job of portraying all aspects of modern capitalistic American ideology free of any potent criticism or hints of injustice in the ideology and systems. . . . [The presentations] have largely been the basis for how I would construct an animated fantasy world as a kid, which in part was the way I perceived reality and would decide what I wanted to do in the future.

More typical, if less thought-provoking, was the conclusion of a twenty-one-year-old white male: "Disney has added a fun element, an American institution that binds Americans in a common experience."

The consistency of answers on virtues, vices, and ideology indicates that Disney presentations possess the definition necessary to have considerable effect on the individual and the social system. That conclusion can be combined with the Surgeon General's research, which partially establishes a causal link between media exposure and subsequent belief and behavior. No one has yet proven that Disneyland, other Disney offerings, and similar "entertainment" media and messages do *not* exert influence in the United States and throughout the world. Ultimately, the Disney universe seems to compete with religious, educational, political, economic, and familial forces in setting ultimate standards for reality and behavior.

Disneyland as Moral Educator

The role that visitors play in the Disneyland drama obviously has identifiable characteristics and immerses them in a specific set of values and cultural preferences. What is the most telling categorization for the experience? The Disney experience might be categorized as merely value-free entertainment and escape. Or it might be elevated to the positive category of formal education or the negative category of overt propaganda. Those categories seem extreme and out of balance for Disney, even though elements of each are present. A middle category seems most appropriate: The *morality play* integrates the appeal of entertainment through its dramatic structure and the effect of teaching through its ethical lessons. As a morality play of secular American values, Disneyland utilizes entertainment, education, mythology, and utopianism to typify, strengthen, and spread a patriotic American's idealized vision of nation and world, of the past, the present, and the future.

The central idea of Disneyland shows through as "happiness," and the achievement of happiness has long been the goal of classical Western ethical systems. Aristotle reasoned that the ideal of happiness could best be achieved by living with sufficient material goods, as a participating citizen of the polis, maintaining excellence and moderation in all virtues, and focusing on the pleasures of the mind. The operation of the intellect, Aristotle reasoned in his *Ethics* (X,7), "aims at no end beyond itself and finds in itself the pleasure which stimulates it to further operations; . . . in it must lie perfect happiness." Thomas Aquinas, in a similar manner, defined the goal of life as happiness and then attempted to identify what happiness might be. He discussed at great length the advantages and disadvantages of all the obvious possibilities—pleasure, fame, honor, wealth, and so on—that might bring happiness. He concluded that the means to human happiness was the perfect operation of the intellect contemplating the highest object, God; hence, the "beatific vision" as the goal of Catholic religious life. On a popular and mass level rather than on the sophisticated elite level of Aristotle and Aquinas, Disney presentations generally offer a similar kind of values clarification. Disney has added the skills of the artist and dramatist and offered an actual experience of what he understood and felt as happiness. At the same time, like Aristotle and Aquinas, he suggested the virtues and vices that enable one to achieve a life of happiness.

Morality plays normally serve a particular religion, as, for example, *Everyman* did for the Christianity of the late Middle Ages. Questionnaire responses indicate that Disney's ethical dramas seem to serve the "civil religion" of America, which combines the strains of the Puritan theocrats and the republican Founding Fathers. Disney presentations lack the "ultimacy" necessary to be considered religious. Nevertheless, to the rootless youth of southern California, Disney becomes an important reality-adjusting mechanism; the Disney universe offers a larger-than-life ground and source of beliefs about life and people and society. The Disneyland morality play reflects the larger American civil religion in its *creed*, the mythological pantheon of ultimates personified in Disney characters; in its *code*, the socially approved "good" Puritan behaviors and their opposites; and in its *cult*, the regular ritual communion with the larger national civil religion available to participants through television, movies, comic books, parks, and similar media. The conclusion to every Mickey Mouse Club program—"M-I-C. See you real soon. K-E-Y. Why? Because we *like* you!"—was like a final blessing at the end of a religious service. An individual performer in a Hollywood studio pronounced that the scattered anonymous millions were "liked." Every viewer was told that he or she was personally approved by Jimmy Dodd and, by extension, all Mouseketeers, Uncle Walt, the Disney corporation, and presumably whatever gods may be. The expression may have been partially a con, partially a zen-like statement that "what is, is good," and partially a foreshadowing of the American hunger to be reassured that "I'm okay; you're okay."

Disney never considered himself a religious leader, but he did occasionally refer to himself as an educator. He generally avoided associating himself with audio-visual pedantics and with the traditional formal classroom that McLuhan calls "an obsolete detention home, a feudal dungeon."[52] Contemporary formal schooling generally avoids the techniques such as folk tales, communal rituals, imitative role playing, and, for productive tasks, working apprenticeships. In the United States, pluralism prevents the direct teaching of ethics, metaphysics, or theology in the public schools. This leaves a vacuum for students—one not always filled by familial religious-ethnic interpretations of behavior and values. Mass-mediated culture is available to fill the void.

Disney presentations, of course, are not *only* morality plays. But using the genre of morality play to study Disney illustrates how mass-mediated culture impinges on basic definitions of reality and behavior. Even natural, immediate experiences are filtered through the lens of mass-mediated culture. One questionnaire respondent admitted, "The first time I slept along the Mississippi River in Louisiana I said, 'Wow! This is just like on the first part of Pirates of the Caribbean.' "

Disney and American Society

Looking at the Disney universe as *system-specific* both confirms and transcends the numerous aesthetic and political critiques of Disney. As the first chapter noted, a structural symmetry connects mass-mediated culture—in this case, Disneyland—with internal consciousness—in this case, personal values and ideology. On the other side of mass-mediated culture, a structural symmetry connects mass-mediated culture with the political-economic institutions that organize material life in society—in this case mass democracy within a capitalist framework. The economic evolution of the Disney empire illustrates this latter dimension of the isomorphism among structures of *consciousness, communication* (including mass-mediated culture), and *institutions*.

Before World War II, Disney enjoyed great success aesthetically and internationally, but not economically. He produced the first animated cartoon with sound in 1928; the first animated cartoon in color in 1932 (by gaining exclusive cartoon rights to Technicolor's three-color process); the first feature-length animation, *Snow White and the Seven Dwarfs*, in 1937; and the first stereophonic film, *Fantasia*, in 1940. Disney characters were international celebrities. Mickey Mouse was first banned and later tolerated by Nazi Germany; expelled from Yugoslavia; denounced as meek and then accepted as satire by the U.S.S.R.; viewed enthusiastically by King George V, Queen Mary, Franklin Delano Roosevelt, Benito Mussolini, and other world leaders; immortalized in wax by Madame Tussaud; worn as a neck charm by remote tribesmen; used to merchandise products worth many millions of dollars; and recognized as one of the most universal symbols in the history of humankind. During this period, David Low, an English political cartoonist, made his famous assessment of Walt Disney:

> I do not know whether he draws a line himself. I hear that at his studio he employs hundreds of artists to do the work. But I assume that his is the direction, the constant aiming after improvement in the new expression, the tackling of its problems in an ascending scale and seemingly without aspirations over and above mere commercial success. It is the direction of a real artist. It makes Disney, not as a draftsman but as an artist who uses his brains, the most significant figure in graphic art since Leonardo.[53]

But the ambition and perfectionism of Walt's projects prevented his brother Roy, the business manager of Disney enterprises, from turning a profit. In 1940 an employee strike against low wages disillusioned and embittered Disney. In the same year, debts from building a new studio in Burbank and the high production costs of *Snow White* and *Fantasia* forced the Disneys to become a corporation and sell stock. Disney experimentalism was curtailed by "the bankers," as Disney termed his new overseers. *Fantasia* was cut from four hours to two without his consent or cooperation. During World War II, 94 percent of the studio's output was in the form of 4,000 low-return propaganda and educational films supporting the war effort. The next decade produced the True-Life Adventure series of nature films, which drew praise but little profit.

Disney had been dreaming of an amusement park for two decades by the time he managed to get around the bankers in 1954 and found financing for it. Disney signed a seven-year contract with the struggling ABC television network to produce a weekly television program in return for ABC's purchasing 34.48 percent of the shares of Disneyland, Inc. Within six months of its opening, the park had attracted more than a million paying customers, and Disney enterprises found financial security for the first time. Disney Productions expanded from a gross income in 1950 of $7 million to $50 million by 1959. Since the theft of his Oswald the Rabbit in 1926, Disney had kept complete legal and economic control over his creations. In the contract with ABC was an option for Disney to buy back ABC's shares of Disneyland; when the park turned large profits, Disney immediately exercised the option and regained total control of the park.

Roy's economics and Walt's imagination combined again in the last major project of the Disney brothers, Walt Disney World. Disneyland had returned $273 million to the Disney corporation in its first ten years but had returned $555 million to others who owned Anaheim hotels and tourist facilities. To avoid such profit sharing, the Disney organization quietly bought up 27,500 acres—an area twice the size of Manhattan Island—near Orlando, Florida, for a second park. On his hospital death bed, Walt was planning the park and, adjacent to it, a last utopian dream, a Disney-planned and Disney-built city of 20,000 people enclosed in a climate-controlled glass dome, called the Experimental Prototype Community of Tomorrow (EPCOT). Walt died in 1965, EPCOT was scrapped, and Walt Disney World opened on schedule near the time of Roy's death, in 1971, as a larger copy of the Anaheim park. It was expected in its first ten years to bring $6.5 billion in economic benefits to the state of Florida.

As the financial world applauded Disney successes, the art world backed off. *Fortune* and *Forbes* praised Disney; Walt was selected among the ten greatest men of business in American history; the Disney empire moved to the fringe of the list of the 500 largest corporations; and hundreds of millions around the world patronized Disney movies, television, comics, records, and merchandise while the amusement parks competed with professional baseball and football for total volume of paid attendance each year.[54] But in the world of art criticism, John Ciardi dismissed Disneyland as "Foamrubbersville." Desmond Fisher quipped that a spoonful of sugar makes the medicine go down—or makes the medicine go away. Pauline Kael felt Disney turned good children's stories "rotten." When Rafferty called Disney the greatest educator of the century, Frances Clarke Sayers responded that sexy little Tinker Bell with her oversize buttocks, together with the waif's creator, had been "too long at the sugar bowls."[55] Richard Schickel, in the definitive critical biography of Walt Disney and his work, chronicled the Disney shift from earlier creativity to later commercialism, from aesthetic idealism to ideological narrowness, from the development of refreshingly immediate *folk* delights to the marketing of bland *mass* cultural expressions.

The system of capitalist mass production gradually supplanted elite or other aesthetic standards as the Disney yardstick of achievement. That pressure increased Disney's natural tendency to identify with the middle-class mainstream of American culture. "He never developed that kind of contempt you sometimes find in people in the advertising and publicity business," noted a colleague.[56] Perhaps no one in this century came to understand better than Disney the directions and limits of popular American taste and, through that understanding, to cater more successfully to them.

Disneyland was an ultimate expression of Disney's ideals and, through him, of the ideals of a numerical majority in the United States and countless millions elsewhere. Schickel described a structural symmetry between the park and Walt himself:

> Disneyland, to him, was a living monument to himself and his ideas of what constituted the good, true, and beautiful in this world. It was a projection, on a gigantic scale, of his personality . . . . an extension of *a* man in the way that the pleasant grounds of Versailles were an extension of The Sun King. It has none of the discreet impersonality of, say, Rockefeller Center. It was, and is, a statement containing, in general and in particular, conscious expressions of everything that was important to Disney, unconscious expressions of everything that had shaped his personality and of a good many things that had, for good and ill, shaped all of us who are Americans born of this century.[57]

Walt Disney appreciated that he exercised considerable social influence. He was once quoted by a reporter as saying, "I don't even want to be President of the United States. . . . I'd rather be the benevolent dictator of Disney enterprises." On another occasion, when Ray Bradbury suggested that Disney run for mayor of Los Angeles, he replied, "Ray, why should I run for mayor when I'm already king?"[58] A Disney official, John Hench, traces Disney's success to his instinct for exploiting very old human survival patterns. Hench suggests that human aesthetics and a sense for pleasure, which have been carried in DNA chains for 20 million years, distinguish pleasurable experiences as those that boost survival potential, and unpleasant experiences as threatening to survival.[59] Disney himself was less theoretical, often repeating variations of the statement, "We make the pictures and then let the professors tell us what they mean."[60]

The Meaning of the Disney Universe

"The Disney universe" has been used as a label throughout this chapter for three reasons. First, the Disney organization itself uses such labels. It began with animation, then created a Disney "land" followed by a Walt Disney "world." The only more inclusive representation left for Disney to construct is a "universe." Second, "the Disney universe" brings to mind the *universality* of Disney's worldwide spread. Pervasive in the United States, Disney products are widely available throughout the American sphere of influence in the world and have penetrated Third World countries and even revolutionary socialist societies. Third, the encompassing Disney message creates an identifiable *universe of semantic meaning*. The semantics of Disney are conveyed through syntactic structures and issue in behavioral praxis, as in a formal language system. This unity of meaning, more or less consistent in all Disney presentations, makes possible a generalization from Disneyland to other Disney media and messages and makes Disney an ideally self-contained illustration of mass-mediated culture.

Ample evidence in responses of visitors to Disneyland supports the two original hypotheses. Disney seemed clearly to *attract participants into mass-mediated utopian typifications*. Questionnaire responses also verified that Disney *instructs through morality plays that structure personal values and ideology*. Lurking behind the evidence of those hypotheses was a further thesis that Disneyland is *not value-free*. Moreover, the historical evolution of Disney seems to indicate that the priorities of the American political economy helped trim and shape the ethnocentric contours of the Disney message.

Various critical interpretations have been applied to Disney over the years. Herbert Schiller summarizes the suppressive quality of the Disney message as: "Behold a world in which there is no social conflict."[61] From Australia, Patricia Edgar and Hilary McPhee observe

> Walt Disney comics are some of the most sexist publications that can be found. Female characters, when they appear, are aggressive, materialistic and typically stupid. Witness the behaviour of Minnie Mouse or Daisy Duck when they attend a shop sale, smash the car or keep escorts waiting.[62]

E. L. Doctorow's *The Book of Daniel* develops a frequent aesthetic/ideological critique. It ponders Disneyland's lack of natural authenticity, subtlety, and complexity in substance, and charges the park with historical reductionism and political totalitarianism.[63]

In this study of Disney we have tried to emphasize *understanding* rather than *judgment*, by focusing on the *system-specific relativity* of Disneyland. As the Super Bowl case study will further illustrate, the most popular expressions of mass-mediated culture recapitulate in microcosm the larger social system. If these expressions were aesthetically elite or politically critical—failings for which critics castigate them—they could never become the most popular expressions of a mass, democratic, capitalistic system that is itself neither aesthetically elite nor politically self-critical.

To illustrate the system-specific relativity of Disney, both Disneyland and Disney comic books can be contrasted with examples from an opposite ideological perspective. For example, the possibilities of an amusement park exemplifying revolutionary socialism would sharply contrast with Disneyland. The revolutionary park could provide a multimedia wrap-around version of a participatory morality play developed around the themes of movies like *The Battle of Algiers, Z, State of Siege, The Murder of Fred Hampton, Hearts and Minds,* and other expressions of the critical left. The ideals of Marx, Lenin, and Mao would be expressed in highly dramatic and involving ways. Writers like Frantz Fanon, Herbert Marcuse, and James Baldwin could develop themes, Costa-Gavras and Felix Greene could translate them to dramatic forms intensified into socialist-realist art, and architects and engineers from the People's Republic of China could construct the park in perfectionist detail. The dominant feeling would be one of "happiness" achieved by eliminating capitalism and replacing it with a responsive and productive socialist-communist people's republic on a global scale. In Moscow, in fact, the Exhibition of Economic Achievements, a vast park with "theme" buildings, and the Museum of the Revolution are pale reflections of the

possibilities of utopian, multimedia environments exemplifying revolutionary socialist ideals. Such "propagandistic" parks would relate to the
Soviet or Chinese systems in precisely the same manner that Disneyland
relates to the United States system.

Comic books in the People's Republic of China provide another
contrast with Disney's system-specific relativity. New China's comic books
are carefully planned and are widely available to be read and passed
around in trains, buses, factories, markets, schools, and barracks. They
unmistakably endorse collective action in the interests of the masses
rather than individual activity in the interest of only one's self. For example, the story of one popular comic revolves around a ninth-century
peasant revolt in which the leader of the peasants lacks an ideological
line, becomes selfish, and dies in the end. In another, a woman wishes to
use a pail full of manure for her small private garden rather than the
collective field; her altruistic husband and fellow villagers convince her
otherwise and in the end she thanks them for opening her eyes. The
comics reinforce, in fact often duplicate, the stories in New China's plays,
films, novels, and operas. The Great World of Shanghai, an enormous
recreation area for family groups with simple tastes, provides entertaining revolutionary education.[64] The messages are far removed from the
Hulk, Mandrake, and Mickey Mouse.

A powerful critique of the Disney universe was developed by Ariel
Dorfman and Armand Mattelart during the period of the Allende democracy in Chile. As we mentioned previously, they evaluated 103 issues of
Disney comic books from a Third World and Marxist perspective. In
Chile Disney comics were eighteen times more numerous per capita than
in the United States and were published by a government-owned printing
house. Globally, Disney comic books are published in twenty languages,
distributed in sixty-seven countries, and have a monthly circulation of
nearly 19 million. The monthly circulation in countries like Brazil and
West Germany is higher than in the United States, despite their much
smaller populations.[65] Dorfman and Mattelart's critique stirred controversies in South America and elsewhere; Disney prevented a North American edition and, for a time, prevented the importing of an English-
language edition through United States customs.[66]

Dorfman and Mattelart's thematic content analysis found that Disney comic books symbolized (a) *consumerism*, in the constant search for
treasure by Donald Duck and others, the theme of more than three-
fourths of the stories; (b) *colonialism*, in their stereotyping of residents
of remote countries, where half the stories occurred, as either good children or savages; (c) *classism*, in their portrayal of those who resemble

manual laborers as criminals; and (d) *imperialism*, in the seizure and removal of foreign treasures by Donald and others. Uncle Scrooge's exorbitant accumulation of wealth is represented in the comics as eccentricity not exploitation; money becomes not the expression of a relationship between haves and have-nots but merely a fetish object. The comics studied and reprinted in the book pictured protestors as dangerous and absurd; Latin American and Southeast Asian revolutionaries as lazy, tyrannical villains; and business*men* and "the good old Navy," as Donald called it, as heroes. Dorfman and Mattelart argue that Disney's utopian picture serves the interests of the privileged few wealthy classes and nations (and the male sex) by creating a false consciousness of social realities. They conclude that Disney comic books "mask the web of interests which form a socially and historically determined and concretely situated system: North American imperialism."[67] That, in rather more pointed language, is what *system-specific relativity* is all about.

The Disney universe structures "meaning" in life, as does mass-mediated culture in general. It offers a paralanguage for speaking experience in meaningful patterns, a semiological system that organizes and controls what its signs represent: the immediate experience of living existence. Popular mass-mediated cultural expressions "fix" reality both by receiving and transmitting dominant patterns of perception, structures of feeling, cognitive maps, and cultural norms. They represent the "central zone" of a cultural system.

The significance of popular culture may be underestimated or misconstrued because of popular culture's *anomalous* character; it is neither literature nor folklore, neither elite art nor folk art. It is not even business only or entertainment only. But, as Joseph Arpad argues, popular culture's anomalous quality makes it an appropriate and important *mediator* for the contemporary sense of reality. Following William James, Arpad notes that the preconscious mind reduces data input by allowing into consciousness only information *continuous* with our sense of reality. Repressed *contiguous* information must be mythically mediated as sacred to be incorporated into our stable sense of reality, as Lévi-Strauss argues. Arpad concludes that popular consciousness, following its own traditions and conventions, mediates between continuous and contiguous phenomena and produces the complex American national character that is known throughout the world for its popular culture.[68]

Disneyland and Walt Disney World qualify as the popular culture capitals of America, as Margaret King has suggested.[69] They are the largest single visitor attractions in the United States, receiving 16 to 18 million people each year—more than visit Washington, D.C. In its first ten years, Disneyland attracted a quarter of the United States population and numerous foreign visitors and dignitaries. According to King, Disney's parks are America's quasi-religious Mecca and are the most technically advanced entertainment centers in the world. They humanize technology by creating enclosed environmental artworks through the technique of "animation in the round." They have been called in the *New York Times* "the most important city planning laboratory in the U.S."[70] Perhaps illustrating Disneyland's appeal, an octogenarian widower, Millard Jones, visited the park three times a week for many years following his wife's death in 1971.[71]

The themes, symbols, and spatial structure of Disneyland constitute a utopia. Utopias reify an ideology and a morality. An *ideology* is a system of representations of the imagined relationship between real persons and the real conditions of living. A *morality* provides rules of conduct for acting out the ideology. A utopia is not a complete universe. In the Disneyland utopia, for example, it is impossible to consider without shock the gory death of an employee in the Tomorrowland attraction "America Sings." During the first days that it was open in 1974, a female hostess unthinkingly leaned through an opening to call to a friend and was crushed between the moving walls designed as the Carousel of Progress. Employees report that it took several days to eradicate her remains from the machinery.[72]

Disneyland's morality play "typifies" by drawing from a fundamental set of images, myths, and reflexes that form the dominant substratum beneath the worldview, self-image, and life-values of an amorphous majority in the United States.

The park is a total medium exercising an awesome degree of social control. Even beyond the "feelies" of Huxley's *Brave New World*, Disneyland involves *all* the senses of the visitor by controlling the entire environment that feeds into the senses. Disneyland may recall popular impressions of brainwashing techniques and Skinnerian social engineering. The park thoroughly exercises both body and imagination in reprogramming the human biocomputer. A visitor is removed from the normal environment, thereby suspending usual reality-testing mechanisms. Persuasive techniques disguised as value-free entertainment actively involve the visitor in the on-going themes and symbols of the park, creating a group consensus around these central themes and symbols. Preparation for and reinforcement of these individual and group norms is provided for months and years before and after the visit by similar messages transmitted to the visitor anywhere in the world via television, films, comics, and other media.

The compelling power of the park and the Disney universe in general stems from its imagination, its perfectionism, and its feel for where the feelings and limits of the masses already are—as opposed to elitist or radical criticism concerned with where the tastes and consciousness of people could be. Disneyland does not point higher aesthetically or politically; it extrapolates from, confirms, and beautifies the status quo. In this, the park is the ultimate mass democratic capitalist blend of entertainment, education, and business. Whatever credentials Walt Disney might once have been granted in folk, elite, or popular art circles, his achievement was in the end the most perfect entrepreneurial realization imaginable of the at once extremely limited and extremely vast potential of contemporary mass-mediated culture.

The visitors disengage themselves from their role by trudging back up Main Street, U.S.A., moving through the turnstiles and past the ticket booths where the tape-recorded voice still welcomes new members to the cast. They find their car in the vast parking arena, exit onto the busy Los Angeles freeways, and feel the "real world" reassert itself. They sense that they have been for a time in a different world, a utopian universe of happiness where everyone knows what goodness is and goodness always wins. And they have been. Its influence may remain with them more subtly and for longer than they ever realize.

Notes

1. Christopher Finch, *The Art of Walt Disney: From Mickey Mouse to the Magic Kingdom,* with a special essay by Peter Blake (New York: Harry N. Abrams, 1973), p. 393.

2. For example, Irving Goffman, *The Presentation of Self In Everyday Life* (Garden City, N.Y.: Doubleday, 1959).

3. Leo Lowenthal, "Biographies in Popular Magazines," in Paul Lazarsfeld and Frank Stanton, eds., *Radio Research 1942–43* (New York: Duell, Sloan and Pearce, 1944); see also Gaye Tuchman, ed., *The TV Establishment* (Englewood Cliffs, N.J.: Prentice-Hall, 1974). Paul F. Lazarsfeld and Robert K. Merton, "Mass Communications, Popular Taste and Organized Social Action," in Bernard Rosenbert and David Manning White, eds., *Mass Culture* (New York: The Free Press, 1957), pp. 457–73. C. Wright Mills, *The Power Elite* (New York: Oxford University Press, 1956).

4. Mills, *The Power Elite.*

5. William Flint Thrall and Addison Hibbard, *A Handbook to Literature,* revised and enlarged by C. Hugh Holman (New York: The Odyssey Press, 1960), p. 293.

6. "Disneyland Facts and Figures," fact sheet by Walt Disney Productions, Disneyland Division, Anaheim, Calif., 1974.

7. Lloyd Shearer, "How Disney Sells Happiness, *Parade,* March 26, 1972, p. 4.

8. Ibid., p. 5.

9. Ibid.

10. Ibid.

11. Personal interviews with various former Disneyland employees, 1974–75.

12. Margaret J. King, "Disneyland and Walt Disney World: Traditional Values in Futuristic Form," paper presented to the Comparative Popular Culture Research Seminar on Traditional Media, July–August, 1975, Honolulu, Hawaii.

13. Edwin Black, "Brave New Tomorrowland," *New Times*, December 13, 1974, p. 51.

14. *Walt Disney's Disneyland: A Pictorial Souvenir* (Anaheim: Walt Disney Productions, 1974), p. 3. © 1974 Walt Disney Productions.

15. Richard Schickel, *The Disney Version: The Life, Times, Art and Commerce of Walt Disney* (New York: Simon & Schuster, 1968), p. 323. All quotes from *The Disney Version* copyright © 1968 by Richard Schickel. Reprinted by permission of Simon & Schuster.

16. Finch, *The Art of Walt Disney*, p. 432.

17. Louis Marin, "Dégénérescence Utopique: Disneyland," Chapter 12 in *Utopiques: Jeux D'Espaces*, with quotations in English taken from informal abbreviated translation by Marin delivered as a paper titled, "Utopia and Ideology: Disneyland," p. 8.

18. Ibid.

19. *Disneyland Souvenir*, p. 25 © 1974 Walt Disney Productions.

20. Marin, *Utopia*, p. 13.

21. Peter Blake in Finch, *The Art of Walt Disney*, pp. 431–32.

22. *Disneyland Souvenir*, p. 21. © 1974 Walt Disney Productions.

23. Frances Clarke Sayers, *Los Angeles Times*, May, 1965: reprint of the original Sayers letter and an extended interview with Ms. Sayers of UCLA appeared in *F.M. and Fine Arts*, August, 1965, and was reprinted as "Walt Disney Accused," *The Horn Book Magazine*, December, 1965, pp. 602–10.

24. Richard Schickel, "The Films: No Longer for the Jung at Heart," *Time*, July 30, 1973, p. 39.

25. Ibid.

26. Marin, *Utopia*, p. 6.

27. William McReynolds, "Disney Plays 'The Glad Game,'" *Journal of Popular Culture* 7, no. 4 (Spring 1974), p. 787.

28. Gilbert Seldes, quoted in Schickel, *Disney Version*, p. 223.

29. William F. Lynch, S.J., *The Image Industries* (New York: Sheed and Ward, 1959), pp. 27–28.

30. Sayers, "Disney Accused," p. 602.

31. Schickel, *Disney Version*, p. 323.

32. Dick Gregory, *No More Lies*.

33. John G. Cawelti, *The Six-Gun Mystique* (Bowling Green, Ohio: Bowling Green University Popular Press, 1973).

34. Will Wright, *Sixguns and Society: A Structural Study of the Western* (Berkeley: University of California Press, 1975).

35. Joseph Arpad, "Between Folklore and Literature: Popular Culture as Anomaly," *Journal of Popular Culture* 9, no. 2 (Fall 1975), pp. 403–22.

36. T. C. McLuhan, ed., *Touch the Earth: A Self-Portrait of Indian Existence* (New York: Pocket Books, 1972), p. 45.

37. Finch, ed., *Art of Disney*, p. 367.

38. Schickel, *Disney Version*, pp. 343–44.

39. Carl Bernstein and Bob Woodward, *All the President's Men* (New York: Warner Paperback Library, 1975), p. 176.

40. Richard A. Maynard, *The Celluloid Curriculum: How To Use Movies in the Classroom* (Rochelle Park, N.J.: Hayden Book Co., 1971), pp. 139–47.

41. Edmund Carpenter, "Film, Primitive Man, and Reality," *Media Ecology Review*, 1973.

42. Marin, *Utopia*, pp. 13–14.

43. Marshall McLuhan, "Classroom Without Walls," in Edmund Carpenter and Marshall McLuhan, eds., *Explorations in Communication* (Boston: Beacon Press, 1960), p. 3.

44. Marin, *Utopia*, pp. 12–13.

45. Ariel Dorfman and Armand Mattelart, *Para Leer al pato Donald: Communicacion de masa y colonialismo* (Buenos Aires: Siglo Veintuno Argentian Editores, 1972), p. 85.

46. Pauline Kael, lecture-discussion, University of Illinois (Urban, 1967).

47. Schickel, *Disney Version*, p. 335.

48. Finch, *Art of Disney*, p. 402.

49. Ibid.

50. Leo E. Litwak, "Fantasy That Paid Off," *New York Times Magazine*, June 27, 1965.

51. Schickel, *Disney Version*, p. 335.

52. Marshall McLuhan, "Five Sovereign Fingers Taxed the Breath," in Carpenter and McLuhan, eds., *Explorations*, p. 207.

53. Schickel, *Disney Version*, p. 190.

54. Herbert I. Schiller, *The Mind Managers* (Boston: Beacon Press, 1973), pp. 94–95.

55. Sayers, "Disney Accused," p. 602.

56. John Hench, Vice-President of WED, in Finch, ed., *Art of Disney*, p. 422.

57. Schickel, *Disney Version*, p. 315.

58. Ibid., pp. 158, 364.

59. Finch, ed., *Art of Disney*, p. 409.

60. Schiller, *Mind Managers*, p. 78.

61. Schiller, *Mind Managers*.

62. Patricia Edgar and Hilary McPhee, *Media She* (Melbourne: William Heinemann Australia, 1974), p. 19.

63. E. L. Doctorow, *The Book of Daniel* (New York: New American Library, 1971), pp. 301–9.

64. Endymion Wilkinson, trans., and Gino Nebiolo, intro., *The People's Comic Book: Red Women's Detachment, Hot on the Trail and Other Chinese Comics* (Garden City, N.Y.: Doubleday, 1973), pp. viii–xv. Some other books on the nature and role of comics are: Arthur Asa Berger, *The Comic-Stripped American;* David Kunzle, *The History of the Comic Strip;* Jerry Robinson, *The Comics: An Illustrated History of Comic Strip Art;* Les Daniels and John Peck, *Comix, A History of Comic Books in America;* Mark James Estren, *A History of Underground Comics.*

65. Circulation figures are cited from a display case in the Disneyland Emporium on Main Street, U.S.A., August, 1974.

66. The controversy over the study is described in the prologue to *Para Leer*, "Donald y las Politica," by Hector Schmucler. The refusal of U.S. Customs to release the English-language version is described in the circular of Green Mountain Editions, Oshkosh, Wisconsin, January, 1976. Printed in Great Britain, the English-language edition, *How to Read Donald Duck: Imperialist Ideology in the Disney Comic*, is available from International General, P.O. Box 350, New York, N.Y. 10013, U.S.A.

67. Dorfman and Mattelart, *Para Leer;* see also Armand Mattelart, "Mass Media in the Socialist Revolution: The Experience of Chile," in George Gerbner, Larry Gross, and William Melody, eds., *Communications, Technology, and Social Policy* (New York: John Wiley, 1973), p. 428.

68. Arpad, "Between Folklore and Literature."

69. King, "Disneyland."

70. Paul Goldberger, "Mickey Mouse Teaches the Architects," *New York Times Magazine* (October 22, 1972), p. 92.

71. King, "Disneyland," pp. 10–11.

72. Interview of employees in "America Sings," Disneyland, December 25, 1975.

Sports

Play-action, cheerleaders, massive stadiums, and the rest of football from homecomings to the Super Bowl reveal a great deal about American society.

3

The Super Bowl: Mythic Spectacle

Why is the Super Bowl the most lucrative annual spectacle on
American media?

When were electronic media wedded with spectator sports?

How do mass-mediated cultural events resemble ancient mythic rituals?

How does the Super Bowl fulfill contemporary mythic-ritual functions?

What is the essential internal structure of North American football,
and how does it parallel structures in American society?

Are there sexism, racism, and authoritarianism in the Super Bowl?

How does Super Bowl football compare with other sports in the West
and with sports in contrasting non-Western cultures?

How can the Super Bowl be both a propaganda vehicle serving a power
structure and an enjoyable choice of viewers?

NBC Television Sports "proud" presentation of Super Bowl XI to perhaps 85 million Americans from the Rose Bowl in Pasadena, January 9,
1977, ushered in a popular spectacle of intriguing cultural significance.
Gilbert Seldes notes that the instant fame of Lord Byron upon the publication of "Childe Harold's Pilgrimage" reached some 2,000 people, while,
in the era of mass culture, Lassie's first film meant for the dog "adoration
on the part of ten million."[1] A quarter century later, in 1969, when Joe
Namath led the New York Jets to victory in Super Bowl III, announcing
the coming of age of the American Football Conference and the end of
the Green Bay Packer dynasty, four or five times Lassie's original followers
saw it all in their living rooms while it happened. And by 1974, when
the Miami Dolphin line and Larry Csonka moved through the Minnesota
Vikings for a 24 to 7 victory, more Americans watched than had seen the
first man walk on the moon and only slightly fewer than the record 95
million who watched the funeral of President Kennedy.

What makes the Super Bowl the most lucrative annual spectacle in
American mass culture? To answer that question this case study utilizes
the 1974 Super Bowl VIII telecast on videotape as a data bank of cultural
indicators and a para-literary text for exegesis, and then interprets that
data to explain both the inner structure and the social function of the
Super Bowl as a total mass-mediated cultural event. Methodologically it
draws on a variety of communications-related disciplines to achieve a
balance between Anglo-American emphasis on empirical data and Continental interest in philosophical implications. The thesis that emerges
is this: The Super Bowl combines electronic media and spectator sports
in a ritualized mass activity; it structurally reveals specific cultural values

Two Weeks of Ballyhoo; Seven Minutes of Action

Possibly because he owed it to his muse, or out of clinical obligation, an assistant professor of communications at the University of California at San Diego was inspired to put the stopwatch on the telecast of Super Bowl VIII on Jan. 13, 1974.

Offhand, this would seem an odd way to squander an afternoon, but there really isn't much to do in January in San Diego once you've seen the zoo.

But the good professor has a blockbuster hidden here. His clockings indicate that the 23 percent recorded as scoreboard time is deceptive. Every football game contains dead time in which the players hold hands in the huddle, the quarterback petitions the center for the ball, and other dramas occur. During these moments, the clock is moving—but the ball is not.

Thus, in a telecast stretching nearly four hours (including all the pre- and postgame coverage), the football was actually in motion for approximately seven minutes.

Before Super Bowl of 1969, Joe Namath found the answer to tensions in a thrifty manner that avoided any fines. He confided that he had spent the night before the game in his room—with a blonde and a bottle of scotch. Regrettably, Michael Real, the assistant professor of communications, was not on hand to clock the drama.

Condensed from an article by Melvin Durslag in *TV Guide*, XXIV:3 (January 17, 1976), pp. 14–16.

proper to American institutions and ideology; and it is best explained as a contemporary form of mythic spectacle. A cross-cultural mythic approach to Super Bowl VIII indicates why the annual Super Bowl may not be culture with a capital *C* but is popular with a capital *P* surrounded by dollar signs and American flags. In doing so, the study shakes cobwebs off academic theories of myth and raises questions about media, American culture, and mythic ritual.

Sports and Electronic Media: A Marriage Made in Heaven

By successfully blending electronic media and spectator sports, the Super Bowl has become the capstone of an empire. Even oddsmakers agree it is the number-one game[2] in what 1972 public opinion surveys found was the number-one sport in America.[3] The president of the United States concocts plays and telephones them to coaches in the middle of the night; astronauts listen in orbit; cabinet members, top corporate executives, and celebrities vie for tickets to attend the game in person. In its first eight years, the Super Bowl surpassed the one-hundred-year-old Kentucky Derby and the seventy-year-old World Series as the number-one sports spectacle in the United States.[4] Commercial time on the Super Bowl telecast is the most expensive of the television year, surpassing even the Academy Awards presentation. These are the figures on Super Bowl VIII:

Live attendance: 71,882

Television audience: 70 to 95 million

CBS payment to NFL for television rights: $2,750,000

CBS charge for advertising per minute: $200,000 to $240,000

Total CBS advertising income from game: over $4 million

Estimated expenditures in Houston by Super Bowl crowd: $12 million

Words of copy sent out from newsmen: over 3 million[5]

Curiously, this mass cultural impact revolved around a telecast that was composed of a distribution of elements as illustrated in Figure 3–1. The excitement seemed to be about a football game, but the total play-action time devoted in the telecast to live football was less than ten min-

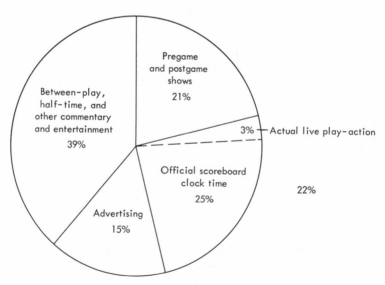

FIGURE 3–1   Distribution of Elements in the Super Bowl Telecast

utes. How has the combination of spectator sports and electronic media evolved into such curious and powerful expressions of mass-mediated culture?

Super Bowl VIII was only a recent climax in the sacred union of electronic media and spectator athletics. The courtship began with Edison's film of the Fitzsimmons-Corbett fight in 1897 and was consummated nationally in 1925 when the first radio network broadcast Graham Mc-Namee's description of the World Series, and in 1927 when the first cross-country radio hook-up carried the Rose Bowl.

Three qualities made the union fruitful. First, the *physical* nature of athletics met broadcasting's need for events capable of colorful visual representation and/or aural description. In the 1974 Super Bowl, when Alan Page charged through the line to throw Jim Kick for a loss and the crowd roared, the tangibly physical event fit broadcasting in a way that exclusively intellectual or verbal activities do not. Second, a sequential and cumulative *dramatic* structure issuing in heroes and happiness, losers and tragedy, distinguishes spectator sports from participatory exercises and leads to mass spectacles able to attract and hold the interest of large crowds. Super Bowl VIII was like the staging of a medieval fable pitting a band of Vikings against an army of Dolphins. Third, unlike formal drama, sports are *self-determining* and take place live in real time. In Super Bowl X directors Chuck Noll and Tom Landry and actors Terry Bradshaw and Roger Staubach could no more foresee the outcome than the viewer at home who saw the drama unfold as it happened.

An absolute difference in maintenance of suspense and feeling of participation separates reading a post factum print medium report from following live events unfolding on electronic media. A sports page, no matter how skillfully written, can only approximate the participatory suspense of watching the closing minutes of a half when a Viking two-minute drill combined with a Tarkenton hot hand is capable of creating an emotionally draining frenzy reminiscent of a Tchaikovsky finale. It is not the print medium and not the books of Lombardi, Plimpton, or Meggysey, however interesting they may be as spin-offs, that account for the striking success story of professional football in the third quarter of the twentieth century. Rather, it is television's system of sight, sound, and simultaneous delivery that enables fans to share in sports history in the making: "Remember in the '76 Super Bowl when I bet you Staubach would hit Pearson with the bomb on third and . . ." What was received throughout the country from Houston between 2 P.M. and 6 P.M. on January 13, 1974, as a communications experience combined the audio-visual sensations of film, the dramatic structure of experimental theater, and the currentness of news. The "psyched-up" viewer feels like everything except what he is, a passive consumer, when in a Super Bowl telecast an instantaneous and multisensory delivery system joins hands and heart with a complex, high-pressure sport to give birth to an audience experience qualitatively (for the individual) and quantitatively (for the society) distinct from previous cultural experiences.

The marriage, one is tempted to say, was made not in heaven but somewhere between Wall Street and Madison Avenue. The combination of television and sports has created substantial incomes for each, spilling into major corporate coffers. In addition, the viewing experience of the Super Bowl, taken in mythic perspective, has become peculiarly appropriate to life in the Wall Street–Madison Avenue dominated advanced industrial state. Of course, big-time football was not the only offspring of the wedding of electronic media and spectator sports. Over two and a half years in advance of the events, ABC had sold its television commercial time for the 1976 Summer and Winter Olympics for $62 million.[6]

Mythic Functions of Media Sports

Although mass-mediated culture tends to profane a civilization's most sacred and powerful words and images, in the process it manages to elevate otherwise mundane events of no real consequence to the status of spectacles of a powerful, quasi-sacred myth and ritual nature. The Super Bowl telecast conveys this feeling of larger-than-life drama. Before the 1974 game announcers proclaimed: "We fully believe that this game will live up to its title Super Bowl. . . . We expect this to be the greatest Super Bowl ever." The screen was filled with images of vast crowds, hulking superheroes, great plays from the past, even shots from and of the huge Goodyear blimp hovering over the field. During the game all-time records were set: Fran Tarkenton completed eighteen passes to break Joe Namath's record for Super Bowls, and Larry Csonka broke Matt Snell's Super Bowl record by gaining 145 yards in his 33 rushing attempts. The actual game was one-sided and boring. *Sports Illustrated* led its coverage with "Super Bowl VIII had all the excitement and suspense of a master butcher quartering a steer."[7] But after the game the one-sidedness itself became the occasion for historic superlatives: "Are the Dolphins the greatest team ever?"

A productive analytic framework for diagnosing the psychic involvement generated by live mass-mediated culture comes from philosophers and anthropologists who study the function of myth in preliterate societies.

Generally speaking, *mythic activity* is the collective reenactment of symbolic archetypes that express the shared emotions and ideals of a given culture. Among nonliterate peoples, mythic beliefs and ritual activities cement together the social whole, while literacy frequently limits the role of obvious myth to formalized and secondary dimensions. The first chapter noted that Ernst Cassirer placed myth among the six basic symbol systems through which humans express and control their environment.[8] Mircea Eliade emphasizes the role of myth and ritual in classifying the experience of time and space into functionally separate units designated as "sacred" and "profane" and in identifying the role of the archetypal hero.[9] Claude Lévi-Strauss has outlined the mental structures of the archaic mind, which works concretely and mythically.[10] More empirically, Roy Rappaport's field studies of New Guinea tribesmen specify the ecological functions of myth as the regulatory and directing mechanisms for living in harmony with the environment.[11] These perspectives shed new light on the interpretation of the Super Bowl.

The multisensory, simultaneous experience of Super Bowl viewing resembles reading a sports report as an isolated individual—the "print experience"—less than it resembles standing on the edge of a ring of Dakota Sioux dancers, like Black Elk, hearing, watching, and feeling the collective energy unleashed by participation in ritual activities rooted in mythic beliefs—the "aural experience."[12] McLuhan, Carpenter, and others have stressed the parallel between preliterate aural communications and "post-literate" electronic communications in creating a tribal consciousness that lives collectively, mythically, and in depth, in contrast to the individualism, rationalism, and linear segmentation of "book culture."[13] The case of the Super Bowl clarifies such claims. Whether constructive or destructive of the total ecology, modern, mediated, myth-with-a-million-members spectacles, like their ancient predecessors, do perform important functions for the spectator-participant and the larger human ecosystem.

Why do people watch the Super Bowl? Among a survey sample of roughly a hundred subjects, primarily university students, more than one-half of the males and one-fourth of the females watched Super Bowl VIII. The conscious motivation expressed varied from fanatic enthusiasm to bored escapism. Viewers explained

they watch football regularly (40%)

there was nothing else to do (18%)

this one is the big game (16%)

they were fans (12%)

they had bets on the game (10%)

it was the in thing (2%)

their boy or girl friend would have it on (2%)

If the game were to be cancelled, 4 percent reported that they would be happy, while 25 percent reported that they would be very upset.[14]

But such conscious, overt, individual motivation is only the tip of the iceberg. Harry Edwards begins to move below the surface of motivation when he describes the "social balm" effect of sports:

The circus of sport offers not only social stability but balm for individual stresses and anxieties. The sports fan, for example, finds that the success of his favorite team or athlete reinforces his faith in those values that define established and legitimate means of achievement. He returns from the game to his job or his community reassured that his efforts will eventually be successful. So when he is cheering for his team, he is actually cheering for himself. When he shouts "Kill the umpire!" he is calling for the destruction of all those impersonal forces that have so often hindered his own achievement.[15]

Attributes of Mythic Function

An in-depth analysis of the interests of viewers and the social functions of the Super Bowl reveals that it functions in a manner very similar to traditional mythic activities. The symbolic forms of myth provide personal identification, heroic archetypes, communal focus, spatial and temporal frames of reference, and ecologically regulatory mechanisms.

Personal Identification. Individual participation in the spectacle of Super Bowl VIII was aroused by a variety of stimuli within the telecast that evoked subjective associations within the viewer. The mechanism is similar to but more direct than the "commodity fetishism" through which consumers identify with advertised automobiles, liquor, and similar symbolically manipulated products. For example, individual performers in Super Bowl VIII awake viewer ideals. Former college or sandlot quarterbacks can identify with Fran Tarkenton or Bob Griese; laborers can appreciate the unsung heroes of the interior line like Larry Little; white collar workers can identify with Don Shula's management strategy as coach or with Pat Summerall's commentary; as Edwards points out, "the black fan naturally identifies more directly with the black athlete," such as Mercury Morris or Paul Warfield.

As viewers are drawn into the role of vicarious participant, they become partisan by choosing one team and putting their feelings and maybe some money on the line. A Purdue graduate picks Miami because Griese is his fellow alumnus; a Baltimore fan picks Miami because he liked Shula as Colts' head coach—or picks Minnesota because he resents Shula's abandoning *his* team; those who favor underdogs side with the Vikings; the seekers of perfection and "history's greatest" bless Miami with their support. Even "trapped" viewers (predominantly females) who watch only by default select a favorite team early in the telecast. The epic and its outcome then take on meaning to each individual. As Jacques Ellul argues, face-to-face relations are substantially displaced by the technological society: the individual, as well as the state, comes to *need* the modes of participation, identification, and meaning given to individual and collective life by what Ellul calls mass propaganda.[16]

Heroic Archetypes. The prototypical role of the sports hero is the most frequently considered mythic function of American athletics. Recalling Orrin Klapp's studies of American heroes, Ronald Cummings describes the idealism/disillusionment archetype of the hero of Super Bowl III, Joe Willie Namath:

> Joe Willie was American innocence and idealism equipped with nothing more than the myth of Arnold Palmer. You can come from twenty strokes back and win on the last hole. You can win the Super Bowl with a last place team. You can conquer racism, war and poverty. You can purge evil from the world. You can be free. And then, the all-American thud, the crying outside the commissioner's office, saying how much he loved football; the assassinations, Kent State, the bombing at Wisconsin.... Americans continue to emerge from the virgin woods and lose their manheads.[17]

Super Bowl super heroes become almost primordial Jungian figures as their exploits are praised in the press and worshipped by youth. Holy places are established to which pilgrimages can be made. The football Hall of Fame in Canton, Ohio, commemorates the location in which George Hallas sat with others on the running board of a car and planned professional football almost half a century ago. Lévi-Strauss notes how such contemporary historic sites function like primitive mythic foci: "Nothing in our civilization more closely resembles the periodic pilgrimages made by the initiated Australians, escorted by their sages, than our conducted tours to Goethe's or Victor Hugo's house, the furniture of which inspires emotions as strong as they are arbitrary."[18]

Communal Focus. The feeling of collective participation in the Super Bowl is obvious in interviews with viewers and studies of viewer conversation and traffic patterns.[19] The majority of viewers saw the game in a group setting, used it as a social occasion, talked and moved at prescribed times during the telecast, and discussed the Super Bowl with acquaintances before and after the day of the game. Especially for the more than half of the adult males in America who watched the game it was a source of conversation at work, in the neighborhood, at shops, and wherever regular or accidental interaction occurs.

A communal myth may use more than one medium to spread its mystique, and the print medium thoroughly prepared for and supplemented television's live coverage. From Sunday, January 6, through Monday, January 14, 1974, New York's three daily newspapers devoted 4,075 column inches, including pictures, to the Super Bowl.[20] Allowing space for advertisements, that means some 50 newspaper pages of information were available on Super Bowl VIII in one metropolitan area. In addition, publications as diverse as *Ms.* and *Rolling Stone* reported on the Super Bowl. By game time the viewer-participants *know* they are joined with people in the room, in the stands—all over the country—in following this spectacle. As Cassirer and others point out, the essence of mythical belief and ritual activity lies in the feeling of collective participation and sharing of concerns and powers beyond the potential of the individual human. Adrenalin flowing, the fan glued to the Super Bowl telecast is communally joined to great forces no less mystically than is the tribal dancer calling forth success in the hunt.

Marking Time and Space. These are functions that sports have partially taken over from nature itself. Ronald Cummings observes,

> Nature has disappeared from most contemporary lives, shut out by gigantic buildings, train and walkway tunnels, a densely populated atmosphere. We have restructured our environment and our relations to it, and the artificial turf and Astrodome are physical symbols in the sport realm, a realm which has historically been associated with the "outdoorsman."[21]

"Seasons" are now commonly spoken of as football season, basketball season, and baseball season as much as fall, winter, spring, and summer. Far more newspaper space and broadcast time are given to sports than to weather even in rural areas of this country. Many males, isolated from weather all week by an office or plant, spend Saturday and Sunday afternoons not enjoying the elements but watching a ballgame. The seasons are orchestrated to provide overlaps, not gaps. As early spring grass begins to stir to life under the last film of snow, denatured American attention turns slowly toward baseball spring training while basketball season peaks toward its NCAA and NBA conclusion. National holidays are as closely identified with sports as with religious or historical meaning. Thanksgiving and New Year's Day mean football; Memorial Day, auto racing; the Christmas season, basketball tournament; and so on. Sports overlay the sacred cycle of mythic time to provide a needed psychic relief from the tedium of Western linear time.

In a similar vein, regional markings traditionally associated with family and neighborhood can, in the atomistic absence of such traditions, be regrouped around city and regional athletic teams. The Chicagoan may identify more with the Cubs, Sox, Bears, Hawks, or Bulls in a neighborhood bar, at a place of work, or throughout the Daley fiefdom than he does with his neighborhood, his work, or his political representatives themselves. In these terms, Oakland did not exist prior to 1967, but now with professional teams in football, baseball, basketball, and hockey, it is clearly on the big league map. The Vikings, in fact, widened their designation beyond a city and called themselves a "Minnesota" team. The fact that all major professional sports are basically American national sports, even when playoffs are called the "World" Series or the "Super" Bowl, may account for more than a small part of the national cohesion and identity.

Without exaggerating these time and place markings made by sports, one can parallel their mythic functions with the traditional distinction between "sacred" and "profane" time and space in the study of comparative religions by Mircea Eliade and others.[22] From the undifferentiated flow of experience, archaic societies separated out certain objects, events, times, places, and persons and endowed them with special significance. These "sacred" poles of existence contrasted with everyday "profane" existence and were identified through cyclic ritual activities with the renewal of primordial events and archetypes. As such, they provided ultimate meanings and were the central focus for the organization of social and personal life.

In a manner psychically similar to the traditional Maori Islanders or Yaqui brujos, the contemporary American uses "sacred" events of the Super Bowl type to escape the uncertainties of "profane" existence. In a secularized society, sports fill a vacuum left by religion. Anyone familiar with "sports fans" would be unsurprised to learn that typical Twin-Citians approached the afternoon of January 13, 1974, with more of the excitement that Black Elk felt for his Dakota Sioux rituals than those same Twin-Citians had felt that morning attending religious services. For many Americans, Sunday afternoon televised sports are more socially approved, publicized, and exciting than is Sunday morning church-going. Richard M. Nixon's interest in the Washington Redskins was more apparent than his interest in Quakerism, and his choice of the "sacred" refuge of televised college football over the "profane" world of antiwar demonstrators during the October, 1970, moratorium was symbolically significant. The cycle of games and seasons, culminating in the annual Super Bowl, provides crucial "sacred" markers breaking the "profane" monopoly of secular time and space in the advanced industrial, technological society of the United States.

Ecologically Regulatory Mechanisms. Myth-ritual patterns may function as central control systems of the total ecological environment as Rappaport established in his study of ritual in the ecology of a New Guinea tribe, *Pigs for the Ancestors*. He described in detail how

> Tsembaga ritual, particularly in the context of a ritual cycle, operates as a regulating mechanism in a system, or set of interlocking systems, in which such variables as the area of available land, necessary lengths of fallow periods, size and composition of both human and pig populations, trophic requirements of pigs and people, energy expended in various activities, and the frequency of misfortunes are included.

He argues that while Tsembaga rituals "are conventionalized acts directed toward the involvement of nonempirical (supernatural) agencies in human affairs," the twelve- to fifteen-year cycles of mythic events *de facto* regulate crop rotation, game distribution, mating patterns, population, warfare, trade, and virtually all of the environmental relationships of the tribespeople.[23]

One of the directly regulatory functions of the Super Bowl as an American myth-ritual is to move goods within the economic system. The Super Bowl VIII telecast, including the pregame and postgame shows, included 65 advertisements, of which 52 were structured 30- and 60-second commercials and the remainder were brief program or sponsor notices. Advertisements occupied slightly more than 15 percent of the Super Bowl VIII air time and were sponsored by 30 different companies. The number of advertisements for each category of product were

7—automobiles
7—automobile tires
4—automobile batteries
4—beers
3—wines
3—television sets
2—insurance companies, credit cards, railroads, banks, NFL
1—hotels, retail stores, airplanes, locks, movies, copiers, foods

The advertisements for New York Life Insurance and Boeing were constructed on sports themes, as were notices for upcoming CBS sports programs. Tire and battery advertisements emphasized strength and dependability, virtues helpful in both winter and football. Liquor appeals included traditional glamor, gusto, and fun. The fuel shortage was evident in the emphasis of automobile advertisements on economy and efficiency. Consumer unrest was reflected by promotion of general corporate images as well as specific products. "Don't be fuelish" public service notices were included in keeping with the Nixon administration's approach to fuel shortages, and a plug was inserted for NFL players going on a trip for the Department of Defense.

In general, commercials and announcements managed to promote specific products and services, strengthen corporate images, and subtly support domestic and foreign policy. At the same time that conservation of energy was encouraged, an energy-consuming form of transportation was promoted: Ford and Goodyear advertised most. Further, the nonautomobile products advertised as part of the "good life" of the Super Bowl society bore little direct relationship to basic necessities such as food, clothing, shelter, or health. The overall impression of the Super Bowl VIII advertising fit the pattern of a post-scarcity, created-need economy by supporting the institutional status quo and promoting "super" consumerism. Presuming companies do not spend more than $200,000 a minute without results, the regulatory mechanism of Super Bowl VIII advertising, on the specific level, stimulated the purchase of particular products and, on the general level, maintained the consumer ethic developed by lifetimes of exposure to continuous, pervasive advertising.

Inside Super Bowl VIII: A Structural Analysis of Football

Myths reflect and make sacred the dominant tendencies of a culture, thereby sustaining social institutions and life-styles. What are the common structural constituents that underlie both the parent American society and its game-ritual offspring, the Super Bowl?

Cummings takes a step toward a structural, semiotic analysis of American sports when he writes

> The essential aspects of American sport are basic expressions of the American cultural pattern. . . . The very forms of our sports indicate dominant temporal and spatial national features. If the hunt was the central expression of sport in pre-industrial, state-of-nature America with its expansive landscape and assertion of a primal relationship between man and nature, then baseball, football, basketball and the like are the central expressions of an urban, technological, electronic America reflecting its concern with social structure and interpersonal relationships. . . . Since industrial America severed work from a sense of fulfillment, we have turned more and more to sport as an accessible means of self-contemplation. This is the reason for the cheer and sense of release when the batter sends the ball soaring out of the park; the pleasure of the stuff shot, the break-away; the satisfaction of the bomb, the punt return, the long gainer. Our modern sports are attempts to break out of an artificially imposed confinement.[24]

But such surface observations do not touch the deep structure of any single sport. Football is not a mere parable or allegory of American life. It is not a story outside and about a separate referent. Rather, it is a story that is also an activity and a part of the larger society. Moreover, it relates organically to the larger whole. As such, the Super Bowl is a formal analog of the institutional and ideological structure of the American society and culture it is "about." *In the classical manner of mythical beliefs and ritual activities, the Super Bowl is a communal celebration of and indoctrination into specific socially dominant emotions, life-styles, and values.*

Characteristics of the Game

Territoriality. Endless statistics were available on Super Bowl VIII: Miami completed 6 of 7 passes and gained 196 yards on the ground; Minnesota completed 18 of 28 passes for 166 yards, but were penalized 65

yards to Miami's 4. Other figures on total yardage gained, time of possession, kicking games, and third down conversions were on the air and in
the papers. But the *essential* datum was Miami 24, Minnesota 7. What
those figures meant was that Miami had been able to occupy progressively
enough of the 100 yards of the Rice Stadium playing field to move the
ball on the ground, in the air, or by foot into the Minnesota end zone for
three touchdowns, three conversions, and one field goal, against only one
touchdown and conversion in return.

Football centers around winning property by competition, as does
capitalism. Moreover, in football the winning of property means nothing
unless one wins all the property, that is, backs one's opponent into his
own valueless end zone. Points go up on the electronic scoreboard, as on
a stock market read-out, only when the opposition is driven off the field.
This all-the-way quality of football scoring replicates the ultimates of
laissez-faire economics and the "game" of monopoly capitalism. We can
begin to see why Hunter S. Thompson found "God, Nixon, and the National Football League" inseparable in his mind.[25]

Time. The scoring drive by Miami in the opening minutes of Super
Bowl VIII took 10 plays to cover 62 yards. The series used up 5 minutes
and 27 seconds on the official clock but took 9 minutes of real time and
only 42 seconds of live play action from the snap of the ball to the whistle
ending the play. Football consists of very brief bursts of physical activity
interspersed with much longer periods of cognitive planning and physical
recuperation. It is strictly regulated by an official clock and ends, not
organically, as does baseball when the last batter is retired, but through

external imposition when the clock runs out. Professional football is as segmented temporally, and almost as technological, as the firings of a piston engine or the sequential read-outs of a computer. The periods of action have an intensity appropriate for a hyped-up, superconsumerist society, far removed from the leisurely sun-filled afternoons of an early twentieth-century baseball park. And, in a society where virtually everyone wears a timer around the wrist, we are clock-watchers not in order to dally through work hours but because we know that only a limited amount of time is available feverishly to achieve, achieve.

Labor. Sexually, male domination of the Super Bowl is total. Of the hundreds of players, coaches, announcers, personalities in commercials, halftime entertainers, celebrities in the crowd, and others transmitted into million of homes across the nation by Super Bowl VIII, only two halftime entertainers—Miss Texas and Miss Canada—and a small handful of anonymous actresses in commercials and faces in the crowd were not male. The Super Bowl is covered by newspapers whose sports and business pages are both about as predominantly male as are society pages female.

Racially, dozens of black players and several black announcers, although no black anchormen, were visible during Super Bowl VIII. But, more significantly, no head coaches, no team owners, and few of the super-wealthy Rice Stadium crowd were black. The Super Bowl telecast seemed to confirm the claims by sociologist Harry Edwards of parallels between black athletes and Roman gladiators. From 1957 to 1971 black football players increased from 14 to 34 percent among the professional leagues.[26] But, the black 10 to 15 percent of the American population still assumed a large part of football's "menial labor" with the managerial levels remaining largely closed to them.

Social roles within teams are divided between offense and defense. Psychiatrist Arnold Mandell hired as a consultant despite his knowing nothing of football, studied the San Diego Chargers for a season and discovered that the categories are mislabelled. Offensive players tend to be defenders of a system while "defensive players are offensive in their attempts to destroy." The offensive personality protects the structure and is basically passive, while the defensive player is highly aggressive and gets "joy" out of destroying the structure. Mandell began developing these categorizations when he noticed that lockers of offensive personnel were neat, whereas defensive players tended to sling equipment about.[27] Interestingly, offensive heroes like Csonka, Warfield, or Griese, if Mandell is correct, symbolize law-and-order cops or western sheriffs. Along with other mass-mediated defenders of the establishment, they tend to be ushered more quickly into the upper reaches of the American "star" system than the outlaws of defensive teams, like Nick Buonoconti or Jack Scott.

Management. The organization of personnel in professional football is almost a caricature of the discipline of a modern corporate military-industrial society. Teams developed by years of training and planning, composed of forty-eight men, each performing highly specialized tasks, compete in the Super Bowl. Books by former players stress, whether approvingly or disapprovingly, the organizational discipline on and off the field.[28] David Meggyesy came to resent his authoritarian coaches; Jerry Kramer idolized his mentor Vince Lombardi; and Pete Gent described his coach, Tom Landry, as a cold technician. Gent emphasized the role of professional football as a metaphor of American society even to the point of employers moving employees, that is, teams trading players around the country for the good of the corporations without regard for personal preference or welfare.[29] Super Bowl coaches such as Shula and Grant appear on television like cool corporate executives, or perhaps like field marshalls directing troops trained in boot camp, aided by scouts, prepared for complex attack and defense maneuvers with the aid of sophisticated telephone, film, and other modern technology (*la technique,* in Ellul's sense). In an enterprise in which strict disciplinarians like Vince Lombardi, Don Shula, and Woody Hayes have created the powerful empires, the primers for coaches might be military manuals and for players *The Organization Man.* In fact, the Super Bowl trophy, dedicated to Lombardi, is a thick silver fist rising out of a block of black granite; in the top of the base is carved a single word: *Discipline.*

The imposition in April, 1974, of fines totaling $40,000 against San Diego Charger players and management for violation of NFL drug rules reflects the management structure. NFL Commissioner Pete Rozelle fined eight players, the coach, and the franchise apparently for such things as the smoking of marijuana by individuals in the privacy of their homes. The president of the Chargers, Gene Klein, immediately accepted the fine saying:

> If I quarreled with that, if I started to pick at that, I would dilute the strength of the commissioner. I want a strong commissioner for both the clubs and the ball players, for football. I think Pete is a strong commissioner.

Of course, management, on a first-name basis with its coordinator Rozelle, wants a completely authoritarian structure for professional football. On the other side, labor, represented by Ed Garvey and the NFL Players Association, called the move "an outrageous action and decision" and pledged to fight it to the end.[30] The action bypassed the more difficult question of the alleged widespread use of painkillers and amphetamines by teams and seemed only a step removed from censoring players' sex lives.

American executives find themselves thoroughly at home with professional football. The admiration of former Whittier College third-string end, Richard M. Nixon, for Lombardi seemed very like his well-publicized admiration for George C. Scott's portrayal of Patton. Former college star Gerald Ford even used clumsy football metaphors in his speeches:

> I only wish that I could take the entire United States into the locker room at half time. It would be an opportunity to say that we have lost yards against the line drives of inflation and the end runs of energy shortages. ... [But] we have a winner. Americans are winners.[31]

According to detailed accounts in *The New Yorker* and *Rolling Stone,* [32] top corporate executives from Ford, Shell, Xerox, and other giants of industry inundated Houston for Super Bowl VIII. The Alan R. Nelson Research firm of New York reports that 66 percent of those earning $20,000 or more like pro football "quite a lot," while only 42 percent say the same of major league baseball. The vice president of NBC sports, Carl Lindemann, Jr., says, "I'd be hard-pressed to name a top executive who doesn't follow football avidly."[33]

In short, if one were to create from scratch a sport to reflect the sexual, racial, and organizational priorities of the American power structure, it is doubtful that one could improve on football. In its use of both time and space, the action of football is more compressed and boxed in than is the former national pastime, baseball. Both sports are sequenced around a single ball, require large teams, and are regulated by numerous rules and rule enforcers. But, as even the simplest play diagram reveals, football's temporal and spatial confinement demands the most regimented and complexly coordinated forms of activity. The segmentation of time and space recalls the predictable regularity and externally imposed demands of other familiar American sights—assembly lines, tract homes, and superhighways.

Cross-culturally, the most absolute contrast with such industrial-military use of space, time, and labor can be seen in yoga and similar oriental exercises with their fluid continuity in time, their adaptability to any location, and their flexibility for indivdual or collective expression.

Action. Many sports, such as tennis or chess, provide no physical contact between participants. Some sports, like baseball, allow occasional contact. A few sports, like boxing and football, have physical contact as their base. In the Super Bowl, two opposing teams with members averaging roughly six feet two inches and 225 pounds in bulk line up facing each other repeatedly to engage in various kinds of body-to-body combat. Super Bowl VIII's pregame show briefly referred to "the pit," an area extending several yards on either side of the line of scrimmage and reaching from tackle to tackle along the interior line. "The pit" resembles what among densely overcrowded rat populations is called "the behavioral sink" wherein all manner of antisocial behavior abounds.

Both statistics and participant observations help identify the physical nature of football competition. Statistically, the television on-camera coverage of a typical Super Bowl VIII play showed an average of roughly 7.5 physical encounters between players per play. The extremes for any one play were a minimum of 4 and a maximum of 14 of what ranged from short-range physical contact to head-on, full-speed collisions. On an extra point conversion, 20 of the 22 players on the field participate in such physical contact, normally exempting only the kicker and his holder. The full flight collisions of kick-offs recall the charge of the Light Brigade. Participation on these special teams for punts and kick-offs or "bomb squads" according to Meggyesy "requires nothing but a touch of insanity, some speed and a willingness to hit."[34] When Jake Scott fumbled a Mike Eischeid punt in Super Bowl VIII, at least 14 separate physical encounters took place on screen before all the blocking, downfield coverage, and scrambling for the ball was completed.

Participant observations of and about injuries reveal more of the physical nature of the game. Jim Mandich's broken thumb and Paul Warfield's pulled hamstring did not prevent their playing in Super Bowl VIII, although Milt Sunde's injuries prevented his participation at the last minute. Bob Kuschenberg, Miami offensive guard, broke his left arm four weeks before Super Bowl VII. A steel pin was inserted inside the bone for protection and he played, as did four other Dolphins with metal pins holding various limbs together. For the 1970 Super Bowl, the rib cage of Kansas City defensive back Johnny Robinson was "swollen and mushy" and he was in "misery." His roommate, Len Dawson, reported

> Wednesday of that week, I was sitting there thinking there's no way he can get out on a football field. . . . He got a local anesthetic just to see what it felt like and it made him woozy. So then they got a thoracic surgeon to go in and shoot him a different way. I don't know how they shot him or where, but they were able to deaden it and leave his mind clear.[35]

Jerry Stovall reported, when he retired after nine seasons as a St. Louis Cardinal safetyman,

> In my years in football I've suffered a broken nose, fractured a right cheekbone, lost five teeth, broken my right clavicle, ripped my sternum, broken seven ribs, and have a calcium deposit in my right arm that prevents me from straightening it. I've also had 11 broken fingers. And I hurt my right foot so bad I almost lost it, injured my right arch and broke my right big toe three times. . . . The injuries hurt on rainy days—sometimes even on sunny days.[36]

Pete Gent, formerly of the Dallas Cowboys and author of the football novel *North Dallas Forty* says, "My back is so sore I can't sit still for long.

I've got arthritis in my neck from butting people with my head, and if I walk too far my knees swell. But I know plenty of guys who are hurt worse."[37] Merlin Olsen, defensive tackle for the Los Angeles Rams, described the experience of getting injured:

> I played 12 games in 1970 with a bad knee and I kept aggravating it. I knew it required an operation—both for torn ligaments and cartilage.
>
> [Then, in the 1971 Pro Bowl] I was hit directly on the kneecap and my knee bent the wrong way about 15 degrees. The minute that contact was made I could feel things starting to tear.
>
> I tried to get the foot out of the ground and couldn't. I couldn't stop my momentum, either. I was like slow motion. I could feel each muscle and ligament popping. Once I was on the ground the pain was about as intense as anything I've ever felt. But the pain was with me only about 30 seconds. Then it was gone—totally.
>
> When I went in at halftime the doctors examined me. They'd pick up my foot and the knee would stay right on the table. I got off the table and went into the shower and the knee collapsed backward on its own. A couple of coaches were standing there and they turned white and almost passed out.[38]

Olsen was lucky. He had a cast on the knee five weeks, cut the cast off, walked away, and played the next season apparently as strong as ever.

Other professional football knees make equally grisly stories. After four operations on Joe Namath's knees, one doctor estimates, "He'll barely be able to walk by the time he's forty."[39] When Dick Butkus, the Chicago Bears' middle linebacker, developed a bad right knee in the 1973 season, he continued to play. The following September he went to one of the nation's most prominent orthopedic surgeons. The surgeon reportedly called it "the worst-looking knee I have ever seen," and told Butkus, "I don't know how a man in your shape can play football or why you would even want to." The doctor advised Butkus that, if he must play, he should spend all of his time from the end of one game until ten minutes before the kick-off of the next either in bed or on crutches. The surgeon thought there was no danger of ruining the knee further by playing, because there wasn't that much left to ruin. Butkus, needless to say, finished the season and reportedly considered the installation of a metal knee after his playing days were over.[40]

Such descriptions of injuries bring out, despite immensely sophisticated and thorough padding, how physically brutal football is as a sport. Only the low number of actual fatalities preserve it against public outcry and distinguish it from outright warfare.

The Super Bowl is a paramilitary operation, according to a UPI story of November 9, 1972. The article stated that for Bud Magrum, a University of Colorado lineman, the Vietnam war was a training ground for his play on the football field. A double Purple Heart recipient decorated for bravery under fire in Vietnam, Magrum said, "You go to war on the football field. Every time you line up, you've got a job to do. You've got to go hard the whole time." And when Magrum hits someone, he likes to make sure they know they've been hit.[41] Rocky Blier went from Vietnam hero and casualty to 1975 Super Bowl hero.

North American football's violent action contrasts with other possible entertainments like dance or various noncontact sports that predominate in much of the world. Perhaps in a society that devotes over a third of its prime-time television to shows concerned with murder and violent crime and that rates explicitly brutal and gory films as G or PG, it is not surprising that its most popular sport and most lucrative media spectacle should be violent.

Motivation. In some settings, football is played for fun. But the Super Bowl is far removed from such motivation. Members of the winning team in Super Bowl VIII each received $15,000; the losers $7,500.[42] There may be a surface "thrill of combat," "test of masculinity," "search for glory and fame," and even "love of the game," but underneath there is one motive—money. When Duke Snider, a center-fielder for the Brooklyn Dodgers, published an article in the *Saturday Evening Post* in the middle 1950s admitting "I Play Baseball for Money," there was a tremor of scandal that ran through the American public, as if a clergyman had said he did not much care for God but he liked the amenities of clerical life. But when Mercury Morris was asked on national television after the Dolphins' one-sided Super Bowl VIII victory, "Was it fun?" he replied, "It was work," and no one batted an eye.

Even though professional football is played by a team, Pete Gent argues that the motivation is strictly individual. The opposition is the other team, but an individual may lose his job to, or be hurt or let down by, anyone on his own team, and any of those misfortunes might cut his reward, the salary, more than a team loss would.[43] Meggyesy adds that the player "is a commodity and he is treated with unbelievable cynicism."[44]

Even nonprofessional football has a heavily commercial base. Penn State collected $1 million from televised football in the 1973 season— $650,000 from the Orange Bowl and $350,000 from regional and national appearances during the regular season. Oklahoma's NCAA probation that same season cost them $500,000 in television revenue. Ohio State University led the nation with an average of 87,228 paying customers in each of its expensive seats at six home games in 1973. The 630 football-playing four-year colleges in the United States attracted over 31 million spectators in 1973, averaging over 10,000 for each game played in the nation.[45] The figures increased in succeeding years. An unsuccessful coach is more than a *spiritual* liability to his school. A college player, even if his scholarship and employment "ride" does not make all the sacrifice and pain worthwhile, can hope for a return on his investment by making it financially in the pros. In fact, the feeder system, which culminates in the Super Bowl, reaches down to any mobile, oversized high school or junior high player, drawing him on with the dream of fame and the crinkle of dollars.

Infrastructure. The institutional organization of professional football is not *like* American business; it *is* American business. Each team is normally a privately owned company or corporation with shareholders and top executive officers, including a president, who is frequently the principal owner. Each corporation employs hundreds, including secretaries, public relations personnel, doctors, and scouts, all of whom the public seldom hears. Employees, including players, receive salaries and bonuses and are hired and fired. Team corporations enter into multi-million-dollar television contracts and rent stadiums, which may have been financed by publicly voted bonds but leased at moderate fees to the privately owned football enterprise. A franchise in the National Football League sells for many millions of dollars. The coordinated management of the teams under the superstructure of the League and its Commissioner Pete Rozelle is matched by an increasingly powerful player's union. Without qualification, professional football is big business.

The Super Bowl itself becomes a "corporate orgy of excess and exploitation," according to *Rolling Stone*, with individual companies like Ford, Chrysler, and American Express each spending up to $150,000 hosting executives, salesmen, and customers through the weekend. A two-page article by Frank Lalli in *Rolling Stone* described Super Bowl VIII's "$12,000,000 Businessman's Special" in awesome detail. He quoted Jimmy the Greek who said that for corporate executives, the Super Bowl "is bigger than a political convention. Everybody tries to be here." Super Bowl tickets are "allocated" and NFL broadcast coordinator Robert Cochran estimates that 80 percent wind up in corporate hands. Jean Seansonne of *Newsday* said of Super Bowl VIII, "This game is for the royalty to attend and for the peasants to watch on TV, a situation that does not cause the NFL . . . any guilty feelings."[46]

Packaging. The Super Bowl as a commodity to be consumed from the television "box" receives careful packaging via the 21 percent of the broadcast devoted to pre- and postgame shows and the 39 percent between kick-off and final gun devoted to commentary and entertainment. The 1974 telecast opened with a pregame half-hour show featuring Bart Starr's analyses of filmed strengths, weaknesses, and strategies of each team and concluded with a panel of fifteen CBS sportscasters interviewing heroes of the day's game. In between, there were striking multicolor visuals with a rapid, dramatic score opening each section of the telecast; there were grandiose adjectives and historical allusions by announcers, an endless reciting or superimposing on screen of statistics and records, the pregame pageantry, the half-time extravaganzas and "Playbook," and, of course, the 52 advertisements for everything from tires to next week's CBS sports offerings.

The nationalism of American sports is made explicit with the National Anthem at the beginning of virtually every competition from Little League baseball to the Super Bowl. Super Bowl VIII offered an ideal popular singer for middle America, Charley Pride, who is both black and country-western–working-class American, Archie Bunker and Fred Sanford, all rolled into one. The CBS announcer had the right country but the wrong song, when he proclaimed that Charley Pride would now sing "America, the Beautiful." (After Pride finished the "Star Spangled Banner," it was correctly identified.) Further appeal to middle America was evident when the six officials were introduced as "a high school teacher in Ohio . . . a paint company official . . . a medical supplies salesman. . . ."

Half-time entertainment, which in a viewer survey proved generally to be scorned by male viewers but preferred over the game by some female viewers, is interesting in unintended ways. The martial music, precision drills, uniforms, and massive formations faintly recall Hitler's Nuremberg rallies, specifically as immortalized by Leni Reifenstahl in *Triumph of the Will*. Super Bowl VIII featured the University of Texas marching band with Miss Texas playing a hoe-down style fiddle. They were followed by a three-ring circus with Miss Canada as ringmistress. Female roles in America's number-one spectacle are "strictly cheesecake," as one woman commented. The telecast then cut to the American Express "Playbook" with Bud Grant, Don Shula, Tom Brookshire, and Bart Starr, followed by the live, on-field finals of the Ford punt and pass competition for boys from across the country.

Announcers between halves and throughout the game made the audio portion sound like an amalgam of the wartime rhetoric of Winston Churchill and the dry objectivity of Dow Jones averages as they praised heroics and cited statistics. They rhapsodized over Larry Csonka's running, which looked, especially in slow motion, like nothing so much as the charge of a bull across the ring in Madrid. They described intricacies of play, sometimes erroneously, throughout Super Bowl VIII and narrated no less than 44 instant replays, a television gimmick ideally suited for both the connoisseur and the inattentive. "Monday Night Football," which was ABC's highest ranking show for that fall season, coming in eighteenth with a 21.3 Nielson rating, topped CBS's Super Bowl coverage in both use of statistics and show-business style, but a technological obsession with the spectacular and the statistical were still unmistakable in television and press packaging of Super Bowl VIII.

Spectacle. What is the relationship of this packaged experience to the concrete lives of viewers and the surrounding political-economic system? The Super Bowl, like the bulk of mass-mediated culture, is at once a celebration of dominant aspects of a society and a diversion from unmediated immersion in that society.

Despite all the Super Bowl's overt and latent cultural significance, it is popular as a *game,* that is, the formal competition itself has no overt functional utility. It is apart from the viewers' work, from bills, from family anxieties, from conflicts in the community, from national and international politics. Total psychic involvement becomes desirable because the game is enjoyed for its own sake, unlike most activities in the deferred-reward world of laboring for salaries, home, and self-improvement, or eternal salvation. In contrast to wars or family problems, the viewers are aware that they can enjoy or even opt out of the Super Bowl with the same free choice that they entered into it because "it's only a game." In this manner, the Super Bowl is typical of mass-mediated culture in arousing all the emotions of excitement, hope, anxiety, and so on, but as a displacement without any of the consequences of the real-world situations that arouse such feelings.

For the viewer, the Super Bowl, like much of television and mass culture, provides a feeling of a "separate reality." Despite its mass standardization, it has something of the magic and awesome appeal of the "nonordinary states of consciousness" by which Yaqui brujo Don Juan Matus gradually transported Carlos Castaneda beyond a mechanical life of recording anthropological field data.[47] The satisfaction that viewers seek in the Super Bowl is born in a hunger not unrelated to the search for ecstasy and comprehension around which mystic and esoteric traditions have been built. In the Super Bowl, however, the yearning is arrested at a low level, subject to what Lynch calls the "magnificent imagination" that fixates rather than challenges the human capacity for creative imagery and symbolic formulations.[48]

Criticizing the Spectacle. Historically, the Super Bowl parallels the spectacles of the Coliseum in Rome where the spoils of imperialism were grandiosely celebrated. As a game, the Super Bowl is not a simple, traditional diversion in the way that playing a hand of cards is. As a human and collective experience, the Super Bowl is rather a "spectacle" of the type that Guy Debord attacks politically and philosophically in *Society of the Spectacle.* Debord claims

> The entire life of societies in which modern conditions of production reign announces itself as an immense accumulation of *spectacles.* Everything that was directly lived has moved away into a representation. . . .
>
> The spectacle, understood in its totality, is simultaneously the result

and the project of the existing modes of production. It is not a supplement to the real world, it's added decoration. It is the heart of the unrealism of the real society. In all its specific forms, as information or propaganda, advertisement or direct consumption of entertainments, the spectacle is the present *model* of socially dominant life.[49]

Charges that the Super Bowl is a spectacular opiate for an aliented society recall the "vast wasteland" analyses of American television and gain strength from a distinction made by Claude Lévi-Strauss, who states that rituals have the *conjunctive* effect of bringing about a union or even communion between initially separate groups of profane and sacred, living and dead, initiated and uninitiated. Games, on the other hand, have a *disjunctive* effect, issuing in the establishment of a difference between players or teams into winners and losers where originally there was no indication of inequality. Lévi-Strauss concludes that games, like science, produce distinct events by means of structural patterns and "we can therefore understand why competitive games should flourish in our industrial societies."[50] In such an analysis the Super Bowl appears unlike myths and rituals because it uses mental structures to direct events that result not in reconciliation, but in the separation of groups and inequality between them.

A globally cross-cultural perspective recalls the following generalizations in critically evaluating the Super Bowl as a cultural indicator:

70 percent of the world population is unable to read

Only 1 percent has a college education

50 percent suffers from malnutrition

80 percent lives in what America defines as substandard housing

The American 6% of the world population possesses over half the world's income; lives "in peace" only by arming itself against the other 94%; spends more per person on military defense than the total per person income of the rest of the world.[51]

In such a context it is not surprising that dominant popular ritual has nationalistic and militaristic overtones. In contrast, the Hopi Indians lived on roughly the same plateau in the southwestern United States for some 5,000 years in ecological balance with their environment while "Western civilization" went through the violent rise and fall of countless empires. Yet the average Super Bowl viewer may likely condemn as superstitious and savage the Hopi rituals that regulate their relationship with the environment.

Dave Meggyesy's seven years as a linebacker with the St. Louis Cardinals led him to thoroughly negative conclusions.

It would be impossible for me not to see football as both a reflection and reinforcement of the worst things in American culture. There was the incredible racism which I was to see close up in the Cardinals' organization and throughout the league. There was also violence and sadism, not so much on the part of the players or in the game itself, but very much in the minds of the beholders—the millions of Americans who watch football every weekend in something approaching a sexual frenzy. And then there was the whole militaristic aura surrounding pro football, not only in obvious things like football stars visiting troops in Vietnam, but in the language of the game—"throwing the bomb, being a field general," etc.—and in the unthinking obligation to "duty" required of players. It is no accident that some of the most maudlin and dangerous pre-game "patriotism" we see in this country appears in football stadiums. Nor is it an accident that the most repressive political regime in the history of this country is ruled by a football-freak, Richard M. Nixon.[52]

An understanding of contemporary media, the functions of mythic rituals, and the structural values of professional football in a cross-cultural framework takes one sufficiently inside the Super Bowl to explain why 85 million Americans watch it and, at the same time, provides the aesthetic distance to question the Super Bowl's global significance. The Super Bowl recapitulates in miniature and with striking clarity certain dominant strains in the society in which it was born and that takes such delight in it. As a mythic spectacle, the Super Bowl has developed as a perfect vehicle for reinforcing social roles and values in an advanced industrial state.

The structural values of the Super Bowl can be summarized succinctly: *American football is an aggressive, strictly regulated team game fought between males who use both violence and technology to win monopoly control of property for the economic gain of individuals within a nationalistic, entertainment context.* The Super Bowl propagates these values by elevating one football game to the level of a mythic spectacle that diverts consciousness from individual lives to collective feelings, and completes the circle by strengthening the very cultural values that gave birth to football. In other words, the Super Bowl serves as a mythic prototype of American ideology collectively celebrated. Rather than a mere diversionary entertainment, it can be seen to function as a "propaganda" vehicle strengthening and developing the larger social status quo.

While the critics may overstate their case, viewing the Super Bowl can be seen as a highly questionable symbolic ritual and an unflattering revelation of inner characteristics of mass-mediated culture in North America. Nevertheless, to be honest, for many of us it still may be a most enjoyable activity.

Whatever the judgment, the next time a network "proudly presents" a Super Bowl or its mass-spectacle successor, it may well be ushering in a communications event more culturally and symbolically significant than even the traditional American icons of apple pie, motherhood, and the flag.

Notes

1. Gilbert Seldes, "Communications Revolution," in Edmund Carpenter and Marshall McLuhan, eds., *Explorations in Communication* (Boston: Beacon Press, 1960), p. 198.

2. Jimmy "The Greek" Snyder of Las Vegas said of the 1974 Super Bowl in Houston: "The entire season boils down to this one game. . . . This is bigger than a political convention. Everybody tries to be here." Frank Lalli, "And Now for the Pre-Game Scores," *Rolling Stone* (February 28, 1974), p. 40.

3. Gallup and Harris polls cited in Anton Myrer, "The Giant in the Tube," *Harper's Magazine* (November 1972), p. 40.

4. Roger Angell, "Super," *New Yorker 59* (February 11, 1974), pp. 42–43.

5. Data summarized and rounded off from figures cited in Lalli, Myrer, and Angell above, and in *Variety* and *Broadcasting*.

6. *Los Angeles Times*, January 10, 1974.

7. *Sports Illustrated* (January 21, 1974), p. 14.

8. Ernst Cassirer, *Essay on Man* (New Haven: Yale University Press, 1944); Ernst Cassirer, *The Myth of the State* (New Haven: Yale University Press, 1946); Ernst Cassirer, *Philosophie der Symbolischen Formen* (Darmstadt: Wissenschaftliche Buchgesellschaft, 1958).

9. See especially Mircea Eliade, *The Sacred and the Profane*, translated by Willard R. Trask (New York: Harper & Row, 1959).

10. Claude Lévi-Strauss, *The Savage Mind* (Chicago: University of Chicago Press, 1966).

11. Roy A. Rappaport, *Pigs for the Ancestors—Ritual in the Ecology of a New Guinea People* (New Haven: Yale University Press, 1968).

12. Black Elk, *Black Elk Speaks—Being the Life Story of a Holy Man of the Oglala Sioux*, as told through John G. Neihardt (Lincoln: University of Nebraska Press, 1961).

13. Carpenter and McLuhan, eds., *op. cit.*

14. Survey by the author and assistants during week of January 13, 1974, at University of California at San Diego.

15. Harry Edwards, "The Black Athletes: Twentieth Century Gladiators for White America," *Psychology Today 7*, no. 6 (November 1973), p. 44. See also Harry Edwards, *Sociology of Sport* (Homewood, Ill.: Dorsey Press, 1973).

16. Jacques Ellul, *Propaganda: the Formation of Man's Attitudes*, translated by Konrad Kellen and Jean Lerner (New York: Alfred A. Knopf, 1966); see especially chapter 3.

17. Ronald Cummings, "The Superbowl Society" in Browne, Fishwick, and Marsden, eds., *Heroes of Popular Culture* (Bowling Green, Ohio: Bowling Green University Popular Press, 1972), pp. 109–10.

18. Lévi-Strauss, op. cit., p. 244.

19. Observations by author and assistants in various residences on January 13, 1974.

20. Linda Scarborough, "Four Thousand Inches of Super Bowl Blitz," *More* (February 1974), p. 12.

21. Cummings, op. cit., p. 104.

22. Eliade, op. cit.

23. Rappaport, op. cit., pp. 3–4.

24. Cummings, op. cit., pp. 103–4.

25. Hunter S. Thompson, "Fear and Loathing at the Super Bowl," *Rolling Stone* (February 28, 1974), p. 28.

26. Edwards, loc. cit.

27. Matt Mitchell, "The Last Outpost of Civilized Warfare—Dr. Arnold Mandell on Pro Football Players," *Sports Digest* (October, 1973), pp. 11–13.

28. David M. Meggyesy, *Out of Their League* (Berkeley: Ramparts Press, 1970); Chip Oliver, *High for the Game*, Ron Rapoport, ed. (New York: William Morrow, 1971); Jerry Kramer and Dick Schaap, *Instant Replay* (New York: Norton, 1968); Jimmy Brown with Myron Cope, *Off My Chest* (New York: Doubleday, 1964); see also George Plimpton, *Paper Lion* (New York: Harper & Row, 1965) and Vince Lombardi, *Run to Daylight* (Englewood Cliffs, N.J.: Prentice-Hall, 1963).

29. Peter Gent, *North Dallas Forty* (New York: William Morrow 1973); also interview NBC "Today" show, October 9, 1973. The use of technology and managerial techniques is similar to that described in Jacques Ellul, *The Technological Society*, trans. John Wilkinson (New York: Alfred A. Knopf, 1964).

30. *San Diego Union*, April 28, 1974, pp. 81 and 88.

31. *Newsweek*, February 25, 1974, p. 30.

32. Angell, op. cit.; Lalli, op. cit.

33. Lalli, op. cit., p. 40.

34. Meggyesy, op. cit., p. 127.

35. Dwight Chapin, "Playing in Pain," *Los Angeles Times*, February 10, 1974, III, p. 9.

36. Ibid., p. 8.

37. Ibid.

38. Ibid., p. 1.

39. Ibid., p. 8.

40. Dave Nightingale, "Butkus May Get Metal Knee," *Los Angeles Times*, February 10, 1974, III, pp. 8–9.

41. "Football Magrum's Own War" (UPI) *San Diego Union*, November 9, 1972.

42. "Facts and Figures on Super Bowl VIII," *Los Angeles Times*, January 13, 1974, III, p. 6.

43. Gent interview, loc. cit.

44. Meggyesy, op. cit., p. 44.

45. "TV Giveth and TV Taketh Away," *Chicago Tribune*, December 23, 1973; also "Ohio State Tops Nation in Football Attendance," (AP) *Chicago Tribune*, December 23, 1973.

46. Lalli, op. cit.; Angell, op. cit.

47. Carlos Castanada, *The Teachings of Don Juan* (Berkeley: University of California Press, 1968); *A Separate Reality* (New York: Simon & Schuster, 1971); *Journey to Ixtlan* (New York: Simon and Schuster, 1972).

48. William F. Lynch, S.J., *The Image Industries* (New York: Sheed & Ward, 1959).

49. Guy Debord, *Society of the Spectacle*, unauthorized translation (Detroit: Black and Red, 1970), paragraphs 1 and 6.

50. Lévi-Strauss, op. cit., p. 32.

51. American Friends Service Committee, "Bulletin," December, 1973.

52. Meggyesy, op. cit., pp. 146–47. Myrer, op. cit., reaches a similar conclusion: "But of course football is *not* a sport, any more than Vietnamization has meant peace in Vietnam. Football is a symbol, a mass entertainment, a heavy industry, a way of life—a kind of upside-down morality play in which might is right and viciousness is its own reward, where the talented and vulnerable are maimed and the brutish survive and are increased."

Health

Marcus Welby, the retired chief of staff of television medicine, and his colleagues express culturally dominant images of health and drama.

4

Marcus Welby
and the
Medical Genre

What makes up the genre of medical drama and its popular picture of health?

What are the standard conventions of setting, character, and plot in televised medicine?

How do dramatic and documentary medical programming compare?

How do commercials relate to health?

What is the potential of mass media for health education and service?

How does the mass-mediated medical genre express and shape a network of cultural priorities in both health care and the larger political-economic system?

"Marcus Welby, M.D." represents a category of popular entertainment concerned with the medical profession and the struggle of health and life against disease and death. Popular portrayals of medical practice run from children playing doctor to novels of student nurses to the infamous doctors Jekyll and Frankenstein and on to "Ben Casey" and "Medical Center." These portrayals constitute a *genre* of dramatic conventions focused around the important issue of a culture's image of physical health and of systematic means for maintaining it.

Genre and Formula in Popular Culture

The analysis of genre and formula has proven a productive methodology for classifying and understanding such mass-mediated popular culture as westerns, detective fiction, romantic love stories, comics, science fiction, and other identifiable groupings.

John Cawelti defines a *genre* as "a conventional system for structuring cultural products."[1] He distinguishes *conventions,* in the form of certain favorite plots, stereotyped characters, or similar elements known beforehand by both creator and audience, from *inventions* uniquely imagined by the creator. Popular writers, directors, producers, and performers employ genres in the form of conventional formulas. The formulas provide standardized settings, situations, characters, and patterns of action. Such conventional systems in turn reflect patterns of games, rituals, dreams, symbols, and myths in the present and past of the larger cultural system. Genre or formula analysis draws from social science approaches such as content analysis and from literary approaches to settings, characters, plots, and similar dramatic conventions.

Behind the analysis of genre and formula in popular culture is the literary approach to myths and symbols as, in the words of Cawelti, "the key to unlock the secrets of culture through an analysis of the dialectic between literary expression and the realities of society."[2] In this approach, the mythic image is seen as a mode of perception as well as a reflection of reality. It *expresses* all that a culture attaches to an object or idea and *shapes* the perceptions of those who share it. By identifying the basic patterns in a conventional formula and in several formulas, genre analysis searches for the "network of assumptions" that express the basic values of a culture or subculture in a particular era.

This chapter investigates the genre and formulas of medicine and health in popular culture as they are pictured in their most widespread representations, namely on television, including documentary nonfiction and spot announcements as well as dramatic fiction. What can a survey of the popular genre of medical fact and fiction reveal about the dramatic conventions of commercial media; the actual delivery of health care today; the potential for the dissemination of health information; and the cultural system of which all this is a part?

Televised Medical Dramas

Horace Newcomb pioneered the study of the medical (and legal) genre on television in his chapter on "Doctors and Lawyers: Counselors and Confessors" in *TV: The Most Popular Art*.[3] He traced a major part of the appeal of Marcus Welby to the fatherly compassion of the figure played by Robert Young who had previously starred in the series "Father Knows Best." Newcomb concluded that Welby, as counselor and confessor as well as medical specialist, solved fictional problems in the show's plot while directing to the audience advice that embodied traditional American values in a more-or-less explicitly didactic way.

"Marcus Welby, M.D." became the chief of staff of the medical genre through its consistently high television ratings from 1969 to 1976. Welby's creator and executive producer, David Victor, also developed "Dr. Kildare" a decade earlier. "Dr. Kildare," like its contemporay "Ben Casey," centered around the relationship between the younger star and his older medical mentor. Welby reversed the emphasis by focusing on the older doctor who guides his assistant, Dr. Steven Kiley, toward competence, trustworthiness, and compassion. Producer Victor ascribed the program's continued popularity to the fact that, as family practitioners, Welby and Kiley saw the entire spectrum of human drama. Victor noted, "You get yourself painted in a corner, dealing only with hospital cases."[4] The star, Robert Young, received an average of 5,000 letters a week seeking medical and emotional advice.

The Welby formula employs as its setting a private practitioner's offices and connected home, a situation featuring a single patient and his or her family in each episode, and a plot in which Welby and Kiley treat medical problems, provide emotional support, and often heal broken family structures.

A sample of nine programs[5] featured these patients: a superstar tennis player and his wealthy mother; a teacher; a wealthy financier and his social columnist wife; the wife of a wealthy politician; a wealthy young lawyer and his heiress sister; a middle-class couple; and two other wealthy patients whose occupations were not specified (see Table 4–1). Seven of the nine patients were wealthy. Six of the nine were missing a close relative—father or mother, husband or wife—for whom Welby and Kiley provided emotional substitutes. Most of the episodes pictured initial resistance by the patient to treatment, efforts by the doctors to help the patient face the disease, and a flawlessly correct use of therapy and medication. Minorities and women were cast in traditional roles with most doctors played by white males (none were women), nurses primarily played by white females (none male), and integration primarily in roles played by orderlies (although two young interns were black). Contrary to medical reality, patients were often portrayed as being perfectly well one minute and seriously ill the next. In the end of each episode, the lives of each patient and his or her family are usually happier and more satisfying

TABLE 4–1. Socioeconomic Status and Absences of Family Members for Nine Episodes of "Marcus Welby, M.D."

SAMPLE	DATE OF BROADCAST	OCCUPATION/STATUS OF PATIENT AND/OR FAMILY	ABSENCE OF FAMILY MEMBER
1.	1/28	Superstar tennis player, rich mother	Father (husband)
2.	2/04	Teacher	Wife
3.	2/11	Well-to-do	Father (husband)
4.	2/25	Well-to-do politician's wife	None*
5.	3/04	Well-to-do	Father (husband)
6.	4/08	Rich financier, social columnist wife	None
7.	4/29	Well-to-do young lawyer,	Both
8.	5/06	rich heiress sister	Parents
9.	5/13	Middle-class couple	None

*At the end of this program the husband is serving a prison sentence while the wife is being counseled by Dr. Welby.

through the intervention of Dr. Welby, even when medical cures are impossible.

The standardized setting, characters, and plot resolution in "Marcus Welby, M.D." create and satisfy formulaic dramatic expectations among viewers. Their impact may also carry over into real life.

Dr. Michael Halberstam notes, "Focusing on one problem patient and his family per episode, Welby and Kiley seem to be running a two-man Intensive Care Service, in which they not only attend to their patients' medical problems, but take them to ball games, serve them elaborate dinners, stop by their jobs, and attend their weddings." Halberstam concedes that for dramatic purposes the condensation is justifiable but warns that exaggerations may lead 46 million viewers to expect superhuman medical care.[6] More malpractice suits may be one result.

Viewers are warned that money helps in acquiring quality medical treatment. In the nine-program sample of "Marcus Welby, M.D., the preponderance of wealthy patients added the dramatic appeal of the prestige and glamor of wealth. Its "incidental learning" also supported the scramble for money and reflected the class-bias of American health care in which quality treatment is a privilege for the wealthy and not a right for all, despite the range of governmental and private medical insurance and subsidy programs.

"Marcus Welby, M.D." consistently portrayed the scientific and emotional aspects of disease and health care with sophistication and precision. However, the program generally avoided sensitive or complex ethical and political problems such as the socialization of medicine, doctors' strikes and slow-downs, doctor shortages in rural and inner-city areas, institutional abuses, malpractice controversies, and the importance of continuous preventive measures as well as episodic curative medicine. The program's caution generally favored established power and stereotypes. One episode, "The Outrage," dealt with the sexual assault of a fourteen-year-old boy by his male science teacher. Protests against the episode from the National Education Association, the City of New York Human Rights Commission, the Atlanta Board of Education, the National Gay Task Force, the American Psychiatric Association, and others pointed out that homosexual child molestation was no more common than heterosexual and that the program may have damaged both homosexuals and public educators.[7] Since Welby's audience ratings remained high, ABC was little bothered by the complaints.

The ultimate priority for Welby and other programs in the medical genre is audience size and consequent advertiser income, but scripts are checked for medical authenticity. Since 1955, the Physicians Advisory Committee on Television, Radio and Motion Pictures (PAC), formed by the American Medical Association, has been the official medical advisory body working in conjunction with American mass media. In 1966, the PAC chairman described the role of its nine members in Hollywood and four in New York: "The PAC's prime function is to maintain medical accuracy. It should be thoroughly understood that it in no way acts as a censor of storyline material. If this were attempted, the door of the media would be quickly closed to them. The sole purpose of the Committee is to give corect assistance."[8] PAC reviewed each Welby script for technical accuracy and provided two on-site physicians as technical advisors. In addition, the American Academy of Family Physicians (AAFP), a nation-wide organization of 35,000 family practitioners, checked the Welby scripts through its Public Relations Committee to ensure accurate portrayals of primary care family medical practices.

Despite its limitations, "Marcus Welby, M.D." easily surpassed in medical authenticity most of the remainder of television's medical staff. The 1960s offered "The Nurses," "Ben Casey," "Doctor Kildare," and similar melodramas. The 1970s brought "Medical Center," "Police Surgeon," "Emergency," Danny Thomas in "The Practice," and others. Continuing from the 1950s, in fact from the heyday of radio soap operas, the daytime serials have abounded in doctors and nurses. "As the World Turns," "Days of Our Lives," "Love of Life," and the other daily melodramas virtually all feature doctors and medicine as frequently as does their competitor, "The Doctors," which is ponderously dedicated each afternoon to "the brotherhood of healing."

As an example of the cruder dimension of the medical genre, "The Nurses" played on television for several years beginning in 1962. It used two registered nurses as consultants, one on scripts and one on the set. The American Nursing Association volunteered its services, but the producer selected his own nurse consultants and, if one acknowledged that a given incident was *possible*, it was left in the script. Of course, "The Nurses" became deeply involved in the private lives of their patients. Executive producer Herbert Brodkin defended outlandish dramatic devices by saying, "A nurse's job is to prevent dramatic episodes from happening so the climactic situations are in a sense artificial. But without these dramatics we wouldn't have a show."[9] Many real-life nurses wrote letters complaining of the ineptness of the student nurse in the program, failure to show her in a student role, overly dramatic presentations of hospital life and the nurse's role, and portrayals of nurses as alcoholics, reactionaries, and neurotics. The escapist diversions of "The Nurses" tended to illustrate Herbert Schiller's thesis in *The Mind Managers*: "The aim to television and radio programming . . . in a commercial society is not to arouse but to lessen concern about social and economic realities."[10]

Among other dramatic medical programs, "Medical Center" featured the steely-blue-eyed Chad Everett as Dr. Joe Gannon, who seemed to have been certified in all twenty of the medical specialty fields of the American Medical Association. Despite exterior shots of the grounds and buildings of a modern urban research, education, and clinical medical facility (UCLA's in fact), the program featured standard "hospital television" and was most popular with female viewers, especially adolescent girls and women over fifty.[11] A Canadian series, "Police Surgeon," resembled low-budget, action-adventure movies more than a medical show. "Emergency" was little more than a fireman-rescue program, which made it number one in popularity among children under twelve.[12] Danny Thomas as Dr. Jules Bedford in "The Practice" alternately healed and yelled at his patients on the West Side of Manhattan; like Welby, he even made house calls—a note of pure nostalgia for most viewers.

As a whole, dramatic programming in the medical genre on commercial television capitalizes on the immediate emotions and drama of the struggle against death and disease, the threat of severance from loved ones, the aura of science and technology, and the ideals of human compassion and service. The shows maximize the dramatic potential of medicine with minimal attention to instruction concerning health and medicine. These dramatic productions are the most popular formula in the medical genre because, despite the wishes of narrow rationalists, they present myth and drama broadly conceived more than information and education in a formal sense.

Documentary Televised Medicine

Medix. The "Medix" documentary series was created by the Los Angeles County Medical Association (LACMA), whose members sensed a need for public health education and, in conjunction with an independent film production company, created "Medix" as a local program for the Los Angeles area.

After receiving consistently high ratings, the half-hour show was syndicated and eventually appeared on 75 stations available to approximately 65 percent of the nation's population.[13] In 1972 and 1973, it received an Emmy award from the Hollywood Chapter of the Academy of Television Arts and Sciences for achievement in a Community Affairs Series. It received three other Emmy nominations as well as numerous awards and commendations for distinguished public service broadcasting from such major health organizations as the American Heart Association, the American Medical Association, the Red Cross, and the March of Dimes.[14]

Ideas for programs originate with members of the Medical Association. The scripts are then prepared by the show's executive producer and are reviewed by a member of LACMA's Public Information Committee. Joseph F. Boyle, M.D., Trustee of LACMA, explains the function of his physician's group in the show's production: "We have a clear understanding that our role is to see that the information is accurate and clear, but we exercise no editorial control beyond that. Whatever the good or bad aspects of medical practice which may turn up in a 'Medix' story, it is understood that it will be presented in a fair and open fashion. We also have an understanding with both our producer and the television station that we will not attempt either overtly or covertly to sell the medical profession to the public."[15]

Most of the installments combine footage filmed on location with studio segments hosted by a young newsman. The format of the "medical knowledge" programs features documentation of a disease or condition, its prevalence among the population, and the frontiers of research now being explored to combat it.

A breakdown of the topics of the first 26 syndicated shows (see Table 4–2) reveals that four major health subject areas were *not* covered: cancer, nutrition, sex education, and issues in health care delivery.

When the producers desired to make the show available nationwide,

TABLE 4–2. Topics for the First 26 National Broadcasts of "Medix"

I. *Medical Knowledge* (13 programs):	Disaster Drill
The Seeing Eye	Objective: Healthy Babies
Sleep and Dreams	A Fitness Fun-for-All
Count Backwards from 100 . . . Pain	You're Being Asked (to give blood)
How Do You Hear?	
When Kidneys Fail	III. *First Aid* (3 programs):
So Old the Pain (Arthritis)	What to Do at an Accident
The Physical	With a Little Health from our Friends
Autistic Children	This Is an Emergency
The Day of Two Doctors	
The Complete Heart	IV. *Alcoholism* (2 programs):
Chalk Talk with a Jock Dock (sports medicine)	The Deadliest Drug
	How Drinking Affects Driving
The Difference Is—Now They Can Walk	V. *Quiz* (2 programs):
If Your Child Were Deaf	Health Quiz
	What Do You Know About Teeth
II. *Health Advice (preventive, etc.)* (5 programs):	VI. *Other* (1 program):
How to Take It Off (dieting)	Youth Gives a Damn

the Burroughs-Wellcome Pharmaceutical Company agreed to sponsor the effort. Burroughs-Wellcome had been involved in progressive medical developments through annual donations of hundreds of thousands of dollars for the development of clinical pharmacology programs in various medical schools. Their sponsorship of "Medix" made the show available to individual local stations free of charge. Burroughs-Wellcome received two of the five minutes of commercial time, and the station could then sell the remaining three or use them for public service announcements. In addition, the drug firm invited local and state medical societies to participate in sponsorship at no expense to themselves.[16] As "public service programming," it promises less income for stations and is broadcast outside prime audience hours. For instance, in San Diego "Medix" was aired Sunday nights at 11 P.M., when, according to Nielsen, only 23 percent of homes with television sets had them turned on.[17]

Today's Health. "Today's Health" was modeled after the AMA's magazine of the same name. The half-hour offering was planned for syndication in 50 markets throughout the country in the spring of 1974, but it never got off the ground. The show's format was divided into three segments: (a) documented medical news shorts; (b) an interview with a celebrity about his or her personal medical experience; and (c) a discussion with an expert on some field of health care. The program was moderated by a young male M.D. and an actress with experience in consumer affairs. On the pilot broadcast they discussed such topics as varicose veins and a new cure for hiccups. Another segment featured a general practitioner discussing the doctor-patient relationship with aid of staged vignettes. The discussion concerned such down-to-earth matters as why a patient may have to wait hours to see a physician for a few minutes. In the celebrity interview portion, comic Peter Sellers explained life after a coronary.[18]

"Today's Health" attempted to cater to the expectations of the American viewing audience: happy-talk hosts, a rehash of superficialities, no complex issues of health and health care delivery, skirting of socially accepted antihealth practices such as preservatives in and processing of commercial foods, and a celebrity interview, which was potentially effective and has been utilized in several "Medix" installments. However, lacking vitality, the program was never widely syndicated.

Feeling Good. "Feeling Good" was first offered in 1974 as an hour-long "variety show." When critics attacked its sloppiness, it was taken off the air for "revision." It was then shortened to a half-hour show and focused on just one issue each week.

"Feeling Good" was created by the Children's Television Workshop, originator of "Sesame Street," which had raised children's programming above the quagmire of Saturday morning cartoons. "Feeling Good" broke from tradition by addressing pressing health problems and involving non-whites in a realistic manner. The program was conceived as having a vast potential for delivering health education to all segments of the population, largely due to its freedom from commercial interests. However, the program's initial effect was watered down by its adherence to a "variety show" format: an hour of skits, routines, and musical numbers complete with stylishly designed studio sets.

The newer "Feeling Good" abandoned this piecemeal approach by shortening the broadcast, dealing with only one topic per program, and engaging television personality Dick Cavett as its host. Cavett, in introducing, narrating, and concluding, gave a warm human touch to each installment, balancing wit and gravity. Each program either featured a distinguished cast in a dramatization of a problem or offered a well-crafted documentary film. At the close of the program, "Feeling Good" listed telephone numbers of various agencies in the community for further information or assistance. Bradley Greenberg's research study of one episode, "VD Blues," found an encouragingly high percentage of exposure, increased information, and greater ease in dealing with this frequently taboo topic as a result of the program.

Commercials and Health

Health-related short spots on television promote drug consumption and tend to provide little helpful information concerning health. Researchers at the Wayne State University School of Medicine watched one Detroit station for an entire week—130 hours—and found that 70 percent of the health material broadcast was inaccurate, misleading, or both. They reported that many major health problems were virtually ignored with the four major causes of local deaths receiving very little attention. In addition, the topic of disease prevention merited only 16 minutes out of the 130 hours logged, and only one 3-minute spot appeared concerning mental health. They compared the number of "pro-drug" messages urging the consumption of a pill or other ingested remedy to those assuming an anti-drug stance and found that the pro-drug statements outnumbered the others by a margin of greater than 10:1, providing ample support for the national pattern of extensive legal and illegal drug usage. The researchers concluded that "very few of the health categories actually contain health information—in fact, only anti-drug, anti-smoking, prevention, mental health and others could be said to contain any at all. The rest are primarily profit-oriented, and contain health information only to the extent necessary to justify the particular product or service being advocated."[19]

In another study, Joan Gussow found that the nutritional message of children's television advertising was blatantly antinutrition. The study, which was presented as testimony before the Subcommittee on the Consumer of the U.S. Senate Commerce Committee, observed that over 82 percent of the network commercials aired during children's broadcasts were for ingestable items. In decreasing order of frequency, the foods advertised were breakfast cereals, snacks, vitamins, beverages and beverage mixes, frozen waffles and toaster tarts, canned pasta, canned desserts, frozen dinners, fast food restaurants, peanut butter, and oranges. The researchers noted that the four basic food groups were very poorly represented and that the vast majority of the commercials were for food products, not for the foods themselves.

Two related studies of the impressionability of children underscore the importance of the above. In one, preschool children were given two food substances and exhibited a marked preference for one of them. However, after being read a story in which the hero enjoyed the overly sweet, originally unpalatable taste while their favorite was portrayed as tasting bad, the children reversed their initial preference for several days. Another report showed that a group of fifth and sixth graders believed 70 percent of health-related commercials and that belief in and use of related products was higher in children with lower socioeconomic status.[20] Joan Gussow remarks, "For every advertiser, the decision on what and where to advertise is, of course, based on marketing wisdom, not nutritional wisdom. Unfortunately, the combined impact of all these *marketing* decisions delivers a rather stunningly counternutritional message to our children." She concludes that "the attitude of some American food manufacturers toward food, that it is just one more of the world's raw materials to be played with and manipulated for our amusement and for the greater delight of that 'consuming prince,' the American, is immoral."[21]

Another segment of the population specially affected by television advertising is the elderly. A random sample of 100 commercials found that a majority of the ads promised youth, youthful appearance, or energy to act youthful (often by implying an improved sex life), while 43 percent of them featured young and attractive characters. This indicates that television commercials dictate that youth is the model by which to measure one's self. As Scott Francher, a geriatrician, states, "The gap between the physical and social self as experienced in reality and the television self, the model the viewer is directed to incorporate, may be so great that a loss of self-esteem is a natural consequence. Such occurrences as thinning hair, failing eyesight, dentures, and a more measured, less action-oriented life style are not accounted for by the social model; indeed, their very existence is met with denial."[22]

The importance of the televised image of age is magnified when conjoined with the theory of Dr. Muriel Oberleder of the Bronx State Hospital, who maintains that senility is not caused physiologically but is a function of the anxiety related to the *cultural* stresses placed on the elderly juxtaposed with the usual life crises of the aged, such as forced retirement, loss of spouse, and the like.[23] The televised rejection of the elderly, perhaps reflecting a societal fear of aging and death, may be connected with the fact that the elderly spend the least money on advertised goods of any consumer group.

While taking advantage of children and ignoring the elderly, television advertisers in general sell a materialistic, commodity-based life-style founded on *consumerism*. An examination of the commercials shown with two medical dramatic series, "Marcus Welby, M.D." and "Medical Center," illustrates this. (See Tables 4–3 and 4–4.) The data point to at least two trends: a heavy reliance on cosmetics, nonnutritious foods, and over-the-counter drugs, and a paucity of public interest or community service messages.

TABLE 4–3. Advertisements Appearing on Nine Episodes of "Marcus Welby, M.D."

I. *Cosmetics* (18 total)
   A. Baby Oil 2
   B. Hair Coloring 5 (3)
   C. Deodorant 4 (2)
   D. Skin Creme 3 (2)
   E. Eye Shadow
   F. Pantyhose
   G. Mouthwash
   H. Hair dryer

II. *Food Products* (10 total)
   A. Soft drinks 2 (2)
   B. Instant Drink Mix
   C. Instant Soup Mix
   D. Fast-food outlet
   E. Flavored peanut spread
   F. Cake Mix
   G. Crackers
   H. Cereal
   I. Wine

III. *Health Related* (19 total)
   A. Pain Relievers 11 (5)
   B. Toothpaste 3

   C. Soap 2 (2)
   D. Tampons 2
   E. Asthma Reliever

IV. *Household Items* (16 total)
   A. Dog Food 4 (4)
   B. Cleansers 4 (2)
   C. Oven cleaner (2)
   D. Laundry aids 2 (2)
   E. Carpeting
   F. Paint
   G. Vacuum cleaner
   H. Dishwasher

V. *Other* (4 total)
   A. Motel 2
   B. Bank
   C. Felt-tip pen

VI. *Community Service* (1 total)
   A. Free blood check

See Table 4–1 for dates. Number after product indicates the total number (if greater than 1) of each type of ad. Number in parentheses indicates number of different companies (if greater than 1) represented.

TABLE 4–4.   Advertisements Appearing on Four Episodes of "Medical Center," April 28–June 2, 1975 (See Table 4–3 note)

I. *Cosmetics* (10 total)
  A. Deodorant 3 (3)
  B. Make-up 2
  C. Beauty soap
  D. Perfume
  E. Mouthwash
  F. Shampoo
  G. Pantyhose

II. *Food Products* (11 total)
  A. Tea 2
  B. Spaghetti sauce 2
  C. Soft drinks 2 (2)
  D. Chewing gum
  E. Fast food outlet
  F. Gelatin dessert mix
  G. Automatic coffee maker
  H. Vegetable oil

III. *Health Related* (2 total)
  A. "Sex-appeal" toothpaste
  B. Aspirin

IV. *Household Items* (11 total)
  A. Cleansers 5 (5)
  B. Laundry aids 3 (2)
  C. Dishwashing liquid
  D. Cat food
  E. Plastic trash bags

The many cosmetic advertisements reflect the youth obsession discussed above. In addition, most of the items displayed represent a learned compulsion to anoint the body with artificial products without giving thought to their possible long-range side effects. For example, many commercials present products as "the natural way" when they are in actuality highly processed, synthetic substances. Also, the Food and Drug Administration does not require cosmetic manufacturers to establish the safety of their products before marketing and advertising them.

Health-related items account for a large portion of the commercial time on "Marcus Welby" and "General Hospital." These are the same advertisements that form the bulk of the pool labeled "inaccurate and misleading" in the Detroit study. Claims that "four out of five doctors" recommend the product, that "hospital testing" has proved its value, or that it "contains the ingredient doctors prescribe most" are aired without mentioning, for instance, the size or inherent bias of a survey, or the difference in treatment of a condition requiring a prescription and one that can be controlled with over-the-counter nostrums or with no drugs at all.

The tensions between advertising and health are not new. During the late eighteenth century, an Englishman named Sir John Hill regularly published a journal, probably the most potent advertising medium of the time, that was the equivalent of television today. It carried ads for his herbal remedies, which he claimed to be infallible panaceas, his poetry, which was comparable to contemporary jingles, and a weekly "lay sermon." The sermon was apparently designed to convince readers of his honesty in the same way that an actor portrays a doctorlike "expert" sitting behind an official-looking desk and removes his glasses to "level with" the viewers. Television viewers may share the antagonism toward medical advertisers that prompted one of Sir John's contemporaries to send him these lines.

"Thou essence of dock, valerian and sage,
At once the disgrace and pest of this age.
The worst that we wish for thee, for all thy crimes,
Is to take thy own physic and read thy own rhymes."[24]

Television commercials may be the single most powerful persuasive medium in the world today. They could be used directly to promote health, education, creativity, understanding, and the general welfare instead of serving merely sales and profits. But 60 seconds of commercial time on the Welby show costs $75,000, above and beyond the tens of thousands of dollars in production costs for making the advertisements. As a result, few community service announcements or health-for-health's-sake messages are aired during the program or throughout prime time from 8 to 11 P.M. when viewing is heaviest and profits are greatest.

Television's Potential

American television has great potential for transmitting health information. What might television do to promote specific public health education campaigns; general health education; special programming for specific groups in the population, such as the elderly; postgraduate education for physicians; and broadcasting that demands active participation rather than the passive deterioration of the viewer?

The simplest television tool is the 30- or 60-second public service announcement (PSA). Since the mid-1960s, the American Dental Association has produced and distributed one-minute cartoon films to over 250 TV stations throughout the country. The spots are intended to be shown during peak mother and/or child viewing hours and cover such topics as the importance of dental health to total health and appearance, brushing after meals, safety, and periodontal disease. Although there has been nó pilot study to monitor the effectiveness of the presentations, a 1965 survey was answered by 60 percent of the stations carrying the PSAs with an average of 12 showings a month per station.[25]

The PSA has also been used in the field of mental health as a tool in primary prevention. In 1970, a series of six-minute-long messages was produced by the Ohio Department of Mental Health and Mental Retardation, employing hand puppets to deal with six stress situations of childhood: the arrival of a new baby brother or sister, a mother's pregnancy, starting school, a death in the family, hospitalization, and parental arguments.[26] The series applies the crisis theory of Dr. Gerald Caplan, who maintains that distressing life situations often result in serious emotional disturbance. If the crisis is successfully resolved, the individual's ability to deal with subsequent crises should be enhanced, thus reducing the probability of serious emotional decompensation under stress.[27] In each of the PSAs, "Bernard the St. Bernard" practices such "crisis intervention" by providing understanding and reassurance to his troubled puppet friends. The aim of the films is to lend guidance to children in such situations before they actually have to encounter them, so that they may be better prepared to handle such problems in real life.

The television spots are presented in conjunction with continuous puppet shows at the annual state fair, as well as the distribution of 10,000 "Bernard" coloring books. A survey conducted 18 months after the initial presentation of the series indicated that 90 percent of the children and 50 percent of the parents questioned were familiar with the films, with an overwhelmingly favorable reaction from both groups.

The short spot announcement can be valuable in any number of health education issues. For example, PSAs could be employed to bring potential cancer victims, otherwise fearful of the disease and its treatment, into their doctors' offices promptly after the first symptoms appear. One recent suggestion along these lines describes "a spot during the time-out of a football game showing a man turning away from a TV set and saying, 'I had cancer of the _____ ten years ago. I went to my doctor when I first noticed that something was wrong. We caught it early and treated it immediately. Now I am in good health, working and enjoying my life. Cancer can be a treatable disease.' "[28] Such "healthy" television seems to be effective. One "Medix" program on "How Drinking Affects Driving" was credited by various law enforcement agencies as well as the Southern California Automobile Club as having a significant influence on the decrease in Los Angeles traffic accidents and fatalities over the 1973 Christmas holiday season.[29] Other programs might offer compensatory information and direction in areas of low doctor-density and could attract more minority members into health careers despite the prohibitive costs of training.

In Canada, a series of four miniprograms on prenatal care was aired on an afternoon discussion program on commercial television with accompanying free literature made available to the viewers. In a follow-up survey, the only major complaint registered by viewers was that they wanted more time devoted to the films, while the producers felt that the use of educational over commercial television would have benefitted the programs.[30] "Consultation," a show originating from the University of

Illinois Medical Center in Chicago, is a weekly half-hour medical information program with an extremely tight budget broadcast on various stations in 35 states.[31] It features the show's host experiencing various treatments and examinations, followed by dialogue with a guest medical professional. Taking this participation concept one step further, a Boston program entitled "Medical Call" consisted of a 20-minute visual and verbal presentation of some health topic, followed by a "live" telephone question-and-answer session among viewers, the physician-host, and his local health personnel guests.

To reach a specific segment of the community, a new type of information transmission, the "narrowcast" on cable channels, is now possible. One such special population group is the elderly. As was described above, commercial television relates a distorted view of the elderly, even though they watch more TV than any other age group.[32] This group has several specific problems in obtaining health care: They are physically or mentally limited in getting to it, they have difficulty in wading through the often complex delivery systems such as social security and Medicaid, and their isolation may leave them ignorant of current and accurate health information. Cable casting to the elderly might be economically beneficial as well. It is estimated that 30 percent of the elderly in nursing homes could live elsewhere with minimal assistance. Since a sizeable portion of Medicaid money is spent on these patients and average rates in nursing homes can be as much as $1,500 a month per patient, considerable sums could be saved by using CATV to enable senior citizens to remain outside full-time facilities.

Another health field that could be stimulated by cable television is the postgraduate education of physicians. Television has been used in this pursuit in Canada[33] and Great Britain[34] and has received a generally favorable response in each country. The major aim of these broadcasts is to keep medical professionals abreast of new knowledge and techniques. On the British program, a specially prepared postscript leaflet includes names of drugs mentioned and recommended dosages with additional information available in a printed supplement to each show.

One final type of health programming is that demanding the physical participation of its viewers, as opposed to the passive inactivity requisite for all other types of TV viewing. An example is "Lilias, Yoga, and You," which is aired at various times during the day over the Public Broadcasting Network. The show features a young woman, Lilias, demonstrating and explaining for home participation the exercises, postures, and rhythms of yoga. She teaches exercise, deep breathing, self-control, and bodily awareness. Indirectly, the program transmits an alternative philosophy, attitudes of self-respect, and an awareness essential to proper health. This program illustrates the valuable and indirectly health-related programming that can exist even within the wasteland that television often is today.

Herbert Schiller summarizes the negative side of both the hope and frustration inherent in the medical genre and throughout modern television: "The lethal combination of intentionally devitalized programming and physically inactivating communications technology is the machinery of contemporary American mind management. Creative efforts to overcome, or at least counterbalance, this passivity-inducing system are desperately needed. An imaginative approach can promote participation and awareness, but it is unrealistic to expect the corporate economy to encourage such efforts."[35]

The Question of Priorities

United States television in particular and Western mass-mediated culture in general reveal the system-specific *priorities* of the multinational society they reflect and instruct.

Health care illustrates the underlying structural symmetry between media image and social reality. The availability and thoroughness of medical care are usually fine for those who can afford it. The medical profession is relatively small but quite prosperous. Sedative and compensatory drugs abound. External cosmetics and flavoring displace internal health and nutrition. Producers and advertisers of consumer goods and services cater to superficial wants that are easily manipulated and exploited and ignore more complex, subtle, and difficult-to-satisfy needs. The educational and persuasive power of the media are used to teach more of the same: how to sell material goods, preserve the status quo in the distribution of power and priorities, and place a low priority on explaining or inspiring healthy living.

The United States has more television sets than bathtubs. Almost 97 percent of the homes have sets and have one turned on an average of almost six and one-half hours per day. What does this great national resource teach and defend as priorities?

Closely related to health, the *international distribution of food* raises questions about the priorities that tend to dominate in mass-mediated culture and, as the last chapter spells out, symmetrically reflect the institutional structure of the political-economic system of private property, capital, enterprise, and profit.

A major international health problem concerns a world food shortage that has been warned of by futurologists and documented by the United Nations and other agencies. According to Michael Rosenzweig, half of the world's 4 billion people are hungry.[36] Perhaps half a billion suffer from severe malnutrition, and more than 10,000 starve to death each week. During a crisis, 20,000 to 30,000 may starve to death in a country like Bangladesh in a single month.[37] Infant mortality in many Third World countries is five times the rate in the industrialized West, and one-half of the death of those under the age of five result from food deficiencies.[38]

The United States, with approximately 6 percent of the world's population, consumes approximately 35 percent of the world's food. It produces its own food supply but does so expensively. For example, the grain that feeds cattle to be consumed as meat by humans could feed many more if consumed directly as grain, meal, or similar nutrients. The United States consumes a quarter of all the precious fertilizer used in the world, and 25 percent of the United States' consumption goes to lawns, golf courses, and gardens.[39]

Yet Americans are taught by televised beer, fast food, dairy, and other commercials to consume more. Alexander Comfort asserts that American diets are based on the prescriptions of poorly informed mothers and inflated in the direction of conspicuous consumption. In restaurants quality foods are served in quantity and often not finished. In an anthropological sense, Comfort notes

> A typical American steak would serve a family, not only in Asia but also in most of Europe, where it would be accompanied by diluent foods (potatoes, rice), which are served in America but commonly left. The anthropologist's impression might be of a chair-borne and car-borne citizen attempting, for fantasy and cultural reasons, to eat a diet appropriate to a log-hewing pioneer.[40]

Comfort estimates that 50 percent of adult male deaths in the United States are precipitated by animal fats and dairy products. These, he adds, are wasteful to produce, are being priced out of consumption, and if avoided would both improve public health and avert shortages. He would develop a new set of priorities in foods and "promote it with commercials."[41]

Unfortunately, the massive power of television and the rest of mass-mediated culture is marshalled in mass capitalist democracies and oligarchies not toward nutritional education and dietary restraint but toward consumption and waste. Commercial media teach buying and consuming as the first priority; diet, health, and equal distribution rank far lower.

Americans spend over $105 billion annually for health care. Yet the United States ranks first in the world in per capita military expenditures but only fifth in health care. It is thirteenth in infant mortality rate and seventeenth in ratio of physicians to total population.[42] Diets are less than ideal and average life expectancy in North America is well below that of many other regions.

The present system of health care delivery contributes to the imperfections. For instance, there is a gross maldistribution of doctors away from rural and inner city areas and a shortage of physicians in the essential area of primary care, because most favor specialties over family practice. There is insufficient utilization of nonphysician members of the health team, such as nurse practitioners, clinical pharmacists, and paramedics. The health insurance system, in conjunction with related economic considerations, calls for extensive restructuring: the medical inflation rate is double that of the rest of the economy. Health care is episodic and not preventive; patients consider their health only after problems become exaggerated, and medicine tends to remove symptoms rather than inhibit causes.

Television and other mass media provide ideal educational forums for improving health attitudes and practices. Proper nutrition, exercise, sexual adjustment, and mental health can prevent many health problems and can be learned through mass media. Unfortunately, the genre of dramatic and documentary medicine on television may be as much a part of the problem as a contributor to solutions. Not only is there a paucity of beneficial programs currently being broadcast, but many of the presentations that do deal with the subjects of disease, medical care, and pharmaceutics promote negative attitudes toward "health" among viewers. American television is a commercial industry run by multinational corporations to promote products and advocate a way of life that tends to value conspicuous consumption, passivity, and external manipulation of the environment; internal awareness and care of the body tend to be devalued (see Chapters 7 and 8). Medicine and health portrayed on television entertain many millions and turn large profits but only partially realize the vast potential of mass-mediated culture for improving and maintaining physical health. The resulting impressions tend to serve the medical profession more than the consumer of health care. Television flatters the medical profession, ignores alternatives such as China's "barefoot doctors,"[43] and continues the monopoly on medical knowledge maintained by well-paid specialists.

The usual genre study investigates cowboy westerns, crime and detective stories, or other conventional formats of popular fiction as they may be expressed in a variety of media such as television, films, novels, poetry, magazines, radio, comics, or theater. This study of the medical genre has been confined to one medium, television, but has moved beyond merely fictional dramatic portrayals to analyze the more directly informational documentary presentations.

While the relation between fiction and fact is invariably subtle, the medical genre on television expresses, reflects, and compensates for practices of formal medicine and health care in the "real world" outside television. Once again, the symbolic expressions of mass-mediated culture reveal an isomorphic symmetry with the material arrangements of society. Media create, extend, and confirm what are then assumed as the "common sense" beliefs and practices of society. Few symbols are of more fundamental importance to a culture than its image and consequent treatment of health, medicine, nutrition, and the body. In the final credits on the balance sheet of the Grim Reaper, Marcus Welby and the medical genre may well be given a grateful acknowledgement.

Notes

1. John G. Cawelti, *The Six-Gun Mystique* (Bowling Green, Ohio: Bowling Green University Popular Press, 1971), p. 29. See also two articles on popular culture methodology in the *Journal of Popular Culture* 9, no. 2 (Fall 1975); they are Donald Dunlop, "Popular Culture and Methodology," pp. 375–83, and David N. Feldman, "Formalism and Popular Culture," pp. 384–402.

2. John G. Cawelti, "Myth, Symbol, and Formula," *Journal of Popular Culture* 8, no. 1 (Summer 1974), pp. 1–9.

3. Horace Newcomb, *TV: The Most Popular Art* (Garden City, N.Y.: Anchor Books, 1974), pp. 110–34.

4. "Health Care for All" (symposium), *The Progressive*, 38:16 (1974).

5. Broadcast by ABC between January and May, 1975, and monitored on KCST-TV, channel 39, in San Diego on Tuesdays, 10 P.M. Pacific time.

6. Michael Halberstam, "An M.D. Reviews Dr. Welby of TV," *New York Times Magazine*, January 16, 1972, p. 12.

7. James Johnson, "AAFP Hedges Answers to Queries on Welby Show," Newspaper of the American Psychiatric Association, December 18, 1974; see also John Spiegel, letter to Roger Tusken of AAFP, September 27, 1974.

8. Dudley M. Cobb, Jr., "Advice on Medical Accuracy in the Entertainment Media," *Western Medicine*, 7:313 (1966).

9. Thelma Schorr, "Nursing's TV Image," *American Journal of Nursing*, 63:119 (1963).

10. Herbert Schiller, *The Mind Managers* (Boston: Beacon Press, 1973).

11. A. C. Nielsen Co., *Nielsen Station Index*, "Viewers in Profile for San Diego," May, 1974.

12. *Today's Health*, 51:22 (1973).

13. Thackara Brown, personal communication, 1975.

14. Thackara Brown, press release, December 11, 1974.

15. Joseph Boyle, "Medix Announcement," December 11, 1974.

16. Thackara Brown, personal communication, 1975.

17. A. C. Nielsen Co., *Nielsen Station Index*, "Viewers in Profile for San Diego," May, 1974.

18. Lester David, "Bringing the Doctor to You," *Today's Health*, 52:6 (1974).

19. Paul Lowinger et al., "Health Information During a Week of Television," *New England Journal of Medicine*, 286:516 (1972).

20. *Pediatrics*, 53:431 (1974).

21. Joan Gussow, "It Makes Even Milk a Dessert," *Clinical Pediatrics*, 12:68 (1973).

22. Scott J. Francher, " 'It's the Pepsi Generation . . .' Accelerated Aging and the

Television Commercial," *International Journal of Aging and Human Development,* 4:245 (1973); see also "The Myths of Old Age are the Myths of the Young: A Symposium," *Journal of Communication* 24, no. 4 (Autumn, 1974), pp. 74–112.

23. Muriel Oberleder, "Emotional Breakdown in Elderly People," *Hospital and Community Psychiatry,* 20:191 (1969).

24. C. J. S. Thompson, *The Quacks of Old London* (Philadelphia: Lippincott, 1929).

25. "Cartoon Films for Television," *Journal of the American Dental Association,* 70:1509 (1965).

26. Ohio Department of Mental Health and Mental Retardation, "Television as a Tool in Primary Prevention," *Hospital and Community Psychiatry* 24:691 (1973).

27. G. Caplan, *Principles of Preventive Psychiatry* (New York: Basic Books, 1964).

28. J. M. Shinkle and Theodore Weiss, "Making Cancer a Household Word" *New England Journal of Medicine,* 290:166 (1974).

29. Thackara Brown, press release, December 11, 1974.

30. *Canadian Journal of Public Health,* 60:315 (1969).

31. Dan Rottenberg, "Keep an Eye on Consultation," *Today's Health,* 50:49 (1972).

32. Carter L. Marshall and Edward Wallerstein, "Beyond Marcus Welby: Cable TV for the Health of the Elderly," *Geriatrics,* 28:182 (1973).

33. S. L. Smith et al., "Physician and Public Interest in Medical Television Broadcasts," *Canadian Medical Association Journal,* 104:1101 (1971).

34. James McCloy, *Proceedings of the Royal Society of Medicine,* 62:399 (1969); James McCloy, "Broadcast Television and Medical Education," *The Practitioner,* 207:99 (1971).

35. Herbert Schiller, *Mind Managers.*

36. Michael Rosenzweig, *And Replenish the Earth* (New York: Harper & Row, 1975).

37. "Food for Whom?" *New Republic,* December 7, 1974, p. 8.

38. Ruth Leger Sivard, "Military and Social Expenditures," *New Republic,* January 4 and 11, 1975, p. 10.

39. TRB, "Stirrings of Spring," *New Republic,* April 5, 1975, p. 2.

40. Alexander Comfort, "The World Diet Revolution," *The Center Magazine,* 1974, p. 35.

41. Ibid.

42. Sivard, "Military and Social Expenditures."

43. The People's Republic of China has developed a number of effective alternatives in health care. See, for example, Dr. Joshua Horn, *Away with All Pests* (New York: Monthly Review Press, 1969); and Senator Mike Mansfield, *China: A Quarter Century After the Founding of the People's Republic,* a report to the Committee on Foreign Relations (Washington: U.S. Government Printing Office, 1975). Since 1949 more than one million "barefoot doctors" have been trained in China. They are usually middle school (junior or senior high school) graduates selected for three months of training, followed by regular refresher courses. They provide primary medical care, first-aid, sanitation, health education, immunizations, acupuncture, and traditional medicine. "Barefoot doctors" also continue regular work occupations as well as performing their medical duties for the people.

Politics

Persuasive media campaigns for selling consumer products, corporate images, or, in this case, political candidates may be as intellectually shaky and mythically titillating as super-hero comics.

5

CRP Media Campaigning: All the President's Ad Men

Are serious political decisions and news information unrelated to popular culture and media?

How are advertising campaigns organized for mass-mediated political and economic persuasion?

What specific tactics and overall strategy are utilized in "propaganda" campaigns such as the 1972 Nixon reelection campaign?

How do mass media and popular culture interact with political sensibilities?

Can mass-mediated persuasion replace rational, liberal democracy and the principle of self-determination?

Political campaigning in mass-mediated capitalist democracies is popular culture par excellence. Bumper stickers, posters, groupies, rallies, jingles, gimmicky ads, glamorized images, balloons, confetti, personality cults, funny hats—throughout the last 200 years presidential campaigns in the United States have provided enough "memorabilia Americana" to warm the heart of every huckster in the land.

Presidential candidates at the peak of their campaigns surpass even rock stars, country singers, movie heroes, and television personalities in the quantity of their media exposure and the fervor of public infatuation. Campaign partisans come to sense the same excitement, suspense, and competition as in the Super Bowl; the same cuteness, simplicity, and predictability as in Disney productions; and the same calculated enthusiasm and idealistic promise as in a Billy Graham crusade. To a large extent the political campaign audience "turns on" with the same uncritical, emotional participation that exists in the rest of popular culture. Contemporary politics and news exist more within than above the world of popular mass-mediated cultural expressions. Walter Cronkite, himself an icon of popular culture, illustrated this from his front-row seat at the 1976 Super Bowl when he invited viewers to join him in July and August at the party conventions for "the Super Bowl of politics."

In a system built on private capital and public elections, successful political candidates, like consumer products and the rest of mass-mediated culture, do not spontaneously arise from the people, nor are they arbitrarily imposed from above. Generally, a trade-off between the preferences of the wealthy and powerful and the needs of the masses provides a modicum of both stability and adaptation in the system. Voters do choose but their choices and motives are structured by mass-mediated information and images, which in turn are structured through the economics of privately owned media and other institutions. Just as a $10 million advertising campaign can generally make a success of a new orange juice, cat food, or toothpaste product, as the pages of *Advertising Age* testify, heavy promotion through mass media can also "sell" political candidates. Proponents of political causes and candidates must therefore accumulate capital to purchase media exposure as a necessary counterpart to traditional political organizing.

How is a mass-mediated persuasion campaign planned and implemented? This chapter investigates the 1972 strategy of the Committee to Re-elect the President (gleefully dubbed "CREEP" by its opponents) as a propaganda campaign played out on the stage of American popular culture. More simple and clear-cut than the campaign of 1976 and many others, the 1972 CRP effort provides a classic prototype of media persuasion by being carefully engineered, immensely successful, and, in retrospect, publicly disclosed by Watergate and related revelations.

The emphasis in this brief historical essay is on the candidate (sender) side of the communication more than on the voter (receiver) side; it is organized around the broadly critical and theoretical framework developed by Jacques Ellul in *Propaganda: The Formation of Men's Attitudes*.[1] It follows Forrest Chisman's call for political communication research on the "information environment" beyond individual voter decisions and takes into account the complex research conducted in the American Association for Public Opinion Research, the American Political Science Association, the American Institute for Political Communication, and the International Communication Association; this chapter also draws on popular sources like Theodore White, Joe McGinniss, Hunter S. Thompson, Timothy Crouse, and Bob Woodward and Carl Bernstein.[2] From prepropaganda and the orchestration of negative images to the final landslide victory, the propagandistic nature of the 1972 campaign illustrates problems of mass-mediated popular politics: the power of advertising techniques; the separation of image and substance; the creation of artificial needs and ignoring of real problems; the subliminal effects of mass culture; the influence of money; and the dangers to the larger system.

Prepropaganda and Control of the Agenda

The first stages of persuasive popular communication related to the 1972 presidential election were concerned with what Theodore White described as "the ongoing fight between the President and the press . . . (for) control of the agenda."[3]

Mr. Nixon's first term in office highlighted some and played down other public "myths and conditioned reflexes," the heart of prepropaganda according to Ellul. His agenda emphasized national security, patriotism, international statesmanship, middle Americans, media bias, and silent majorities over such issues from the previous decade as poverty, racism, or the military-industrial complex. In popular news and mass culture, the symbolically perceived threats inherited domestically from the turbulent 1960s and internationally from the remnants of the Cold War had left battle lines and vocabulary adequate to sustain a definition of the situation that led implicitly to a traditional defense of the status quo. Nostalgia and security became popular commodities, harking back to the 1950s. On a more directly tactical level, anti-Nixon tendencies in the press were neutralized by criticisms and warnings from Vice-President Agnew and other administration spokesmen. The establishment of the White House Office of Telecommunications Policy with Clay T. White-head as director; the appointment of Goldwater's former campaign manager, Dean Burch, as head of the F.C.C.; and shifts in emphasis within the Justice Department and the Supreme Court reinforced warnings that the incumbent would not be kicked around by instant analysis and liberal bias in the news media.

When the "November Group" in charge of the media strategy in the Nixon reelection effort was formed in January of 1972, the situation was yet uncertain. Peter Dailey, a friend of H. R. Haldeman, was placed in charge of a prestigious battery of loyal Nixon advertising executives who had volunteered to serve full time in the Nixon effort for up to one year. As White reported, this November Group was "haunted by the nemesis figure of 43 percent."[4] That was the position Nixon had been holding in the polls for some time. But the visit to Peking in February and to Moscow in May, along with George Wallace's elimination from the race, moved Nixon's support up to 60 percent before the November Group began officially to turn out advertising materials. As a result, coupled with a well-timed presidential calendar, effective prepropaganda had created a climate dominated, in Martin Nolan's words, by "that anonymous, distant, nonpartisan resident of the Oval Office, the walking official portrait on satellite television, toasted by the Chinese and saluted by the Russians."[5] Recognizing this advantage in prepropaganda, the November Group from CRP began with the principle, "We're going to do nothing to bring our man down from the level of the President to the level of the candidate."[6]

In contrast, during the period prior to the general election campaigns, the Democratic primaries and convention were largely counter-productive in identifying and modifying conditioned reflexes and myths that would serve as helpful prepropaganda for the general election campaigns. The negative imaging of Democrat by Democrat, encouraged by difficult to assess "dirty tricks" from outside, left all of the candidates in defensive positions. Even if a candidate won in a primary, his image was permanently scarred by his opponents and, almost invariably, from

Muskie in New Hampshire to McGovern in California, the victory was tempered when polls and commentators predicted greater margins of victory than occurred. The Democratic convention did little to dispel this negative heritage.

Assault Strategy

The testimony of White House speechwriter Patrick Buchanan was one of the few discussions in the televised Watergate hearings that dealt with the overt intent rather than the covert operations of the CRP campaign. Buchanan spoke revealingly of the "Opposition Committee" within CRP, which directed an "assault strategy" built around "attack ads," first against Muskie and later against McGovern. He once described these efforts most appropriately as "offensive ads" and suggested "the negative ads will do more to re-elect the president than positive ads."[7] While campaign commentaries spoke of the CRP campaign as if it were only propaganda of "integration" drawing voters into the positive Nixon platform, the central thrust of the campaign was propaganda of "agitation" against opponents.

The surrogate campaigners, drawn primarily from the cabinet, were especially successful in having their criticism of the Democratic opposition covered in news broadcasts. They were helped by staff-made tapes of their appearances, which, together with similar McGovern staff-made tapes, were used by approximately one-third of the stations covered in the DuPont-Columbia Survey.[8] The budget of the direct-mail campaign—the first Nixon mailing alone numbered more than 12 million pieces—and the telephone and house calls exceeded the budget for radio and television.[9] Much of the copy, especially in its approach to Democrats, attacked McGovern, with or without the presentation of positive alternatives associated with the incumbent. But the most pointedly negative approaches to voters came in the television commercials prepared by the November Group, approved by the White House, and launched September 25, weeks after the Democrats had begun national advertising on television.

The three dominant national one-minute commercials first appeared in early October and focused on defense, welfare, and inconsistency. The commercial on McGovern's proposals to cut the defense budget quoted Hubert Humphrey's attack on the McGovern proposals in the California primary and showed a giant hand wiping away toy representations of half the Navy, a third of the Army, and most of the Air Force. The commercial on welfare and taxes pictured a hard-hatted construction worker high on a girder looking down in helpless chagrin at the other half, the population below, who allegedly would be enabled under McGovern proposals to live unemployed off the hard-hat's taxes. The inconsistency commercial showed McGovern's profile on a weathervane swinging back and forth on both sides of issues. The last was similar to a Nixon profile commercial made by the Humphrey campaign in 1968 but never used.[10] The commercials were mass culture in the worst sense: oversimplified, stereotyped images and formulas capitalizing on crude emotions and fears.

The identification on the anti-McGovern commercials read "Sponsored by Democrats for Nixon." In fact, the commercials were paid for with a "loan" from central CRP campaign funds, were planned by CRP's heavily Republican membership, and in no way arose from independent spontaneous Democratic sources. Covert propaganda, using disguised and indirect sources, gains a quasi-objective strength in media campaigning that is not possible in personalized mudslinging campaigns. When the evening news quoted the Secretary of Defense on McGovern proposals to decrease military spending, the source was indirect and seemingly objective. When a film clip of a rally showed McGovern personally attacking Nixon's economic policies, the source was direct, identifiable, and obviously partisan. Yet, in each case, the message was an attack on the opponent and was planned by the candidate and his campaign committee. CRP's choice of covert sources and media subtlety—surrogate campaigners, misleadingly labelled advertisements, assault strategies—proved effective.

Media Orchestration

Media orchestration, according to Ellul, is the subtle overall integration of varied media exposure necessary for successful propaganda.[11] McGovern's media orchestration fought for maximum exposure and came off "hot." In the final months of the campaign, McGovern made some 300 to 400 live appearances, many of them aimed at media exposure. These were supplemented by McGovern staff-made audio and video tapes of appearances, provided free to local stations, for news shows; endless McGovern appearances on panel, phone-in, interview, and talk shows; ten McGovern fund-raising telethons held in various parts of the country; an estimated 15 million pieces of McGovern direct mail; a series of half-hour prime-time televised McGovern "fireside chats"; and thousands of television and radio spots, ranging from the early "man of the people" Charles Guggenheim productions to the more heavy-handed spots on corruption, tax reform, and law and order by Tony Schwartz.[12] Despite the shift in campaign oratory from early positive proposals, many of which were obscured by emphasis in news reports on internal difficulties in McGovern's campaign, to a later emphasis on corruption in the Nixon administration, the McGovern media utilization was clearly identified and direct. In fact, its focus on one candidate, the explicitness of its messages, and the saturation intensity of its presentation gave it an overbearingly high definition. This "hot" quality did not attract participation and accounted for the "He's talked himself out" response that McGovern precinct workers encountered late in the campaign.

The Nixon campaign, in contrast, was a masterpiece of "cool" strategy in terms of the orchestration of media, if not in its message content. The use of surrogates rather than personal campaigning by Nixon, the emphasis in much publicity, notably the major television spots, on "Democrats for Nixon," rather than a more accurate Republican party identification, the use of radio rather than television for Nixon campaign speeches,[13] the detachment from working for other party candidates—all served not only to shelter Nixon from direct confrontations with potentially unfriendly press or public but also to give what was an intensely calculated and absolutely controlled saturation campaign a feeling of low definition that invited rather than put off participation and support. The orchestration of the 1972 campaign allowed the specifics of the candidate to recede even further into shadows, thus making him a more open receptacle for elements of projection that reside in the receiver rather than the sender.[14]

If we assume that long-term mass culture "propaganda" is implicit in such offerings as prime-time television entertainment shows, the problem McGovern faced becomes clear. From Walter Cronkite, the Waltons, and Hawaii Five-O to the Johnny Carson "Tonight Show," the heroes are organized, white, male adults. But, what appeared on the TV screen during the Democratic Convention was a group of women, minorities, and young people unseating the disgruntled white, male, Democratic establishment. The "new" Democrats did not fit the image of mainstream American "responsibles" as those appear in the dominant popular culture.[15] Instead, the image of elevated presidential responsibility demanding respect and loyalty was favored over the unstable mixture of conflicting interests drawn together by McGovern and the Democrats from outside the standard clichés of popular American television and films.

Mass Culture and Political Sensibilities

One of the most important but difficult to assess effects of strategies like political television commercials is a gradually increasing separation between image and substance, or, as William F. Lynch labelled it years ago in his study of *The Image Industries*, a loss of the ability to distinguish between fantasy and reality.[16] Commercial techniques of emphasis on psychological, subliminal associations of a product—or candidate—

with desirable traits, images, and life-styles allow the intrinsic merit of the product or candidate to recede into the background and de facto unrelated trivialities to gain ascendency.

The Watergate hearings revealed to the public how badly it was fooled by appearances in 1972. President Nixon's drop in popularity in public opinion polls, when the facts became known about the reelection effort, indicated that over a third of the voters would have voted differently had they been aware of the substance of the reelection campaign. Beyond that difference, the Watergate hearings brought home the realization not so much that there were "bad people up there manipulating the electoral process" but merely that there were *people* up there at all. Reassuring to the critics but mildly disturbing to the pious, the hearings lifted the veil of olympian depersonalized detachment and revealed everyday, flesh and blood, human, personal engineering of campaigning and politics in general. Even if the 1972 reelection effort had not been quite so cynically manipulated, the hearings were inevitably disillusioning to a public conditioned by media campaigning to believe in packaged images.

The use of commercial techniques in campaigning separates image and substance in a fashion similar to what Galbraith and others have long warned about as the work of advertising in a noncontrolled, postscarcity economy—the jackass and carrot obsession with *created* needs. In a chamber of horrors recitation, Ellul described how the psychological effects of propaganda replace individual, critical judgment with neurotic, other-directed, hero-worshipping, childishly dependent, collective irrationality. Incidentally, he insists, modern education prepares one *for* rather than protects one *against* propaganda, to the point where the intellectual, with an infinity of contradictory facts within his reach and an inclination to form an opinion on every issue, is the most propagandized individual in society. In Ellul's vision the propagandized individual spends his life in the alienated pursuit of "the artificial satisfaction of real needs or the real satisfaction of artificial needs."[17]

Political campaigns are increasingly modeled after the mass culture style of advertising, rather than the elite style of classical democracies. In 1972 more than $25 billion was spent on commercial advertising in the United States. The machinery is there; the people are trained to accept it; why not use it for political purposes? Nixon's staff was dominated not by politicians but by advertising and public relations specialists. Haldeman had been an executive with the J. Walter Thompson advertising conglomerate, and Ron Ziegler had handled the Disneyland account for the same firm. The use of media to change thinking and influence behavior is not only socially acceptable but is generally considered an essential part of the American political-economic system.

The potential defenses of the individual are eroded by the subliminal effects of popular culture, political propaganda, and mass news. Current television news formats favor shorter snippets of stories in greater abundance, more up-beat features, brighter personalities and side exchanges between newscasters, and a generally "show biz" atmosphere. Such news styles, the vast wasteland of entertainment media, and the disrupting omnipresence of commercial appeals cumulatively flatten out and anesthetize individual ability to evaluate and respond. Ellul, Marcuse, Packard, and others have written about this media desensitization of the masses; Jules Feiffer captured it in a cartoon. He pictured a couple in bed switching their television by remote control to different stations. They flip onto a cowboy-Indian massacre, a murder-mystery shooting, a police shoot-'em-up, the news of Robert F. Kennedy's assassination, and a detective story murder. Without reacting they turn off the set, say good night, and sleep.

The result is that objective reality and genuine approaches to real problems become virtually inaccessible. Mass-oriented popular press, politicians, and pollsters unwittingly conspire to make now national security, now white backlash, now domino theories, now welfarism into *the* issue of the day. White backlash voting is an example. In Sam Yorty's 1968 victory over Tom Bradley for mayor of Los Angeles, David Sears and Donald Kinder have shown in detail how the *symbolically* perceived threat of black power and disruption received through the mass media negatively influenced white voting most in areas where, due to absolute geographical separation, any real, physical threat was least likely.[18] Media campaigns for and against ballot propositions freely exploit fears and manipulate symbolic threats. International trends provide similar examples. Bernard Rosenberg predicted in 1968 that public opinion about the People's Republic of China could be changed overnight if opinion-makers chose to "turn on the faucets of influence" and picture China as a struggling ally rather than as the scourge of the earth; it happened, only a few years after his prediction.[19] The nation's perceptions of the world, or what Walter Lippmann called "the pictures in our head," are at stake. Joseph Lyford speaks of America's "regressively nationalistic" climate, in which media skirt the problem areas of the world just as freeways skirt slums and in which American citizens, living in the plantation house, see the poor of the world working the new cotton fields "through the wrong end of the telescope."[20]

From the infrastructural base that determines CRP campaigns and mass cúlture in general comes the ultimate priority—corporate profit. Money has the power to shape campaigns and popular culture as the cup shapes the coffee. Expenditures on mass media have become the largest single expense in many campaign budgets.[21] Campaign reform acts have eased some fears, but the candidate with more money to spend still has an advantage that has nothing to do with platforms and positions. Moreover, money provides a protective shield around and a connecting link among vested interests in government, industry, and media that C. Wright Mills labelled "the power elite." For example, as Nicholas Johnson pointed out about his own Federal Communications Commission, the regulatory agencies reflect the bias of money and interlocking interests.[22] During the early days of the Nixon administration, the *New Republic* warned that regulatory agencies tend to protect the industries they are supposed to regulate and ignore the public they are assigned to serve. Popular politicians, mass newcasters, and others who have access to mass media cannot criticize this power of money without biting the hand that feeds them.

Generally, "serious" political matters are kept separate from the "lighter" concerns of popular culture. The 1972 CRP campaign illustrates the danger of such compartmentalization. The most disturbing possibility is that CRP and Watergate were not aberrations of American political practices but were typical, if exaggerated, expressions of the use of popular culture and media propaganda in contemporary mass politics.

Political campaigns, specifically as they reach the public through mass media, set the agenda for the nation, give specific focus to the vagaries of public opinion, and point a direction for the allocation of important resources. They are also a mythic battleground and catharsis.[23] Judging from the 1972 CRP campaign, the Surgeon General might well issue a warning: "Political campaigns may be hazardous to your health." Still, campaigns seem to resemble less a disease than the drugs used to hide a disease. The danger is that narcotizing the registration of pain in the central nervous system normally results in deferred but greater suffering in the total body. CRP campaigns, mass culture, and media propaganda can be used to hide injuries, diseases, and pains in the body politic. To the extent that such practices gloss over real problems and substitute fabrications, a nation together with its real allies and enemies will learn the hard way that inaccurate communications are major contributors to deterioration and death. The *responsiveness* of political and economic systems to human need tends to be *inversely* proportionate to the systems' one-way, authoritarian use of mass-mediated culture to manipulate and mislead the people.

Notes

1. Jacques Ellul, *Propaganda* (New York: Alfred A. Knopf, 1965).

2. Forrest P. Chisman, *The Future of Political Communication Research* (Aspen, Colorado: Aspen Institute, 1974); Theodore H. White, *The Making of the President 1960* (New York: Atheneum, 1961), and sequels 1964, 1968, 1972; Joe McGinniss, *The Selling of the President 1968* (New York: Trident Press, 1969); Hunter S. Thompson, *Fear and Loathing on the Campaign Trail* (San Francisco: Straight Arrow

Books, 1973); Timothy Crouse, *The Boys on the Bus* (New York: Random House, 1972); Carl Bernstein and Bob Woodward, *All the President's Men* (New York: Warner Paperback Library, 1975).

3. Theodore H. White, *The Making of the President 1972* (New York: Atheneum, 1973), p. 268.

4. White, *The Making of the President 1972*, p. 326.

5. Martin F. Nolan, "The Re-Selling of the President" *Atlantic*, September, 1972, p. 81.

6. White, *The Making of the President 1972*, p. 326.

7. Watergate hearings, NBC, September, 1973. See also *Broadcasting*, October 15, 1973, pp. 31–32, and President Nixon's press conference of October 26, 1973, for further details of the administration's approach to broadcast media.

8. Marvin Barrett, ed., *The Politics of Broadcasting: Alfred I. duPont–Columbia University Survey of Broadcast Journalism 1971–1972* (New York: Thomas Y. Crowell, 1973), p. 132.

9. Ibid., p. 138.

10. Ibid., pp. 137–38.

11. Ellul, p. 12.

12. Barrett, pp. 132–35.

13. John Mitchell found radio so effective in the Nixon campaign that he was determined to spend more on radio in 1972. Dan Nimmo, *The Political Persuaders— The Techniques of Modern Election Campaigns* (Englewood Cliffs, N.J.: Prentice-Hall, 1970), p. 134.

14. Ibid., p. 144. See also Kurt Lang and Gladys Engle Lang, *Politics and Television* (Chicago: Quadrangle Books, 1968).

15. Experiments conducted by Paula L. Real with students confirm the existence of this restricted stereotype of presidential potential. When offered a choice of president from among six photographs that included members of both sexes, several races, and varying ages, a majority in each of 6 groups of 30 high school students selected the older white male. Most significantly, replication of the experiment in several different states, with variations in ethnic and other mixtures in the groups, showed the majority preference held constant no matter how other information about the candidates' education, religion, and political philosophy varied.

16. William F. Lynch, S.J., *The Image Industries* (New York: Sheed & Ward, 1960).

17. Ellul, p. 174.

18. David O. Sears and Donald R. Kinder, "The Good Life, 'White Racism,' and the Los Angeles Voter," paper delivered at the fiftieth annual meeting of the Western Psychological Association, Los Angeles, California, April 15, 1970, mimeograph copy.

19. Bernard Rosenberg, "Mass Culture Revisited I," in Bernard Rosenberg and David Manning White, eds., *Mass Culture Revisited* (New York: Van Nostrand Reinhold, 1971), p. 8.

20. Joseph P. Lyford, "The Pacification of the Press," *The Center Magazine* 6, no. 2 (March/April 1973), p. 30.

21. Herbert E. Alexander, *Financing the 1968 Election* (Lexington, Mass.: Heath, 1971), p. 92.

22. Nicholas Johnson, *How to Talk Back to Your Television Set* (New York: Bantam Books, 1970).

23. Marshall Frady observed during the 1976 campaign, "No other enterprise, no other American mystique—whether Hollywood or business or sports—can really challenge politics as the definitive national mythology of power and glory." *New Times* 6, no. 4 (February 20, 1976), p. 19.

Religion

Even if media are the new religion, the old religion of denominations and evangelists like Billy Graham effectively spreads patriotic gospels through television, radio, newspapers, magazines, books, movies, recordings, and other media.

6

Billy Graham:
Mass Medium

Why is Billy Graham so popular?

What do scientific methods of exegesis and ethnography reveal of the cultural role of the Reverend William Franklin Graham, Jr.?

What are the media organization, rhetorical style, and international spread of typical Graham televised crusades?

Was the moralistic Graham a chaplain to the Watergate scandals?

Do Graham and his popular religious parallels write the scenario for life in the advanced industrial state?

How might Karl Marx and Billy Graham evaluate each other?

For more than two decades only one person has been consistently named by Americans among the top five "most admired men in the world" in the annual Gallup poll. First making the list in the early 1950s, the Reverend William Franklin Graham, Jr., ranked with notables such as Dwight Eisenhower, Winston Churchill, and Albert Schweitzer. While presidents, popes, inventors of wonder drugs, and prominent world leaders have come and gone in the fickle world of public popularity ratings, Billy Graham has remained near the top. The company is not always what one might consider flattering: In 1969 Graham ranked second between his friends Richard M. Nixon and Spiro T. Agnew. What brought this gangly, red-haired youth from a farm near Charlotte, North Carolina, to such prominence? What does his prominence reveal about the society that esteems him so highly?

The long development of popular religion, its vast spread, its methods of persuasion, its social role, and its intensely personal quality compel attention but defy easy analysis. When a Jimmy Carter or John Kennedy runs for president, and when abortion and prayer in schools become issues, the popular press debates but seldom resolves questions of religion and society. When more extensive articles, symposia, and anthologies study popular religion as transmitted by mass media, the subject calls forth a pooling of history, theology, anthropology, psychology, and sociology. This chapter attempts to describe major contours of the popular religious landscape by identifying appropriate interdisciplinary methodologies of ethnography, exegesis, and criticism and by applying these methods to an investigation of Billy Graham as the epitome of popular mass religion.

The Reverend Billy Graham has earned a permanent niche in the popular culture hall of fame as a *mass medium* in several meanings of the phrase.

First, Graham has been a "spiritual medium" or evangelistic interlocutor to masses of people. Since 1949, when his Los Angeles crusade first brought Graham headlines in the national press, he has preached to more people, both live and through mass media, than any person in the history of Christianity.

As a mass mediator, Graham stresses that he is not the originator of his message but merely a medium for divine work: "I'm just a Western Union boy delivering God's message."[1]

Second, Graham has achieved and maintained his position of prominence by a masterful use of almost every mass medium of modern communications. In addition to appearing live before many millions at crusades, Graham is heard every day on radio and is read in his syndicated newspaper column, "My Answer." His magazine, *Decision,* goes each month into more than 4 million homes. Graham uses television hook-ups to extend his crusades more widely over a city, and he broadcasts selected crusades nationally and internationally; 292 American stations televised his Australian crusade in 1969. His books, *Peace with God* and *World Aflame,* have sold many millions of copies. He has sponsored and his organization has produced and distributed more than three dozen feature films. By the beginning of the 1970s, according to his authorized biography, Graham was receiving more than 2 million pieces of mail each year, employed more than 400 in his Minneapolis headquarters, and operated the Billy Graham Evangelistic Association on an annual budget of more than $12 million. Billy Graham capitalizes on each mass medium in his role of medium to the masses.

The term "mass" applies to Graham also in regard to the level of culture on which his association operates. The message and style are too uncomplicated to be *elite,* although Graham keeps loosely informed on trends among scholarly theologians. The reach is too cosmopolitan to reflect genuinely *folk* traditions, although Graham's own "decision for Christ" at the age of sixteen took place in a temporary tabernacle of raw pine during an eleven-week revival run by the fiery Mordecai Fowler Ham, a classic representative of the "sawdust trail" of fire-and-brimstone folk revivalism. The vastness of Graham's operation makes his appeal more *mass* than *popular* culture, although Graham does attempt to avoid crass signs of mass manipulation and provide a degree of personal inspiration and supervision over his association in the manner of a popular artist. Nevertheless, the elements of mass culture are extravagantly present in Graham's approach—a standardized product; within the bounds of average taste; aimed at a large, heterogeneous, anonymous audience; and developed not *by* the people but *for* them by an organized marketing operation. Graham himself freely uses the term "mass" in referring to his evangelism. There is an irony in the Billy Graham phenomenon: The modern American assumption that religion exists as a private personal belief secluded in the intimacy of the individual is contradicted by a dominance over contemporary religion by mass-mediated culture.

Why Is Billy Graham So Popular?

To account for the popularity of Billy Graham, an investigation must come to terms not only with Graham's message and media but also with the peculiarities of the receivers that make this particular message so highly valued. In other words, the popularity of this mass culture phenomenon cannot be fully understood without also understanding something of the larger cultural system of which it is a part. As a result, whether one personally accepts, rejects, or ignores Graham's message, one can better understand fundamental insecurities (negative feelings and ideas) and dreams (positive feelings and ideas) of individuals and groups in the modern industrial states of the English-speaking world by understanding the phenomenon of Billy Graham.

Religion is a major subsystem of culture and society, along with the subsystems of economics, politics, sports and recreation, education, and the family. The subsystems are extensive. For example, according to figures compiled by the National Council of Churches, American Christian churches claim a membership of more than 128 million.[2] Each subsystem, such as religion, has its most popular expression, such as Billy Graham, that is more than a "metaphor" or an "allegory" of culture and society. Like the Super Bowl, Billy Graham is not outside and reminiscent of the whole but is an intrinsic component of the larger cultural system. Classical Greek and medieval metaphysics postulated that there is an "analogy of proportion" between the generic essence of a being and its specific existence. In a similar manner, the dominant expression (Billy Graham) of a major subsystem (religion) recapitulates inner characteristics and major directions of the larger system and its mass-mediated culture. Both epistemologically and ontologically, Billy Graham thus serves as a significant indicator of the organization and meaning of contemporary culture, especially as that culture occurs throughout the English-speaking world of the United States, Canada, the British Isles, Australia, and New Zealand.

A full explanation of Billy Graham's popularity, therefore, will also reveal a great deal about the nature of contemporary life. In the words of Emile Durkheim, "The idea of society is the soul of religion."[3] For Durkheim,

> There can be no society which does not feel the need of upholding and reaffirming at regular intervals the collective sentiments and the collective ideas which make its unity and its personality. Now this moral remaking

cannot be achieved except by the means of reunions, assemblies, and meetings where the individuals, being closely united to one another, re-affirm in common their common sentiments.[4]

Textual Exegesis as a Methodology

This study of Billy Graham is centered in *exegesis* of six videotaped telecasts from Graham crusades.[5] Exegesis is a rigorous, developed method for determining the precise *meaning* of a text by identifying its literary genre, the "life-situation" in which it arose, and the intention of the original author. This study attempts to be more faithful to the text and intention of Graham's message than Graham himself is in his exegesis of texts, including the Bible.

In contrast to serious exegesis, Billy Graham's methods are those of a popular preacher. Graham quotes innumerable phrases and anecdotes from the Old and New Testaments, especially in the archaic wording of the King James Version. But his interpretations of the meaning of the texts are generally free extrapolations rather than strict exegesis. Popular applications often do violence to the original meanings. For example, in one videotaped sermon, Graham cited the phrase "they were marrying and giving in marriage" in the story of Noah as meaning "wife-swapping." Genuine exegesis would first look in detail at the phrase in Hebrew in its context in ancient Israel before considering any jumps to parallels with customs in contemporary America. Shortly after the reference to Noah, Graham arbitrarily associated the fourth horseman of the Apocalypse with mass deaths from chemical and biological warfare; no genuine evidence for the association was offered. Graham's use of the Bible for proof texts and for prophecies about current events is especially "free" and a far cry from the strict meaning of exegesis.

In the original Greek, exegesis means to lead the way out of. It has come to refer to the effort to determine the precise denotation and direct connotations of a term or passage in a text remote from the reader in time and space, especially texts from Hebrew and Christian sacred scriptures.[6] Biblical exegesis defines "inspiration" as God's intention to teach what the human author of a passage intended to teach. The text, therefore, does not stand on its own but must be interpreted by going back first to the original setting, rediscovering its worldview, finding there similar uses of the word or passage under consideration, and within that context explaining the meaning of the text more fully but with complete fidelity to the intention of the original author. Certain principles of interpretation constrain this process. As they are applied to interpretations of the Bible, so can they be to interpretations of Billy Graham.

Different forms of literature, such as poetry, history, myth, or science, represent truth in different fashions. Books in the Bible vary in literary genre from poetry (Song of Songs) to historical narrative (Kings), from sayings (Proverbs) to parables and allegories (Daniel's visions), and each presents a truth proper to its genre. Billy Graham's literary genre is that of the mass evangelist, the popular preacher, and serious exegesis cannot fault him for not being primarily a serious scholar or a political scientist. His literary genre addresses itself to the masses and his message and media reflect that.

Ascertaining the specific time and location, period and people, is indispensable in determining what a piece of literature is attempting to teach. For example, the second and older creation account in Genesis 2 portrays an anthropomorphic God placing two persons as caretakers over his garden, while the first creation account in Genesis 1, composed almost ten centuries later by professional priests, describes in sophisticated lyrics a distant, majestic God who creates by speaking the word. The setting of composition makes a difference. Billy Graham can only be understood in the context of contemporary Western mass society composed of alienated individuals and mass organizations. When he is assessed in that context, his *sitz-im leben,* or life situation, he becomes a revealing indicator of the nature of life in that society as well.

The Old Testament author who places rabbits among the cud-chewing animals intends to prescribe ritual and not teach zoology. In other cases, such as the parables, an author may employ colorful details in order to make a single point. The point is his primary intention; all else is secondary. So too, if Billy Graham uses politics or race in strange ways, or engages in propaganda or exploitation, it is because his primary intention overrides all else. Understanding precedes judgment. Interpretations of Graham or any other popular artist or figure must allow for the conscious intention of the author. In the case of mass-mediated culture, the "author" may be an institution such as the Billy Graham Evangelistic Association (BGEA) rather than the individual himself. In undertaking exegesis of a television program like "Good Times," the author may include not only specific writers, the cast, and producer Allan Manning, but also the institutions of Tandem Productions headed by Norman Lear, CBS Television, the broadcast industry, and the political economy of the United States. This may border on *expandium ad absurdum,* but the program is influenced by the goals and order of priorities of each of these "authors."

Textual exegesis, therefore, determines the direct and full meaning of a text by analyzing its content within the boundaries of literary genre, life situation, and intention of the author. Textual exegesis is especially appropriate to the study of mass-mediated culture in at least three ways.

First, on a minimum level, exegesis compels a grounding in empirical, factual data. The rules of evidence obtain in cultural analysis as well as the courtroom and the laboratory; exegesis provides vehicles for observing those rules. Interpretations of Noah, Job, or Billy Graham become more scientific and reliable the more closely they observe the rules of exegesis.

Second, exegesis focuses attention on the point-of-impact "text," whether the text is a printed document, a film, a television program, a sound tape, or whatever. The text is the decisive link between the author and the consumer. A precise ethnographic record (see next section) of the text provides the starting point for exegesis that centers on its message but also relates that to the source, context, medium, receiver, and effect of the text.

Third, because it was developed for use in examining documents remote in space and time, exegesis allows the work under consideration to stand on its own as an artifact but also to be considered in context. The text of a mass-mediated cultural production can be taken on its own terms, apart from the conscious intentions and above or beneath the goals of its creator. This means, for example, that the conscious motives and goals of those engaged in the Super Bowl and its telecast should be taken into account but that the ethnography, exegesis, and interpretation need not stop there. Textual exegesis is, thus, more confined than and prior to symbolic, semiotic, structural, Freudian, Jungian, Marxist, or other associative interpretations, but it yields more incontrovertible results.

To apply these procedures to an investigation of Billy Graham, we use as the text for exegesis the videotaped telecast of a crusade. As background for understanding the text, what are the literary genre, life situation, and intent of the author? In other words, from whence cometh this William Franklin Graham, Jr.?

The Rise and Influence of Billy Graham

Although Graham had been raised a Christian and had made a "decision for Christ" during his high school years, his commitment to preach the gospel came on the eighteenth hole of a golf course while he was a college student. At the time, he was a nineteen-year-old in his second year at the Florida Bible Institute at Tampa. The school enrolled about 75 students and had been a country club before it was purchased cheaply during the Depression and made into a Bible college and conference center. Graham's authorized biography describes the event:

> One night in March 1938 Billy Graham returned from his [regular evening] walk and reached the eighteenth green immediately before the school's front door. "The trees were loaded with Spanish moss, and in the moon-

light it was like a fairyland." He sat down on the edge of the green, looking up at the moon and stars, aware of a warm breeze from the south. The tension snapped. "I remember getting on my knees and saying, 'O God, if you want me to preach, I will do it.' Tears streamed down my cheeks as I made this great surrender to become an ambassador for Jesus Christ."[7]

In future walks on the golf course, Graham recalls catching "the strangest glimpses of these great crowds that I now preach to." He saw himself participating "in what Billy Sunday and D. L. Moody had witnessed—big stadiums, big meetings."[8]

Billy Graham was to become the leading figure in the fourth "great awakening" of American Protestantism. Each of these historic revival periods has been associated with charismatic preachers and has been the manifestation of basic shifts in theological emphasis within popular American Protestantism.[9]

The first great awakening in America extended from 1725 to 1750 under the influence of Jonathan Edwards, George Whitefield, Theodore J. Frelinghuysen, and Gilbert Tennent. It modified Calvinist emphasis on predestination and called for evangelical demonstration of faith. The second awakening, from 1800 to 1835, proceeded further in the same direction with an emphasis on human free will and freely given grace. Charles Grandison Finney, Timothy Dwight, Lyman Beecher, Nathaniel Taylor, and camp meeting revivalists led this shift, which prepared the way for Billy Graham–style, self-reliant, American individualism. The third great awakening, from 1875 to 1915, split into one stream the Social Gospel movement, which moved away from individualism to socially conscious pragmatism, progressivism, and rationalism and, in another stream, the fundamentalist revivals of Dwight L. Moody, Reuben A. Torrey, and Billy Sunday. The fourth great awakening, after World War II, marked a shift from New Deal utopianism to neo-orthodoxy, with a secularistic, anthropocentric view of life. Theological emphasis on individual salvation replaced social gospel concern for "suprapersonal" levels of sin and redemption.

The revivals of the great awakenings contributed techniques of evangelism as well as theological background for Billy Graham. Despite Jonathan Edwards's warning that revivals were "Prayed down, not worked up," Charles Grandison Finney offered practical directives in his *Lectures on Revivals,* used "the anxious seat" to which awakened sinners might walk forward, stressed experiencing religion, moved revivals from frontier towns to become regular institutions in major cities, used advertising techniques, adopted a dramatic preaching style, and employed protracted meetings beyond the usual four-day period. Later in the century, D. L. Moody worked out organizational methods. William McLoughlin writes:

Moody was the first revivalist to advertise his campaigns in newspapers, on billboards, posters, handbills, and placards; he was the first to make detailed advance preparations for publicity, church organization, training of ushers, choir, counselors, and prayer meeting leaders; he was the first to publish audited accounts of the expenses, collections, and donations for his multi-thousand dollar crusades which lasted anywhere from six weeks to six months in one city.[10]

Billy Sunday in turn, before his death in 1935, added a team of professional managers, block seating of prearranged delegations, massive choirs, entertainment features, and headline-catching social and political comments.

The backdrop for Billy Graham's evangelism was the well-developed revival tradition in the United States. Eccentrics were sectarian and criticized established churches, but mainstream revivalism stressed "cooperative enterprise for the good of religion in general."[11] Professional evangelists attacked only sins and evils on which church leaders and members all agreed. To gain maximum support from area churches and business, they maintained a nondenominational, lowest-common-denominator commitment to Christian doctrine and ethics.[12] They tended to equate conservative evangelical Christianity with patriotic Americanism. As a consequence, the professional revivalists almost perfectly represent the spirit of their times and "the old religious and secular ideals which have been the basis of the American dream."[13]

Graham's Education and Early Ministry

Billy Frank, as the family called him, was born in 1918, the eldest of four children of pious Scotch Presbyterian parents on a successful farm near Charlotte, North Carolina.[14] The youthful Billy Frank is usually described as a mildly rowdy boy who loved baseball and read history books. At the age of sixteen he made his decision for Christ at a revival, along with his friend Grady Wilson, who was to be a lifelong professional associate. At the end of his mediocre high school career, Graham spent a very successful summer as a Fuller Brush salesman, convinced, as Graham describes it, that a Fuller Brush was a necessity of life.

With his mother's guidance, Graham's college career began in 1936 at Bob Jones College, a rigid, unaccredited, fundamentalist college in Cleveland, Tennessee. Billy lasted less than a year and transferred for the next three years to the pious but much freer Florida Bible Institute. Without career plans until his eighteenth hole commitment to preach, Graham began occasionally to witness and preach in Florida, was baptized by immersion as a Southern Baptist there, and ordained a minister in 1939. In 1940 Graham enrolled in Wheaton College, a Christian school of nearly a thousand students near Chicago. Because his other schools lacked accreditation, he was accepted as only a freshman. He majored in anthropology, assuming erroneously that he would have time to go on to theological seminary after graduation. At Wheaton, Graham met his future wife, Ruth Bell, and in 1941 became the successful pastor of a small, independent church near the campus. In 1943 Graham graduated from Wheaton, was married, was deferred from a military chaplaincy, and became pastor of a Baptist church in Western Springs near Chicago.

Graham's career soon accelerated. In October 1943, he was asked to take over a 45-minute Sunday evening radio program, "Songs in the Night," on WCFL, one of Chicago's most powerful stations. He persuaded a popular baritone named George Beverly Shea to provide the singing to match his preaching and from its opening in January, 1944, the show was a success. In May, 1944, Graham was invited to preach at the big kick-off rally of the Chicagoland "Youth for Christ." About 2,800 persons were present, mainly servicemen, in the Orchestra Hall next door to the U.S.O. Center, and 42 came forward at the time of the call. After 20 more successful Saturday night rallies, Graham began full-time travel for Youth for Christ, wearing loud handpainted ties and bright suits as part of the organization's motto, "Geared to the Times, Anchored to the Rock."

In 1945 and 1946, Graham preached in nearly every state in the union and every province in Canada. His wife and the first of their five children moved in with her parents in Montreat in the mountains of North Carolina, where the Grahams eventually built a large rambling home on top of a mountain. Billy's pell-mell southern-style preaching had now matured, and in 1946 he preached in England, Scotland, and Ireland and had a Hearst reporter as part of his traveling team. A pleasant trombonist and baritone, Cliff Barrows, became his master of ceremonies, and they held 360 meetings in 27 cities in the British Isles. Hearst had become interested in Youth for Christ because of its popularity in Los Angeles and because he liked its moral stands against juvenile delinquency. Hearst ensured that reports on Graham's European tour would reach American newspapers through International News Service. On his return in 1947, Graham was made president of Northwestern Schools, an agglomeration of several fundamentalist colleges in Minneapolis with an enrollment of fewer than a thousand. He retained the presidency nominally until 1952, although he spent little time there, since he and his team of Shea, Barrows, and Wilson traveled widely, holding adult as well as youth rallies.

A Star Is Puffed

Graham's first major city campaign took place in Los Angeles in September, 1949, and placed him in a national spotlight from which he never retreated. The "Christ for Greater Los Angeles" committee viewed Graham as just their next annual evangelist, and he had to plead with them for a larger tent, cooperation with all possible churches, and a $25,000 budget, which would ensure plenty of publicity. But at the end of the revival's scheduled three weeks, the crusade suddenly took off and ran another five well-publicized weeks thanks to the conversion of several celebrities and an order from Hearst to his editors throughout the country to "puff Graham."

Near the end of the crusade's third week, Stuart Hamblen, a cowboy singer and well-known radio talk show host in Los Angeles, was personally converted by Graham to Christ and away from smoking and drinking, which conflicted with his upbringing as the son of a Texas Methodist preacher. Hamblen announced this on his radio show and additional hundreds flocked to Graham's 6,000-capacity "Canvas cathedral," encouraging the crusade into a one-week extension. Near the end of that fourth week, the bedridden Hearst, drawing on information from his maid, who was a Graham enthusiast, planted his blessing on Graham and the thirty-year-old preacher was suddenly surrounded by reporters and flashbulbs. The following day the Los Angeles *Examiner* and the *Herald Express* carried banner headlines, and their dispatches were carried by Hearst papers across the country and were picked up by the Associated Press. Jim Vaus, son of a Los Angeles minister, but then a prominent underworld figure and favorite wiretapping expert for Mickey Cohen, was converted on Sunday, November 5. Louis Zamperini, Olympic track celebrity and World War II hero who had since become poverty-stricken, followed shortly afterward. *Time* and *Newsweek* both gave space to the "new evangelist." Headlines across the country screamed the stories of the conversions. The crusade finally closed on Sunday, November 20, 1949. The tent, enlarged to seat 9,000, overflowed with the largest revival audience since Billy Sunday's New York campaign of 1917.

The thirty-year-old sensation's preaching style was simple. Avoiding shrill emotionalism, Graham followed the musical warm-ups with intense but flowing sermons heavily interspersed with quotations from the Bible and focused on contemporary public crises and personal problems. The atomic bomb became a favorite rhetorical device representing insecurities, and the spread of "communism" was pictured as an increasing crisis and threat in world affairs. The authorized biography reveals Graham's worldview at the time:

> In 1949 the United States was forging ahead economically, yet lay shadowed by fear. The Cold War was at its height. Russia's atomic bomb test demolished American nuclear security; the swift victory of Communism in China, and the belief which history would substantiate, that Stalin was preparing to expand his empire by military means and subversion, made the future uncertain and drove the more thoughtful, whatever their politics,

to question themselves about the true foundations of the American way of life. Graham brought world affairs right into the "Canvas Cathedral." He preached in the shadow of international crisis, and he preached straight from the Bible.[15]

Graham's emphasis in Los Angeles and afterward was that only old-time religion based on the Bible could recall America from materialism, immorality, and paganism and save the world from destruction. He preached against divorce, crime, gambling, extramarital sex, and false prophets, and warned that Los Angeles was third in line behind New York and Chicago for destruction by the atomic bomb. The "blond, trumpet-lunged" orator, as *Time* described him, reiterated: "I think we are living at a time in world history when God is giving us a desperate choice, a choice of either revival or judgment."[16] The crusade's newspaper and radio announcements advertised "Held Over by Popular Demand" and "Sixth Great Sin-Smashing Week."[17] Attendance totalled 350,000, with 2,703 "decisions for Christ," and support from 450 Los Angeles churches.

Graham followed Los Angeles with a successful eighteen-day crusade in Boston, but the following three-week crusade in Columbia, South Carolina, was more typical of Graham's increasing success. That crusade recorded 5,050 decisions and culminated in a mammoth rally in the football stadium at the University of South Carolina with 40,000 in attendance. Henry R. Luce, publisher of *Time* and *Life*, tipped off by Bernard Baruch, attended the rally on March 9, 1950, and spent several hours with Graham afterward in the governor's mansion. Their meeting resulted in extensive *Life* photographic coverage of the Columbia crusade and Luce's pledge of favorable coverage of subsequent campaigns.[18] During the crusade Graham also addressed joint sessions of the Georgia state legislature and the South Carolina state legislature. Governor Strom Thurmond officially declared the closing day "South Carolina Revival Rally Day."

Graham's star continued to rise through subsequent crusades until in 1952, at the close of a five-week crusade in Washington, D.C., a special act of Congress enabled Graham to address a rally on the steps of the Capitol building in Washington and to have that address carried live by radio and television across the nation. During that period he became a personal friend of such senators as Richard M. Nixon and Lyndon B. Johnson. During 1952 Graham also met personally with President Truman, attended both national political conventions, spent Christmas with American troops in Korea, and was called by President-Elect Eisenhower to meet with him privately in New York shortly before his inauguration.

William Franklin Graham, Jr., had come a long way from that eighteenth green in Tampa less than fifteen years earlier.

Multimedia and International Crusades

Had Graham continued only to lead live crusades throughout the United States, he would have remained a significant American personage, but he would not have achieved his ultimate status as a major international mass-mediated figure of historic proportions. In the quarter century following his Los Angeles triumph, Graham conducted crusades and delivered addresses almost everywhere in the world and disseminated his message through increasingly complex and diversified mass communication media and networks.

In the year following his Los Angeles success, Graham began a one-half hour radio program, "Hour of Decision," broadcast each Sunday afternoon. The Walter F. Bennett advertising agency in Chicago convinced Graham to initiate the show even though he had difficulty raising a $25,000 advance and ensuring a $7,000 a week budget. ABC carried the program to its 150 affiliates, and in five weeks it achieved the highest Nielsen rating ever attained by a religious program. Most of the early broadcasts were live, originating from a current crusade, and followed the format of the crusades—utilizing music, announcements, and scripture reading as a build-up to Graham's sermon. Cliff Barrows always introduced Graham with: "And now, as always, a man with God's message for these crisis days, Billy Graham." Graham's delivery was consciously patterned after the tense, rapid styles of Walter Winchell and Drew Pearson. Each broadcast ended with a prayer and Graham's sign-off, "And now, until next week, good-bye and may the Lord bless you, real good," followed by a Barrows's call for contributions. Within five years, Graham's "Hour of Decision" was regularly heard by as many as 20 million people over 850 stations linked by ABC, Mutual, Yankee, Inter-Mountain, Canadian, and Australian networks, as well as worldwide shortwave.

As the radio program caught on, letters and contributions began to pour in to Graham's Minneapolis office stimulating the development of a nonprofit corporation, the Billy Graham Evangelistic Association, Incorporated (BGEA), and a daily newspaper column. Graham's radio program brought in 178,726 letters the first year and 362,545 letters the second year. Graham's advertising agency came up with the idea of his writing a daily problem column with a title suggested by Eleanor Roosevelt's "My Day." "My Answer" by Billy Graham began in December, 1952, and within a year was reaching 15 million readers through 73 daily newspapers. By the 1960s it was carried in 123 daily newspapers with over 20 million readers in North America alone. Although BGEA employees prepare the drafts, Graham claims "I've never sent a single 'My Answer' in all these years that I didn't redo until it became mine."[19]

During these same years, Graham's organization expanded into other media: books, magazines, and records. Many letters requested copies of Graham's sermons and the music of his team both on recordings and in sheet music. In 1952 the Grason Corporation (*Graham* and George Wilson, the business manager) was established as a mail-order book and record company. In 1953 Graham published *Peace with God*, the first of his many bestsellers. By 1965 more than 1.25 million copies had been sold in English and millions more in translations. Among his other books are: *Calling Youth to Christ* (1947); *Revival in Our Times* (1950); *America's Hour of Decision* (1951); *Korean Diary* (1953); *The Secret of Happiness* (1955) *My Answer* (1960); *World Aflame* (1965); *The Jesus Generation* (1971); and *Angels, God's Secret Agents* (1975). While Graham cannot match the 79 books published by his Catholic popular media counterpart, Bishop Fulton J. Sheen, his writing directly and by ghost has been an essential part of spreading the message. In the magazine field, in 1956 after several years of planning, Graham created *Christianity Today*, a fortnightly journal positioned between fundamentalists and liberals, which eventually reached a paid circulation of about 145,000. In 1960 Graham founded a popular-format magazine, *Decision*, that claims a circulation of more than 4 million each month and is published in five languages. In 1969 Graham became a regular contributor to *Reader's Digest*, the largest circulation magazine in the world. His Grason Corporation distributes books by and about Graham, recordings and sheet music by his team, morocco-bound Bibles and devotional books, the complete New Testament on records, Bible comic books, and a variety of other items, all of which receive heavy promotion over Graham media especially for gifts at Christmastime.

Alongside the printed word, early in his career Graham expanded his electronic media beyond radio to include film and television. The 1950 Portland crusade was filmed as "The Portland Story" but later became "Mid-Century Crusade." The following year Graham created Billy Graham Evangelistic Films, Inc., which later became World Wide Pictures. The company makes documentary films of his major crusades and also produces feature-length fiction films. One of the first Graham films produced was "Oiltown, U.S.A.," centered on Houston, Texas, as "the story of the free enterprise of America—the story of the development and use of God-given natural resources by men who have built a great new empire."[20] World Wide Pictures has produced more than three dozen feature films, which show at rented theaters for an admission charge as well as at church and civic gatherings. They are effectively distributed globally. "Lucia," set during a Buenos Aires crusade in 1962, was filmed originally in Spanish. "The Restless Ones," released the following year, was seen by 4.5 million and resulted in 400,000 decisions to come forward for Christ. A 28-minute film, "Man in the Fifth Dimension," was the central feature of the Billy Graham Pavilion at the New York World's Fair in 1964–65, a pavilion visited by 5 million people from 125 countries. Released in time to be eligible for Academy Awards in 1976, "The Hiding Place" starred Julie Harris, Eileen Heckart, and Arthur O'Connell and was well received by critics as well as commercial audiences.

When his first fiction film, "Mr. Texas," appeared in 1951, Graham was chastised by his fellow evangelists, who warned that Hollywood was the work of the devil. Graham responded, "If we are going to arrest the vast pagan masses of America, our methods are going to have to change. . . ."[21] In 1969 Graham's authorized biography made an impressive claim: "It is reckoned that every thirty-five minutes a Billy Graham film is being shown somewhere around the world."[22]

Television has proven to be the ideal medium for Billy Graham. The authorized biography acknowledges

> Television crusades form Billy Graham's most extensive and effective ministry. . . . The crusade telecasts sponsored and produced by BGEA are the main evangelistic thrust, and have carried his message wider than that of any other preacher in American history. With three or more series in a year, each comprising several one-hour telecasts, Billy Graham can reach nearly every home in America. . . .[23]

In 1951 Graham originated a televised "Hour of Decision" on Sunday nights with limited success. In November, 1953, NBC offered him a lucrative five-year contract to host a daily secular program; he turned it down. In 1957 Graham revealed to a *New York Times* interviewer his idea for a televised "religious extravaganza":

> I would have someone like Fred Waring's orchestra and glee club playing and singing old religious hymns. Then a five to eight minute skit emphasizing a moral or spiritual truth. And then an interview with a famous person such as Roy Rogers or Vice-President Nixon who would tell of his spiritual experience. This would be followed by a five-minute sermon. The program would be produced on the same scale as a major entertainment show.[24]

Despite his flights of fancy, Graham's television success has been closely tied to his live crusades in both style and distribution. Graham's 1954 Greater London crusade from Harringay pioneered the use of post office land-line relays to transmit Graham's voice to rented auditoriums scattered throughout England and Scotland. For the 1957 Madison Square

Garden crusade, the Bennett agency worked up a contract with ABC to broadcast eighteen Saturday night sessions live on national television. The live quality was a great improvement over the 1951 telecasts, and more than 1.5 million letters, including 30,000 decisions for Christ, came to Graham as a result.

For the 1966 London crusade, Graham was frustrated that they could not buy time on BBC television and that television coverage was not always flattering. The Graham team decided to use for television the same land-line relays they had earlier used so successfully for sound. Using recently developed Eidophore projectors, ten regional crusades projected Graham into theaters. On screens 30 feet high and 40 feet wide, Graham's head and shoulders stood 14 feet high. Similar closed-circuit television arrangements were used in the 1967 All-Britain Crusade and for overflow crowds at crusades in London, New York, Australia, and elsewhere. The 1969 New York City crusade was primarily a television event. The ten-day crusade made Madison Square Garden into a television studio. Each of the ten sermons was broadcast three times in New York City and once in a dozen other major cities.

In fact, in the New York crusade the percentage of those coming forward at the call was considerably higher in closed-circuit television relay halls than at the Garden itself. Organizers attributed the difference to the darkened room, larger image, better acoustics, and fewer distractions. Graham's 1969 Melbourne crusade was the first color telecast from Australia.

So great is the role of television in Graham crusades that the order of the service has been changed. Originally, films, videotapes, and telecasts of crusades were fitted around the service. Later, preliminaries in the service were shortened and a strict time schedule observed to fit the requirements of television. Graham's attitude toward media is positive: "Television is the greatest method the church has ever known for getting over its message."[25]

Billy Graham's personal appearances expanded outward from the United States and Canada to include many other nations of the world at the same time as his media usage expanded from live sermons to include radio, newspapers, books, magazines, films, and television. The mass-mediated versions of Graham were constantly supplemented with live crusades before vast numbers in a wide variety of cities throughout Western Europe, Australia, India, Southeast Asia, Africa, South America, and elsewhere. The mass media and mass crusade outreach was then fed into a complex, computerized feedback system that recorded individual decisions, distributed follow-up literature, notified local churches of converts' names and addresses, solicited and recorded contributions, and generally served to coordinate the marketing, distribution, and public relations functions of the BGEA. The personal follow-up system in which an individual counselor goes forward, stands by, and talks with each person who goes forward is indicative of the masterful intermeshing of mass and personal communications systems in the Graham approach.

Graham's Greater London Crusade in 1954 was his first major success outside the United States. It started with controversy and opposition. The preparatory committee in London thought 50,000 pounds extravagant for publicity and were taken aback when the emphasis was on pictures of Billy Graham pasted all over London with the single slogan, "Hear Billy Graham." Another item caused more trouble. A thick illustrated brochure, 12 by 17 inches, was prepared to encourage large contributions. It contained a statement reading, "What Hitler's bombs could not do, socialism with its accompanying evils shortly acomplished." The socialist government of the Labour Party took great offense and there were attempts in parliament to prevent Graham's entry into England. To Graham, "socialism" meant Communism and not a British political party; his public relations man, Jerry Beavan, had replaced the term with "secularism" but the uncorrected draft was printed by mistake. The resulting furor placed Graham on front pages all over England. The hostility slowly turned to begrudging respect during the weeks of the crusade. In all, over 2 million attended, and the closing session brought over 120,000 persons to Wembley soccer stadium. Graham met privately with Prime Minister Winston Churchill. Eighty percent of the London churches cooperated, and 38,000 people officially came forward during the crusade, swamping the individual follow-up and counseling arrangements.

Graham followed that venture with other foreign successes. In 1956 a four-week crusade in India traveled to major cities and was relatively well received in that religiously sophisticated country. In Kottayam, Kerala, in southern India, Graham attracted a crowd of 75,000. The most long-range effect was that Graham's New Delhi interpreter, Dr. Akbar Abdul-Haqq, joined Graham's team and later conducted numerous crusades throughout India and other Asian countries.

Graham's 1959 crusade in Australia and New Zealand was one of his team's most thoroughly successful efforts. In Melbourne crowds of 25,000 consistently filled the Music Bowl for three weeks, and approximately 140,000 crowded the Melbourne Cricket Ground for the closing. Twenty percent of New Zealand's population attended his six-day crusade in three cities. The culmination in Sydney in April and May, 1959, attracted more than 1 million in four weeks and drew more than 150,000 persons to the closing while another 1 million listened by landline or radio. At the final session alone, 5,683 made their decisions, came forward, were individually counseled, and were registered. Before the Sydney crusade 9,400 persons signed up for training as crusade counselors.

In 1960 Graham held crusades throughout Africa, and since then black members of his team have held associate crusades there. In 1963 in West Berlin Graham convened 1,200 evangelists from many countries for a "world congress" on the goals, methods, and meaning of evangelism. In the midst of subsequent crusades throughout North America and the world, Graham spent Christmas in 1966 and 1968 with American troops in Vietnam.

In sum, Billy Graham's education, early ministry, splashy success, and subsequent international multimedia spread provide the cues for interpreting his message or text: (a) His literary genre is that of the mass evangelist, building on the tradition of North American revivalism and steeped in a mixture of Calvinism, fundamentalism, Americanism, and experience religion. (b) His *sitz-im-leben* is the life situation of an international industrial society that enables him to address and mobilize numbers unprecedented in the history of evangelism. In fact, Graham's role and the role of institutionalized religion in such contemporary multinational life provide him with audiences competitive with the most influential politicians and entertainers in the world. (c) The intent of the author is to use whatever media are available to stimulate a "great awakening" of religion in America and other lands throughout the world by calling individuals forward into a decision for Christ and a life led in the spirit of that decision.

Ethnography of a Telecast

The work of ethnography in anthropology and the social sciences is to provide an exact record describing "regularities in human social behaviour . . . within the boundaries of a particular society during a brief cross section of time."[26] Claude Lévi-Strauss defines ethnography as simply "the observation and analysis of human groups considered as individual entities" and its aim as "recording as accurately as possible the respective modes of life of various groups."[27] Anthony Wallace notes that modern ethnographic methods have produced "an increasing awareness that the research operations of the ethnographer produce primarily not naturalistic or statistical descriptions of regularities in overt behavior but descriptions of the rules which the actors are presumably employing, or attempting to employ, in the execution and mutual organization of this behavior."[28] The emphasis in ethnographic studies on *rules* employed by the actors themselves coincides with the emphasis in exegesis on interpretation from within the framework of the *intention* of the original author.

The following ethnography of a Billy Graham telecast attempts to provide as exact a record as possible describing the regularities of behavior unique to it. Six one-hour Graham telecasts were videotaped, time logged, partially transcribed, and averaged into patterns of regularities.[29]

This application of ethnography may trigger several objections. First, a videotaped telecast is not a direct expression of human behavior itself but only a record of an edited and disseminated partial *version* of behavior. Such a methodologically pure objection slights the fact that all behavior is edited, whether from inside the actor or outside, and that increasingly, as mass media infiltrate human communication, the externally edited behavior provided by networks, film companies, wire services, and similar institutions becomes a dominant behavioral influence paralleling direct personal contact. Moreover, the customs, rituals, and culture portrayed in the sounds and moving images coming from speakers and screens, because of their preediting to fit the tastes of and to link together millions, are themselves virtually ethnographic reflections of cultural regularities. A second objection is that the telecast itself is not completely self-explanatory and that only the study of the people making television or receiving it is genuine social science. It is true that intention and social context are important. Nevertheless, the focus of cultural investigation is obviously on that "point of impact" mediated message just as it is on Shakespeare's written work rather than on his private life or the behavior of his audiences. Popular television may present a distorted picture of social behavior, but because the most commercially successful distortions are always toward the mass norm, television offers a view of social behavior that is more, not less, representative of the tendencies and regularities of a society. In that sense, ethnographic records of mass-mediated culture are at least as valid as ethnographic records of nonmediated individual and group culture.

With these clarifications in mind, the following ethnographic record of a Billy Graham crusade telecast emerges. The temporal regularities that recur in Billy Graham crusade telecasts divide the hour as illustrated in Figure 6–1. The average distribution of time in a one-hour telecast can also be described in four categories, as seen in Table 6–1.

Transcript of a Typical Telecast

I. 0:00 to 2:00: Opening title, identification, and music. The camera opens with long shots of the large crowd and/or close-ups of

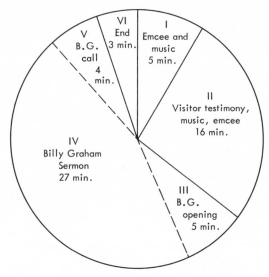

FIGURE 6–1   Distribution of Time in a One-Hour Telecast

singers, while the sound-track carries the gospel hymn music or, in the case of youth nights, the folk music. The camera focuses on the singer(s) and pans slowly over the crowd and the many-hundred-person choir. As the teutonic hymn continues, titles are superimposed over the crowd and singer shots on the screen, identifying the building, city, and state crusade in sequence. For example, one at a time the titles read: "Lobo Stadium," "From Albuquerque, New Mexico," "The New Mexico Billy Graham Crusade."

II. 2:00 to 5:00: Opening by master of ceremonies.   As the music concludes, the camera comes in close on the master of ceremonies, Cliff Barrows, who welcomes everyone to the crusade and telecast, makes introductory remarks, and makes the first sales pitch for Bible-study books offered by Graham.

TABLE 6–1.   Distribution of Categories in a One-Hour Telecast

FEATURE	TOTAL TIME	PERCENT OF HOUR TELECAST
Billy Graham	36 minutes	60%
Master of ceremonies	8 minutes	13%
Visitor testimony	6 to 10 minutes	10–17%
Music	6 to 10 minutes	10–17%

Cliff Barrows joined the Graham team in 1945 at the age of twenty-two. His wife, Billie, also played piano for Graham. Barrows's glad, exuberant voice sets a positive, enthusiastic tone for the crusades. Barrows also directs the choirs, which sometimes number from 1,000 to 1,500 voices.

A typical Barrows' opening line is: "And we do welcome all of you who just joined us on television." He frequently notes something special about the time or place that evening—youth night, "beautiful" Tempe, Albuquerque, or wherever else they happen to be. He may mention something later to come: Graham's topic, a visitor, the music. Barrows usually slips in a plug for the items being widely distributed by the BGEA at that time. In Tempe, it was the "Spiritual Life Packet," including a Bible-study guide. In Albuquerque, it was "Discovery 2," a six-month program of Bible study created by the Scripture Union in Great Britain. It is the sequel to "Discovery 1," which sold out its half million copies. The packet or book is plugged at least twice in each telecast.

III. 5:00 to 21:00: Visitors' testimony, music, master of ceremonies.
In each crusade telecast, an outsider not from Graham's team is given the podium for anywhere from two to ten minutes to localize, make current, or add prestige to the program. Roy Rogers, sometimes accompanied by Trigger, was an early Graham favorite for this role, but it can be anyone of public interest who has made a decision for Christ. In the Southwest several of the crusades have featured Chief Sunny Claus and his family, all Graham associates. Claus awarded Graham an Indian headdress and the high honor of a name, "Warrior of the Great Spirit." Claus is articulate and sophisticated and works among fifteen native American tribes. In the Tempe and Albuquerque crusades, Graham also featured visiting testimony by Bill Bright, head of the international Campus Crusade for Christ; Dr. Ken Tuyan, an Armenian aerospace scientist born in Lebanon and active in Christian youth activities; and Bonnie Barrows, Cliff and Billie's twenty-seven-year-old daughter who had been doing advance work in Albuquerque.

During the twenty minutes of warm-up for Graham at least four or five songs are performed.

George Beverly Shea's deep baritone and rocklike presence have been with Graham since his 1944 WCFL radio broadcasts in Chicago. Dressed in suit and tie, as are virtually all of the males on Graham's team, Shea specializes in old favorites and a few hymns he has composed himself. They are rich in regal imagery and King James language. On the six telecasts he sang, among others, "When Christ Shall Come," "How Great Thou Art," "We Are Climbing Jacob's Ladder," "In Times Like These," and "This Rock Is Jesus." He sang and read the lyrics, or in other ways varied the format, of "The King Is Coming," "I Found a Friend," "What a Frienn We Have in Jesus," and "Rock of Ages." The choih and organ accompany Shea.

Other singers include Myrtle Hall, a relatively sedate black gospel singer who performed in the telecasts such songs as "Holy, Holy" and "Share the Lord by Sharing What He's Done for You." Mark and Diane Yashahara of Hawaii sang "I Have Christ in My Heart" and, of course, "Aloha." Youth nights feature the guitar playing and folk style of Bob and Jane Henley in "Peace and Love . . . , " "Come Let Us Reason Together Says the Lord," and similar rhythmic repetitive numbers. Graham's crusade at convenient locations may feature Jerome Hines, Anita Bryant, Ethel Waters, or Norma Zimmer. Accompaniment is provided by pianist Tedd Smith and organist Don Hustad.

Barrows handles the introductions and commentary throughout these first twenty minutes, never failing to mention that while everything, including the featured Bible-study book and the telecast itself, comes to the recipient free, it is only "your" contributions that make it all possible. The appeal is unambiguous but not pushy.

IV. 21:00 to 57:00: Billy Graham. Billy Graham speaks on camera for an average of 36 minutes during a one-hour crusade telecast. His appearance is broken into four parts: (a) introductory remarks for five minutes; (b) sermon for an average of 27 minutes; (c) call to the audience to come forward, lasting about two minutes; and (d) a separate call to the television audience to follow suit in appropriate ways.

(a) 21:00 to 26:00: Introductory remarks. Graham often begins with a brief moment of prayer, then welcomes the television audience, flatters the location and local people, perhaps drops a name or tells a short anecdote, and finally reiterates the offer of the book being sold and asks for contributions. In the Tempe crusade, Graham flattered Tempe and Phoenix by saying, "My wife will want to move here someday—at least, I hope she will." He promoted the Spiritual Life Packet and asked for contributions for his missionary work. The subsidy was needed, he said, for these telecasts, which "cost more than $1 million"; for a meeting of 3,000 evangelists from 150 countries in Switzerland the following summer; for "The Hiding Place," the highest budgeted gospel picture ever made; and for a gospel exposition in Seoul, Korea. Graham next mentioned "John Conlon, Congressman from here and a longtime personal friend who just read the first psalm." Graham then proceeded into the text of his sermon beginning with a citation of verses from the second psalm.

Graham's opening lines in the Albuquerque crusade further illustrate his adeptness at flattery and sophisticated salesmanship. He began,

I want to welcome all of those that have joined on television as well and tell you that we are at the University of New Mexico in their beautiful, beautiful arena, one of the most beautiful in all the world. . . . They have something to be proud of. In fact, about everything about New Mexico is something to be proud of. (Applause.) I don't want to say too much about New Mexico because I don't think you want everybody pouring in here. (Applause.) . . . It's a treat to be here in the lovely, beautiful, wonderful state of New Mexico. . . .

But now I want to remind you again of what Cliff said about this book, Discovery 2. . . . We want to send it to you free and postage paid, and we want *you* to send some financial help to help us pay for these telecasts, because these telecasts are very expensive and we have a tremendous missionary budget, because we send these telecasts all over Brazil. They go throughout Latin America. They go to the Far East. They go throughout Africa. They go to Australia. They go to all around the world. And in all of those places, we purchase the time—except for a few of them—and we have to pay for it. And that's a missionary responsibility that we believe God has given us. And unless you help us, of course, we cannot continue it. So write to me, Billy Graham, Minneapolis, Minnesota, and we'll send you the book and we hope you'll help us in carrying on this ministry.

(b) 26:00 to 53:00: The sermon.   Graham's sermons are generally structured in three parts: an opening scripture quotation; a statement of a problem in the form of an easily understood social and/or personal threat; and a solution through active belief in Christ. The content of Graham's preaching will be analyzed in the following section; only the external style is described in this section.

This printed page is a difficult medium in which to characterize Graham's live appearances. Graham's use of body and voice resembles dancing and singing. As the above quotations reveal, the style is live and spoken in contrast to the formal reading of a printed text. Television easily conveys these qualities; print does not.

At least three qualities of Graham's live and televised presentation distinguish it from his written work: his appearance, his movement, and his staging.

Graham's personal appearance is carefully attended to and has always been one of his greatest assets. His piercing eyes, square jaw, tall frame, and red hair make him the perfect Hollywood model of an evangelist. He stays trim and tanned with regular rounds of golf. For crusade appearances he dresses impeccably in suit and tie, shunning quasi-religious robes or gowns for himself or any of his team and allowing his youth singers to wear stylishly mod outfits. Graham has long been listed among the best dressed in the United States. When he stands in a light-colored suit jacket with a subtle check pattern running through it and a stylish tie set off by a tie clip and a clip-on microphone (despite the large microphone in front of him on the podium), Graham's figure on the television screen against a darkened background is compelling to any viewer not unfavorably disposed toward his message.

Graham's preaching involves constant movement, hand and body gestures, and continuous variations in vocal intonation and pacing. The resulting rhythm of the presentation, coupled with the anecdotal content, carries the listener/viewer along as do song and dance. Attention is maintained and ideas presented but never in complex or monotonous patterns. On the videotape Graham averaged about 22 full gestures every minute. The variety of such gestures is immense, ranging from the raising of a single finger to flinging both arms out. They are full enough to be visible from remote seats in a mass audience but not so exaggerated as to appear artificial in television close-ups. In Albuquerque at one point Graham compared faith in God to faith in the builders of his speaking platform. To dramatize and visualize the point, he walked back and down 15 feet to the rear, talking all the time. There he pointed with his feet and grabbed the structure with his hands. Then he explained that his "faith" in the carpenters allowed him to strut right up on the platform without doubting or needing to test it—and he strutted vigorously back up to the podium.

The staging of Graham's televised crusades lends impact. The involvement of large crowds and the appearance of hundreds coming forward at the end far surpass the persuasive potential of studio productions in motivating other-directed viewers. The arena in Albuquerque that Graham so effusively flattered was an obvious basketball stadium or fieldhouse. As Graham mentioned the arena, a camera high in a remote corner offered a long shot of the tiers of crowded stands. The large platform for the featured guests and the separate podiums for speakers and for singers rose together near the middle of the court area, set well away from the crowd on four sides. Graham's New York crusades have variously filled Madison Square Garden, Yankee Stadium, and Times Square. The Graham crusades are generally held or at least concluded in stadiums and arenas built for football, baseball, basketball, cricket, or soccer. Such locales highlight the parallels between mass-culture phenomena, in this case mass evangelism and mass spectator sports.

Graham's rhetorical style is clearly popular. He creates a shifting montage of images, examples, and anecdotes. Quotations from the Bible appear every minute or two, usually as a short phrase and sometimes adding no content but conveying a feeling of religiosity through the archaic King James language. Graham cites current events continuously. He frequently quotes "a newspaper," "a Britisher," "the *Los Angeles Times*," "television," or simply "the news" for evidence of current crises, problems, insecurities, or immorality. Drawing on both prestigious and popular sources, Graham may cite Kant, Churchill, or Mao immediately before or after Hank Snow, Charley Rich, or B. J. Thomas. His anecdotes are often stories attributed to members of his team, local officials, or his wife; and his imagery is drawn from the Bible, his youth, mass media, or his travels in other countries.

All of these are woven into the two-part pattern of his sermons—raising a general problem and then showing how belief in Christ solves or eliminates it. The pattern is ancient, almost a classic tragic form. The first part raises the anxiety level of the audience by pointing to a tragic flaw in existence, especially contemporary expressions of irreverent *hubris*, pride. Then with the dénouement comes the saving *catharsis* and a call for *metanoia*, a change of heart. These elements are tied together in a dynamic flow, a unity of plot, that is dramatic and emotional without being shrill or maudlin. Camera pans of the audience show faces politely attentive, almost hynotized in a relaxed, yearning way. Hundreds always come forward in the end. This was achieved in the New Mexico and Arizona crusades by sermons innocuously titled "Hopeless, Yet There Is Hope," "Three Things You Cannot Do Without," "The Storm Is Coming," and "God Plus You."

(c) 53:00 to 55:00: The call to come forward. The culmination of each crusade sermon lies in the call for listeners to make a total decision for Christ and to come forward to the foot of the speakers' platform to express that decision. Rural Methodist circuit riders preaching to frontier camp meetings first developed the practice of calling sinners forward to the "anxious seat" to represent their repentance and forgiveness. A century before Graham, Charles Grandison Finney had made the practice acceptable also in urban revivals, against objections that it was a high-pressure, artificial sales technique. Billy Sunday had labelled the response to the call, "hitting the sawdust trail," in the temporary wooden tabernacles strewn with carpenters' shavings.

Graham's call is quiet but forceful. He has presented the threats and problems of life and has proposed Christ as the solution. For example, his sermon in Arizona on current crises ended with: "The storm is coming. Are you ready? Be ye ready. . . . Turn to Christ by faith, repent of your sins, and receive him into your heart." Then Graham's voice slowed down and he called hearers forward: "I'm going to ask you to come in front of the platform and to say by your coming 'I want Christ; I want to be ready for that hour; I want Christ and to be a new person.'" The previous evening, Graham had begun the call by saying, "I'm going to ask you to stand up and come down here and say a prayer with me." As Graham moved into these lines, the organ and choir began quietly and slowly in the background, reinforcing the special religious feeling of the moment. Graham removes obvious excuses. In Arizona he urged, "Come quickly. Those way up on top, you have plenty of time. We're going to wait." On another evening in Arizona he added, "You may be a member of a church or none."

The call serves several practical purposes. It makes the individual's private decision more tangible and symbolically meaningful. Scholastic theology would identify the call as an expression of the "sacramental principle": an external sign expressing internal grace. Any persuasion is more obviously effective if it influences physical behavior as well as attitudes. Acting on an idea more thoroughly commits an individual to assent to the idea. Persuasion research amply supports the justification for the call to come forward at the end of a service. But the call is also part of a larger organizational apparatus.

Coming forward at the call in a Billy Graham crusade enters the individual convert into an organizational network that begins months before any crusade and continues long afterward. Up to a year in advance of a major crusade, Graham team members come to the contracted target city to hold luncheons with ministers, those in business, and other leaders. Individual churches are affiliated with the crusade, supportive prayer meetings are set up on a weekly basis, youth committees begin promotion, and training classes for "counselors" are established. Vast numbers of persons are thereby "individually" involved in a crusade. For the 1963 Los Angeles crusade, 3,500 churches were involved in one year of preparation; 23,000 church members applied for precrusade training classes; 20,000 personally called on 1 million homes; 80,000 women met in 10,000 homes for prayer meetings before the crusade; youth committees canvassed Disneyland, the beaches, and other tourist and entertainment locations. The final service in 1963 at the Los Angeles Coliseum officially attracted 134,254 persons. On one youth night in that crusade, 3,216 persons came forward at the call.

As Graham folds his arms and reverently bends his head after he makes the call, a follow-up system is already operating around the hundreds quietly moving forward down the aisles. Local counselors are trained weeks in advance of a crusade to meet on a one-to-one basis with each convert who comes forward. They are taught scriptural passages, especially "proof" texts on the divinity and saving role of Jesus, and are taught a few specific questions to ask the new convert. They are to answer any questions the convert may have. If they cannot satisfactorily answer a question, they usher the convert to a head counselor. The counselor introduces himself to the new convert while they are still at the foot of the podium after Graham's last words to the converts assembled. The counselor then proceeds with the convert into the counselling room where the discussion takes place. While there, the counselor helps the convert fill out a card of personal information, which is forwarded to the convert's local church, with a copy to Graham headquarters. The counselor follows up with a visit, call, or letter to the convert within 48 hours.

The pairing of convert and counselor matches persons of roughly the same sex, age, and type, at the same time as it doubles the numbers of those coming forward. The trained counselors are dispersed throughout the audience. When a convert rises to go forward, a nearby counselor as often as possible of the same sex, age, dress style, and other characteristics, at a sign from the counselor's section chief, rises and moves down the aisle with the convert. The counselor follow-up system was fully developed by Dawson Trotman, who had founded a small group apostolate called the Navigators and who was enticed onto Graham's team in 1951.

BGEA statistics on converts reveal that 60 percent are women, 45 percent are persons under eighteen, and 65 to 75 percent are already church members.[30] Follow-up studies disagree on the exact percentage of Graham converts who are, in fact, making their first decision for Christ. Estimates vary from about one-fourth to one-ninth of those who fill out the decision cards. The others making decisions are recovering from backsliding or are rededicating their lives. McLoughlin notes that even by Graham's own statistics, 55 percent of those hitting the trail are not only already church members but are already converted "born-again, Bible-believing" church members.[31] Only 45 percent are "first decisions." These data help interpret the visual evidence of persons coming forward at Graham crusades and telecasts. Given that half are counselors and that more than half the remainder have previously made a conversion, clearly fewer than one-fourth, even by generous estimates, of those pouring down the aisles are making a first decision for Christ. Still more negatively, Pitirim Sorokin's study of Graham converts concluded that, while about half of the converts changed speech patterns to fundamentalist descriptions of changed lives and outlooks, "their outward behavior did not change at all."[32]

Whatever its other effects, the call at the conclusion of a Graham sermon does bring new members into Graham's organization and onto his mailing lists at the same time as it adds a small percentage of new names to local church rosters.

(d) 55:00 to 57:00: The call to the television audience.   Graham stands quietly as the choir continues "Just As I Am" or another invitational hymn and converts come forward. Then he turns to the camera and extends a call to all those watching on television.

The call to the television audience is similar to that given the live audience with the exception that the mass-media audience cannot walk forward to the podium. Other tangible signs are sometimes suggested, and a letter to Graham headquarters is always requested. The videotaped television calls were all variations of, "As you can see, hundreds are coming forward here tonight to say 'yes.' You can make that decision too, if you will." Sometimes, Graham suggests standing up to express the decision. If he can add a historic superlative, he will. For example, in the New Mexico crusade he added, "A higher percentage of young people are coming to Christ here in Albuquerque than, I think, we've ever seen in any American city." On some occasions Graham adds, "You can make that same commitment in your home or in a bar, a hotel lobby, or wherever you may be watching." He always concludes his appearance on the telecast with two items. First, he requests that those who make their decision or wish to help his missionary work write to him, "Billy Graham, Minneapolis, Minnesota." He offers to send to the television converts the same literature that he sends to those coming forward at the crusade. Secondly, he concludes with a "God bless you" and "I hope you'll go to church next Sunday."

V. 57:00 to end: Conclusion and credits.   The music continues for some seconds while the camera shows the podium and crowd. Then the master of ceremonies, Cliff Barrows, comes in with a voice-over repeating Graham's call to the television audience. A typical closing statement at the Arizona crusade ran: "During the past eight days of the Phoenix crusade, many from all walks of life made their decision for Christ. You can too. And, if you do, please write to us—Billy Graham, Minneapolis, Minnesota." A picture of an envelope addressed to Graham fills the screen. Barrows concludes, "This television program has been presented through the auspices of the Billy Graham Evangelistic Association. This is Cliff Barrows. Goodbye and God bless you." Credits superimposed over last shots of the arena credit cameramen, lighting, and other crew members. The last credit is to "Executive Producers—Walter F. Bennett and Fred Dienert." Bennett's advertising agency buys air time around the world for the broadcasts and has handled Graham's lucrative account for a quarter of a century. Dienert, Bennett's associate, first convinced Graham to expand beyond live crusades into radio in 1950.

Exegetical Analysis and Commentary

The preceding ethnography of a telecast outlines the regularities in pattern and rules that determine the basic Graham crusade text. A series of three telecasts forms a single package to be telecast on successive nights. Three such packages from Graham crusades are transmitted during different parts of the year in major American cities and are shown throughout much of Europe, Australia, Africa, and Asia—wherever television time can be bought and Christianity has a foothold. By 1969 Graham's text had caused more than 1 million persons to "come forward" at crusades. Many times that number had heard him live and still many times *those* millions had heard Graham via mass-media relays.

What are the basic ingredients of the message of this successful text, how does that message compare to the multitude of cross-cultural religious possibilities, and what are the theological, ideological, political, and cultural implications of Graham's message?

The Reverend William Franklin Graham, Jr., obviously gives people something they *want*. What is the origin of that want and how does he satisfy it? Graham's own explanation of his success calls on the supernatural and miraculous. Without denying that explanation but simply leaving it in abeyance, we can develop a more mundane explanation.

Both the context and code of Graham's appeal are culture-specific. The context that he draws on and that amplifies his message is the mainstream of popular Western industrial culture, its life experience, values, and symbols. His appeal is to the experience of "alienation" and its manifestations in individual lives and institutional complexities. The code that he utilizes to "solve" that alienation is traditional Christian imagery combined with contemporary American and Western ideals. This is clear in exegesis of his approaches to sex, race, economics, and politics. Since his first "puff" by Hearst and his favored treatment at the hands of Luce, Nixon, and other political and economic leaders, Graham has been a favored child of the American establishment and its allies. Graham has rewarded that assistance and achieved his goal of maximum numerical outreach by remaining carefully within the framework of the dominant cultural assumptions and within the given arrangement of power and the interests of political and economic power elites. Graham's explanation is that his work focuses on the role of Christ as individual savior and all else is secondary. However, as the dominant religious-moral figure in contemporary mass society sustained by personal charismatic influence—as opposed to the formal institutionalized power of the Roman Catholic pope—Graham provides the most powerful endorsement imaginable of the status quo by defining ultimate religious and moral issues as individual, private concerns. Graham's approach to the social order is precisely the dangerously uncritical stance that both Guenther Lewy and Gordon Zahn's studies of Christian churches in Nazi Germany have warned against.

Alongside Graham's culture-bound context and code, the content of his message is also theologically vulnerable when placed in a cross-cultural perspective. The ultimate, the absolute, the first principle, the all, "God" can be defined in three dimensions: (a) history, (b) transcendence, and (c) immanence. Graham is insistent about the historical God of Christianity and His transcendent majesty. But his definition of God lacks immanence; it fails to evoke a sense of the divine as intrinsically, universally present in all that is. Instead, Graham's God is spatially remote (transcendent) and temporally remote (historic) but not immediately present (immanent) except in an *instrumental* way in the particular saving effect of the historical Christ through the action of the Holy Spirit. This instrumental divine presence is strictly confined to individual, internal spiritual activity.

This theological gap in Graham's message becomes obvious when placed in contrast to the most ancient of religious impulses: animism and totemism. Anthropological studies find in nonliterate societies a widespread acceptance of "gods" as life forces immanent in aspects of the immediate natural environment. Formal religions often retain an animistic sense of divine immanence. Hinduism and Buddhism, while deeply spiritual, convey a sense of the divine all-in-all. Zen perceptions and yogic practices emphasize the immediate, as captured in the title of Alan Watts' book on zen, *This Is It*.[33] The same natural animistic spirit is not necessarily alien to Christianity. Yves Congar suggests that a natural rhythm moving back and forth between "engagement" and "detachment" brings into daily Christian life an experience of both the immanence and transcendence of God.[34] William F. Lynch, S.J., has made both a theological and an aesthetic argument for the priority of the incarnational Christic imagination (perceiving God in man) over the escapist Apollonian imagination (seeing God as separate from man, an unattainable ideal).[35] Such awareness, however, is largely absent in American Christianity, especially in the more fundamentalist traditions. The causes are scattered throughout the history of Western Christianity and American Culture.

The result of Graham's disincarnate worldview and theology is an airy nominalism that poses verbal assent to a divine instrument, Christ, as the only solution to an arbitrary, rootless existence. Instrumentalism and nominalism—internal verbal assent to divine intervention through the instrument of Christ and the Spirit—replace the rampant emotionalism that marked God's intrusion in the less sophisticated revival ceremonies. Since nature and immediate experience of life are devoid of God's presence, in Graham's preaching any object or event is only an arbitrary *sign* of something else. "Pagans" mistake these signs for reality, not knowing that the other world of divine spirit proposed by Graham replaces the intrinsic value of vegetation, machines, people, and other proximate reality. The tangible world of objects and events is merely a *sign* to Graham. Certain signs are good, such as marriage and the family. Other signs are bad, such as pornography and war. The most important sign of all to Graham is the Bible. But even the Bible is only a sign: The Old Testament need not be searched for theological truths but only for foreshadowing signs of Christ as he is presented in the New Testament and understood by fundamentalism. Reality-testing for Graham has only one absolute: the internal saving experience of Jesus Christ.

Graham's preaching reflects the above nominalistic worldview. It begins with the assumption, which Graham's rhetoric makes into an emotional experience, that natural existence and finite human life are at best empty and meaningless, at worst negative and miserable. The sole natural exception for Graham tends to be "the American way of life" with its institutional arrangements and traditional virtues.

Graham's Answer

Graham's ethical directives reflect his metaphysical and theological shortcomings. He tends to work within and confirm standard inherited conventions, rather than deepen or challenge or even substantially explain them. His answer on questions of salvation, sex, race, war, politics, and economics illustrate this.

Salvation. Graham assumes that nature is defective. He asks us to "freely acknowledge that there is a defect in human nature, a built-in waywardness that comes from man's natural rebellion against God."[36] As a result, "man's basic problem is spiritual, not social. Man needs a complete change from within."[37] Graham's pessimism is often explicit: "Man, basically, has savage instincts. Even a child—a child has selfishness. He has hates. He needs to be taught to be good."[38] Graham describes this human inadequacy as a characteristic not only of the weak and insecure but also of the strong and confident. He warns,

> I mean that the human mind cannot cope with the problems that we are wrestling with today. And when our intellectual leaders begin to admit that they don't know the answers, and that fact reaches the masses on the street, then they are going to turn somewhere. They will turn to all sorts of escapisms. Some will turn to alcohol. Others will turn to religion in want of security and peace—something to hold onto.[39]

Graham's solution to human shortcomings is biblical conversion, composed of renunciation of sin, an act of saving faith in Christ, and the infusion of divine life into the soul. He states,

> Biblical conversion involves three steps—two of them active and one passive. In active conversion repentence and faith are involved. . . . The third which is passive we may call the new birth or regeneration.[40]

Graham has Americanized the process, insofar as traditional Calvinism saw conversion as at least two-thirds, if not totally, passive on the part of the human individual. The core of Graham's message is simple: "God prescribed the remedy for the ills of the human race. That remedy is personal faith and commitment to Jesus Christ. The remedy is to be born again."[41] Graham's theological roots remain fundamentalist. He distinguishes his position from narrow, bigoted fundamentalism but even more carefully avoids modernism by insisting on the five points of fundamentalism defined by the Niagara Bible Conference in 1895 and expressed in *The Fundamentals.* Graham describes his fundamentalism as acceptance of "the authority of Scriptures, the virgin birth of Christ, the atoning death of Christ, His bodily resurrection, His second coming, and personal salvation by faith through grace."[42]

Graham pours all his energy into being an effective salesman for that salvation message. In the best Fuller Brush tradition, Graham even improves on the New Testament omission of details of the physical appearance of Jesus by describing him as "every inch a He-man." He adds,

> Christ was probably the strongest man physically that ever lived. He could have been a star athlete on any team. He was a real man, with His strong shoulders, His squarish jaw....[43]

Graham also improves the fundamentalist message with Norman Vincent Peale do-it-yourself pelagianism and promises of earthly rewards. After describing how individuals who tithed themselves for the Lord had received back many times their contribution, Graham proposed, "You can't get around it, the scripture promises material and spiritual benefits to the man who gives to God."[44]

"Chaplain to the Watergate Scandal"—Graham's Ethics

Sex. Nowhere is Graham's fondness for traditional small-town, middle-class values more evident than in his position on marriage and the family, the home, and sex. In one of the Albuquerque telecasts Graham spent many minutes describing his idyllic childhood and comparing it to "The Waltons." Homes should be Bible- and prayer-centered; husband and wife should love each other, accept their respective roles in the family, and rear their children carefully. The solution to problems of the family is "prayer and a hickory stick."[45]

Graham's sexual ethics reflect that turn-of-the-century ideal and certain biblical prescriptions. He extracts considerable rhetorical mileage from the effect of the abolition of what has been termed the "triple threat:" fear of infection, conception, and detection resulting from premarital and extramarital sex. He bulls through contemporary confusion by reaffirming traditional absolutes. Graham favors laws against pornography, absolutely opposes adultery, and believes that divorces should be much harder to obtain.[46] He is less likely to extract moral *principles* from the Bible than to cite biblical *rules*. For Graham it is no problem that biblical proscriptions were developed in a Middle Eastern country 1,900 to 3,100 years ago; premarital and extramarital sex are as wrong in today's Tokyo and Toulouse as they were in yesterday's Ur and Qumran. Graham opposes "new" morality. He respects but disagrees with Anglican bishop John A. T. Robinson, author of *Honest to God*. Robinson, in *Christian Morals Today*, argues that the values of the so-called new morality are as firmly anchored in the New Testament as are the rules of the old morality. Robinson summarizes the conflict this way:

Old	New
Law	Love
Fixity	Freedom
Authority	Experience

Robinson pictures morality as a flowing mountain stream strewn with rocks. He suggests that new morality stresses the water and invites one to swim through the rapids. The old morality of the Billy Graham tradition exclusively stresses the rocks and insists that one cling to them. However, Graham's approach to family planning is pragmatic; he disagrees with the Roman Catholic doctrine and accepts birth control, but he shows less fear of population pressures than of a copulation explosion. Graham is uneasy with sex education and disagrees with the Supreme Court ruling against prayers in public schools: "We've taken God out of the schools and put sex in, and I think that this is where many of our problems are coming among young people."[47]

Race. Billy Graham's position on race and similar social issues is less absolute than his position on adultery and similar sexual issues. His individualistic concept of salvation shows through. Nevertheless, Graham is a southern liberal on race. He is too much a child of the South and Baptist fundamentalism to be unequivocally militant and adamant on racial justice and minority demands. But as a southern *liberal*, as the authorized biography notes, he has been "far ahead of his own denomination's position on race."[48]

There is no evidence that Graham tackled the question of racial desegregation and discrimination directly in the first sixteen years of his various ministries. The nation as a whole was ignoring it. Finally, in 1953 Graham refused to provide segregated seating for his Chattanooga crusade and vowed never again to offer segregated crusade arrangements. In his 1953 bestseller, *Peace with God*, Graham stated his position:

> The Christian looks through the eyes of Christ at the race question and admits that the church has failed in solving this great human problem. We have let the sports world, the entertainment field, politics, the armed

forces, education and industry outstrip us. The church should have been the pace-setter. The church should voluntarily be doing what the federal courts are doing by pressure and compulsion. But in the final analysis the only real solution will be found at the foot of the cross where we come together in brotherly love. The closer people of all races get to Christ and His cross, the closer they will get to one another.[49]

There are numerous examples of Graham's moderately progressive ambiguity on race. Prior to 1953 he claimed local committees were responsible for establishing Jim Crow sections of "reserved seats" for blacks at his crusades. When this happened in his 1951 crusade in Greensboro, North Carolina, where no legal restrictions prevented mixed seating, black pastors in the city refused to support his crusade. In 1958, when Governor Timmerman of South Carolina opposed Graham's plan to hold a mixed religious service on the lawn of the state capitol, Graham moved the service to a nearby army camp, provided a platform seat for former governor and leading segregationist James Byrnes, and made no mention of segregation in his address. On the other side of his position, in the late 1950s before the lunch counter sit-ins, Graham advocated an end to segregation in public transportation, restaurants, and hotels. At the private urging of President Eisenhower, Graham worked among religious leaders of the South to encourage both desegregation and patience. At the time of the Freedom Marches, Graham declined to march, saying, "The race question will not be solved by demonstrations in the streets, but in the hearts of both black and white."[50] In 1964 when Alabama was torn by racial conflict in Birmingham and Selma, Graham held peaceful, integrated rallies in Birmingham and throughout the state. Graham cancelled his team's lodgings in London in 1966 when a black team member Howard Jones was rejected. In booking his 1960 series of crusades in Africa, Graham wrote to *Life*: "Because of the race problem, we have turned down an invitation from the churches of South Africa. We feel it will be a greater sermon to them leaving out South Africa from our itinerary."[51] But in 1973 he held crusades in South Africa.

Graham tends toward a patronizingly ethnocentric attitude toward nonwhites and Asian and African nations. He once wrote from Asia,

> What a difference there is between the Christian in India and the average man in the street. The average man in the street seemingly has a fairly hard and dark morbid look on his face. You know the look of heathenism. Yet the Christian is so completely different.[52]

In *Peace with God*, Graham attempted a liberal cross-cultural comparison, which was, nevertheless, built on stereotypes:

> ... It is the same sin that causes an African savage to skulk along a jungle trail awaiting his victim with spear in hand, and a well-trained, educated

pilot to fly a jet plane over that same jungle ready to bomb an unsuspecting village.[53]

Ironically, while Graham directly condemns individual killing as a sin, he does not say the same of those killing in war and refused to make a moral judgment on American involvement in Vietnam.

Graham draws on popular stereotypes and emotional responses to Africa, much as Disneyland does in the Jungle Cruise. In the Arizona crusade, he told a story of how a "British Lord" became interested in salvation only when the plane he and Graham were flying on was threatened by a storm. But with Graham, the setting of the story takes on larger mythic proportions. Slightly abbreviated, the story went

> I remember last year when we were flying out of Africa in a great lightning storm. We took off in East Africa and the storm began to get worse. At first, the British Lord next to me wasn't interested in talking. But as the storm and lightning began to toss us around more, he turned to me and said, "What was that salvation you were mentioning?" (laughter) Finally the plane broke through above the storm and it was calm and beautiful and the moonlight fell over Mount Kilimanjaro and Mount Kenya as we flew back toward Europe.

Africa is associated with dark threats, Europe with civilized security. There is no calculated bias in the story, but Graham's tales of missionary work frequently slip into popular stereotypes of "primitive" peoples and regions.

Indirectly related to Graham's positions on race and political issues is his official membership in the large and wealthy First Baptist Church of Dallas, Texas. There are thousands of Baptist churches closer to Graham's home, but he seems to prefer the "big time" style of 15,000 members and W. A. Criswell, the pastor. Criswell, an ultraconservative fundamentalist, defended racial segregation until 1968 when, as president of the Southern Baptist Convention, he announced that he had been wrong and was changing. Another member of the Dallas church was H. L. Hunt. The church backs numerous conservative causes.

Graham's basic tendency, however, is to play down racial and social issues in order to avoid alienating large segments of potential audiences. While Graham has argued against "legislating morality," he acknowledges the need for laws concerning discrimination. He admonishes, "I think we need laws and I think we've got most of them now. But we are ultimately not going to solve the race problem in America until men truly love each other."[54] He has suggested that America should "clean up the bad slums and housing conditions that breed a great deal of our crime."[55] In the Arizona crusade telecast, Graham even warned that "structures of society are making the rich get richer and the poor get poorer." But generally in these cases he uses these issues merely as *signs*, relatively unimportant in their own right, of the fundamental issue, personal salvation: "That's the reason I concentrate on the individualistic gospel, because I don't think you can clean up a community until you have got men's hearts right."[56]

While in his writings and interviews Graham may occasionally take a position on public issues, he seldom does so in his sermons, despite the fact that he constantly refers to public issues. In both the New Mexico and Arizona televised crusades he recited an inclusive list of current problems. They included: corruption in government, recession, the "crumbling of Southeast Asia," Watergate, atomic stockpiles, demographic pressures, suicide, campus radicalism, "gigantic" famines, radiation pollution, chemical and biological warfare, drugs, alcoholism, urban crime, divorce, pornography, fornication, wife swapping, adultery, rape, sodomy, incest, prostitution. "Everything is wide open," even the possible invasion of insects (*The Hellstrom Chronicle* had just shown on television). After his catalog of horrors, Graham simply moved into the message of individual salvation and never explained precisely how any of the above problems could be solved. Early in his career he railed against the sensuality of Elvis Presley and rock and roll music. He crusades for auto safety but absolves the automobile industry from any guilt for highway injuries and deaths.

Over all, Graham's morality is reductionist. He implies that any problem that cannot be reduced to individual, internal solutions cannot be solved; on larger issues, humans must accept natural pessimism and look to eternal rewards. Of course, ignoring the reality and complexities of the social order generally canonizes the status quo.

Money. Billy Graham's position on money, politics, and ideology fits his personal associations with persons of great economic and political power.

Graham is no enemy of wealth as the membership of the executive committee of his 1969 crusade in New York illustrates. The committee was headed by George Champion, chairman of the board of the Chase Manhattan Bank with its $23 billion in assets, and Elmer W. Engstrom, president of the multinational communications conglomerate, RCA. The treasurer was W. Maxey Jarman, multimillionaire head of Genesco, Inc. The committee was organized by Roger Hull, chairman of the board of Mutual Life Insurance Company, who observed, "Society is becoming too materialistic."[57]

Graham does not exaggerate when he makes statements such as, "Last week I was talking to one of the richest men in the world."[58] BGEA's second feature film pictured the conversion of a Houston millionaire. Rather in contrast to the preaching of Jesus in the New Testament,

Graham's Calvinism emphasizes wealth more than poverty as a sign of godliness. In *Peace with God*, he encouraged detachment from wealth but concluded his explanation of a Christian attitude toward economics by warning that many Christians have "taken a most sinful and damaging spiritual pride in being poverty-stricken."[59]

In financial backing as well as evangelistic conservatism, Billy Graham follows the tradition of successful American revivalists such as Dwight Moody and Billy Sunday. The super-rich, the "robber barons," the Wall Street bankers, and other great financial powers in the United States have generally not been noticeably religious in their behavior—but they have generously supported revivalism. In the late nineteenth century, "the leading captains of industry and finance, men like J. P. Morgan, Jay Cooke, and Cyrus McCormick, served on Moody's committee and donated their time and money for the sake of bringing religion to 'the urban masses.' "[60] In 1917 John D. Rockefeller, Jr., generously supported Billy Sunday's revival in New York City and stated,

> I think Mr. Sunday is a great power for good. I don't think it's any one thing he does or says that counts in particular. It is evident that people are interested and that he gets their attention. And the organization and follow-up work are magnificent. . . . Mr. Sunday is a rallying center around whom all people interested in good things may gather.[61]

It is possible that one of the "good things" attracting wealthy backers to revivalists is the prospect of docile workers and the promise of preaching that comforts the afflicted without afflicting the comfortable.

Billy Graham's finances and personal life appear above reproach. The Internal Revenue Service has raised questions about BGEA tax payments, but no major judgments have been made against Graham or his organization. In 1951 Graham abolished the traditional "love offering" for the evangelist at the end of a crusade, an offering sometimes as high as $12,000. In the same year, Graham paid off the mortgage on his six-room home near Montreat, North Carolina, bought a 200-acre mountain top behind it for $3,200, and accepted an annual salary of $15,000, which was raised to $19,500 in 1963 and $24,500 in 1969, a small part of what he could have asked. In 1955 the Grahams built a large, rambling mansion of antique timber and bricks on their mountain top. There Ruth raised their five children and, when he could, Graham escaped for study, golf, hiking, and family life. Graham's hundreds of thousands of dollars of income from book royalties helped pay for the home and a trust fund for his children. To protect it from souvenir hunters, their Montreat mountain is surrounded by an eight-foot electrified fence and patrolled by guard dogs.

The BGEA pays Graham's travel, lodging, clothing, publicity, and other professional expenses. By 1974 the BGEA's annual budget was over $20 million, and it maintained a dozen offices throughout the world. Its revolving fund finances new Graham ventures until they become self-supporting, and its cross-media salesmanship utilizes television, film, newspapers magazines, radio, books, mail, and other media coordinated by computers. While the average contribution in 1968 was said to be $7.34, large contributions that are separately incorporated and budgeted go to individual crusades, thus obscuring the role of the very wealthy and conveying a sense of an organization built on the average person. The BGEA has never legally or financially embarrassed Graham in any major way, but its commercialism, as William McLoughlin notes, inclines Graham to picture St. Paul as a television preacher, to compare his own work to selling soap, and to promise financial success to his contributors.

Billy Graham's financial connections and political friendships provide the context for interpreting the ultimate ideological implications of his message, implications that are by no means politically neutral.

Political Affiliations

While Graham generally attempts to be politically nonpartisan, his association with political figures parallels his financial orientation. In the New Testament, Jesus and his followers were in frequent conflict with established religious and political authorities. Graham is strictly post-Constantinian in the ease with which he mixes with established world powers.

Billy Graham has met privately with every president of the United States since Franklin D. Roosevelt. While Graham met Harry S. Truman only briefly, he became "spiritual advisor" to Dwight D. Eisenhower during the 1952 campaign and continued through Eisenhower's eight years in office. The vice-president, Richard M. Nixon, began to meet regularly with Graham at public ceremonies. In 1969 Graham visited Eisenhower in the hospital shortly before his death. He came away convinced that the nondenominational Eisenhower, who was named after Dwight Moody, had made a personal commitment to Christ and was looking forward to an after-life.

Graham conversed and played golf with John Kennedy on several occasions and at Kennedy's funeral service was seated among the late president's personal friends. Graham then stayed on in the White House itself for several days to help President Johnson begin his administration. In 1965 in Houston, Johnson became the first president to attend a crusade. Johnson gave Graham rocking chairs for his North Carolina home and Graham spent the last weekend with the Johnson family in the White House and attended church with them on Sunday. The following day he delivered the inaugural prayer for President Nixon, and the Grahams spent the first night in the White House as personal guests of the Nixons.

Billy Graham has been especially close to Nixon. He met him as early as 1952 and in 1955 publicly came to Nixon's defense: "I disagree with those who say that Mr. Nixon is not sincere. I believe him to be most sincere and like the President [Eisenhower] he is a splendid churchman." While Nixon was Vice-President, Graham escorted him to various denominational conventions and summer Bible conferences. Nixon was the featured guest speaker to the more than 100,000 gathered at the final rally in Yankee Stadium during Graham's 1957 New York crusade. During the same period, Graham and Secretary of State John Foster Dulles, united by their opposition to Communism, exchanged endorsements.

In 1960 Graham came as close as he ever has to directly endorsing a candidate in a major partisan election. Graham actually wrote an article for *Life* magazine that endorsed Nixon and was to appear two weeks before the election. *Life's* publisher, Luce, another personal friend of Graham, was delighted. But the night that issue went to press, Kennedy called Luce protesting the lack of a balancing article and Luce pulled out Graham's article. Several governors, southern Democrats, and friends of Graham's had cautioned Graham against the partisan article. Graham claims to be relieved that it did not appear, even though there is a possibility the article might have tipped that close election toward Nixon.

In 1968 Graham played an important role for Nixon. In December, 1967, Nixon called Graham to Key Biscayne for several days to counsel him about running for the presidency. After their long talks on the beach, Nixon decided to run and stated, "Billy Graham had a great deal to do with that decision." Graham gave the benediction at both party conventions that year. Graham knew Hubert Humphrey as an old acquaintance in Minneapolis, but his sympathy for Nixon was obvious. In September during the campaign, Nixon attended the closing afternoon of Graham's Pittsburgh crusade. When former ambasador George W. Ball called Nixon "a man without principle," Graham jumped to Nixon's defense:

> I reacted strongly to a below-the-belt statement last week by George Ball against my long-time friend Richard Nixon. Mr. Ball reflected on Mr.

Nixon's moral character and personal integrity. I've known Richard Nixon intimately for 20 years. I can testify that he is a man of high moral principle. I have not seen one thing in my personal relationship with him that would give any indication that he is tricky.[62]

Graham announced publicly that he had cast his vote for Nixon by absentee ballot in time for newspapers to carry the story prior to election day.

Time noted, in its report on Nixon's early term in office, "Billy Graham's spirituality pervades."[63] Nixon at various times remarked that Billy Graham himself should be president. Graham in turn wrote

President Nixon knows the hearts of Americans. I have known him for many years, and after many conversations with him, I am convinced that his greatest concern is that America shall have a moral and spiritual renewal.[64]

In October, 1971, Graham's hometown of Charlotte, North Carolina, held a special day for the evangelist. Among the honored guests were President Nixon and John Connally. The large bronze plaque placed at the site of Graham's birthplace reads

Birthplace of Billy Graham, born November 7, 1918. World-renowned evangelist, author, and educator and preacher of the Gospel of Christ to more people than any other man in history. "Billy Graham is one of the giants of our time. Truly a man of God, the force of his spirit has ennobled millions in this and other lands. I salute him with deep and profound respect."—Richard Nixon, President of the United States. This marker dedicated on the 15th day of October, 1971.[65]

Graham was at times of direct use to the administration. At one point, for example, Graham selected thirty religious leaders from around the country to come to the White House for a long personal briefing on U.S. foreign policy by Secretary of State Kissinger and President Nixon.

Watergate, the impeachment hearings, and Nixon's resignation placed Graham in a difficult position. When Graham's defenses of Nixon's integrity became inoperative, Graham capitalized on his lack of official connection with the administration and joined in lamenting the spirit of immorality and corruption in big government. Graham was too sophisticated to become irrevocably established as the discredited president's defender in the way that Rabbi Korf allowed himself to be.

How could the moralistic Graham have been virtually the official chaplain to the only president in American history forced to resign because of corruption in the form of break-ins, bribes, manipulation, and (expletive deleted) dishonesty?

Billy Graham maintained, of course, that it was not his influence but a lack of moral and religious influence that created the "Watergate syndrome." In fact, however, Graham's individualistic ethics and chauvinistic ideology may have helped create a Watergate mentality, which encouraged a self-righteous group to use any means necessary to save a system they perceived as sacred from the threat of internally or externally generated change. The Watergate "sin" was not one of private greed and personal corruption, sins of which Graham warns, so much as an extreme application of principles Graham has long expounded: Americanism, authoritarianism, rugged individualism, anti-communism, and anti-intellectualism. This ideological side of Graham's worldview warrants spelling out.

Ideology

From the beginning, Billy Graham's picture of the world has emphasized two parallel levels of conflict and struggle. On the individual level, Christ and Satan are locked in combat over the destiny of the individual human soul. Christ speaks through the Bible, and Satan through all that is secular, sensual, and controversial. On the international level, Christ and Satan confront each other in the power struggle between world powers. Christ is represented by America and her allies, Satan by international communism. By the 1970s Graham no longer spoke for the anti-communist conspiratorial worldview of the late Senator Joseph McCarthy. Nevertheless, his gospel still combined the puritan work ethic and private enterprise, exemplifying Max Weber's thesis concerning the unity of *"die protestantische Ethik und der Geist des Kapitalismus."*[66]

Graham's ideological worldview is rooted in the "rugged individualism" of American neo-Calvinist capitalism. In *The Jesus Generation* in 1971 he wrote, "Idealists in many generations have tried to shape a better world through education, humanitarianism, science, and giveaway poverty programs. All have failed. The individual must be changed." He insists, "Society cannot be changed until we ourselves are changed."[67] In the 1950s Graham frequently spoke of "the rugged individualism that Christ brought" and warned of "the dangers that face capitalistic America," calling on Americans "devoted to the individualism that made America great."[68]

His commitment to individualistic capitalism, Americanism, and religion made Graham from the beginning a militant anti-communist. Communism served Graham the way that alcohol had served prohibitionist Billy Sunday. In a 1953 radio broadcast titled "Satan's Message," Graham explained his understanding of Marx.

> Karl Marx—a subtle, clever, degenerate materialist—authored this philosophy of world socialism. Having filled his intellectual craw with all the filth of Europe's gutters and garbling perverted German philosophies and

half-truths, he spewed this filthy, corrupt, ungodly, unholy doctrine of world socialism over the gullible peoples of a degenerate Europe.[69]

On investigations by Senator Joseph McCarthy and others, Graham said,

> I thank God for men who, in the face of public denouncement and ridicule, go loyally on in their work of exposing the pinks, the lavenders and the reds who have sought refuge beneath the wings of the American eagle and from that vantage point, try in every subtle, undercover way to bring comfort, aid, and help to the greatest enemy we have ever known— communism.[70]

Graham was never quite as fanatic as his confreres Billy James Hargis and Carl McIntyre, but throughout the 1950s his anti-communism was as transparent as it was omnipresent. In 1960 McLoughlin summarized,

> Scarcely one of his Sunday afternoon sermons over a nine-year period has failed to touch on communism and in his regular revival sermons he constantly refers to it to illustrate his doctrinal points. For example, when he delivers his sermon on hell, Graham begins by quoting a *Life* magazine editorial to the effect that Joseph Stalin is doubtless there. If he talks on the Second Coming he compares the end of the world to the chaos that would follow an atomic war with Russia. If he talks of satan he equates communism with Satan's religion. Almost every time he mentions the need or value of a revival he does so in connection with the spread of communism. And several times he has devoted a whole sermon to the death-duel between Christian America and atheistic Russia. It is no exaggeration to say that communism, the atomic bomb, and World War III have replaced the Devil, the battle of Armageddon, and hell in Graham's revivals as the major means of instilling the motive of fear.[71]

In 1966, when asked about urban riots and student demonstrators, Graham responded,

> I think that we have to have understanding and tolerance toward these people, but there are some of them that are not sincere and, of course, there are other groups like the Communists and the Communist-front people who want to manipulate a good cause....
>
> You have all sorts of nuts and cranks and Communist people who come into almost any kind of thing where you have something exciting going on.[72]

In line with his laissez-faire individualism and anti-communism, Graham has made strong statements against labor unions, British socialism, foreign aid, and similar "liberal" causes. In the videotaped New Mexico and Arizona crusades, he several times disparaged the United Nations. Graham cites it as an example of the unsuccessful attempts of men to achieve peace without a firm foundation in Christ. After all, he states, "The United Nations opened without a prayer." Even when Graham decries the hopelessness of the natural world of men, he often exempts the United States. In Albuquerque Graham described the false hopes humankind places in science, pleasure, politics, and radicalism. It was a thoroughly negative indictment until he came to radicalism and described a recent interview with Eldridge Cleaver on "Sixty Minutes." Without mentioning Cleaver by name, Graham explained how "this radical from the University of California" had now come to appreciate that the American system is the best in the world.

Joe Barnhart's thoughtful book on *The Billy Graham Religion* centers on Graham's identification of his Christianity with American patriotism. Barnhart examines the possibility that "Billy Graham is a very popular spokesman of *two* faiths—Evangelicalism and something that might be vaguely described as 'Christian Americanism' or 'Decent Americanism.' "[73] Graham speaks of "freedom" but he lacks general principles for tolerating belief systems and life-styles that differ substantially from his own.

William McLoughlin connects Graham's individualistic gospel with American political conservativism. He writes

> The connecting link between professional evangelists and the Republican party has been a mutual belief in rugged individualism. . . .
> Billy Graham is equally committed to the belief that Christianity and capitalism, like conversion and success, are inseparably linked and that one cannot exist without the other. When Graham speaks of "the American way of life" he has in mind the same combination of political and economic freedom that the National Association of Manufacturers, the United States Chamber of Commerce, and the *Wall Street Journal* do when they use the phrase. And because the Democratic party has, since the 1890's, attacked Big Business and Wall Street and called for government regulation of the economic system in the interests of the general welfare, Graham, like the majority of American Protestant ministers, has cast his influence upon the side of the Republicans (or, in the South, the conservative Democrats).[74]

That was written in 1960. Although the vocabulary has changed slightly since then, the ideological principles have remained intact. In 1972 Barnhart wrote

> In his early years as an evangelist, Graham would extol the ideal of "rugged individualism" and "the American pioneer spirit." This was another version of his theme of Christian stoicism, holding that the new individual can be fully human on the inside, regardless of his external circumstances. . . .
> The phrase rugged individualism is no longer as popular in the United States as it once was. Billy Graham now rarely uses it, although his quasi stoicism and folk existentialism may be seen as the old motif in modern dress. Gradually the notion of rugged individualism seems to be giving way to the notion of a silent majority.[75]

Graham has tempered his anti-communism in the 1970s and even questioned the imposition of an American version of democracy and capitalism on the rest of the world, but Graham still tends to regard the United States as a "messiah-nation." The future of Christianity is tied in with the future of the United States. Barnhart observes that "Christian Americanism" remains an additional fundamentalist doctrine for Graham, despite his travels throughout the world; Barnhart equates it with Shintoism in Japan prior to World War II. In biblical imagery Barnhart concludes

> Graham sees himself as a modern prophet Isaiah in the court of an American Israel. Israel's kings consulted Isaiah about politico-spiritual matters, and politicians and presidents have consulted Graham. Isaiah thought of Israel as God's special and chosen nation to be a light to the gentiles and Graham came very naturally to think of the United States as the major source of light to the heathen around the globe. In some ways Billy Graham has been preaching on and off a gospel of Christian American Zionism.[76]

McLoughlin adds the important critical point that Graham's "Biblical literalism leads inevitably to anti-intellectualism and self-righteousness."[77] In place of the Bible, Graham charged, "so-called intellectuals have substituted reason, rationalism, mind culture, science worship, the working power of government, Freudianism, naturalism, humanism, behaviorism, positivism, materialism, and idealism."[78] Several times Graham has delivered entire broadcasts on "The Sin of Tolerance." As Reinhold Niebuhr wrote, Graham's "pietistic individualism is in danger of obscuring the highly complex tasks of justice in the community. . . ."[79]

The Reverend Graham's myopic view of ethics and morality allowed him to condone even strong-arm tactics by the Nixon administration.

The result of Graham's political consciousness as outlined above is a dangerous tendency toward *totalitarianism*. It was this tendency that was underlined by his White House followers in the Watergate break-in, in unauthorized wire tapping, in the Ellsberg burglary, in the Allende overthrow, in CIA assassination plots, in Russian wheat deal pay-offs, in bribes, in ITT antitrust fixing, in Vesco contributions, and in countless other scandals during the reign of Graham's long-time friend Richard Nixon. Well-meaning despots believe their cause to be just and their means justified, especially when they are morally counselled in individualistic, nationalistic, combative half-truths. Graham's anti-intellectualism breeds inconsistencies that in turn negate firm moral principles or objective political analysis. The Albuquerque videotape contained at least one glaring example. In warning against false, this-world hopes, Graham forecast "anthill civilization" and "sardine can" culture and cried out against Communist China, "regimented, controlled from a central office." Two minutes later he predicted happily, "Christ will be the future dictator of the world." Graham implies that the form of government does not really matter—dictatorships are okay—as long as "our side" is on top.

A Symbolic and Cultural Critique of Mass-Mediated Religion

According to Bronislaw Malinowski, religion as an anthropological phenomenon comprises

> ... the traditional acts and observances, regarded by the natives as sacred, carried out with reverence and awe, hedged around with prohibitions and special rules of behavior. Such acts and observances are always associated with beliefs in supernatural forces. . . .[80]

Malinowski describes the cultural function of religion by noting, "Religious faith establishes, fixes, and enhances all valuable mental attitudes, such as reverence for tradition, harmony with environment, courage and confidence in the struggle with difficulties and at the prospect of death."[81]

What happens to religion when it is transmitted by mass communications media, and what expressions of mass-mediated religion are most popular in the United States?

Parallels to Billy Graham

Billy Graham is the most recognized religious figure in North America,[82] but there are numerous parallels to his combination of religion and media. On radio they have ranged from the controversial Father Coughlin of the 1930s to what William Martin calls "The God Hucksters of Radio."[83] On television there are Oral Roberts, Robert Harold Schuller, Garner Ted Armstrong, Morris Cerulo, and a host of others ranging from faith healers to conservative political commentators. On paperback racks next to Graham's books are Kathryn Kuhlman's *Why I Believe in Miracles*, Hal Lindsey's *The Late Great Planet Earth* and its sequels, Erich Von Daniken's *Chariots of the Gods*, and similar superterrestrial adventures. The denominational press in magazines and newspapers is extremely large.[84] Even comic books such as Spire Christian Comics about football stars, POWs, and other stoic heroes are widely available with the latest Calvinist pieties. Newsletters, pamphlets, and radio commentaries are the specialty of such ministers as Dr. W. Steuart McBirnie, president of the Community Churches of America and conservative political lobbyist based in Glendale, California. As even church attendance itself becomes more "mass" in style, three other Protestant clergymen share Graham's dominance of popular American piety and belief.

The Reverend Norman Vincent Peale—born at the end of the nineteenth century, pastor of Marble Collegiate Church in New York City, and author of fifteen books, among them *The Power of Positive Thinking* —has shared the unofficial White House chaplaincy with Graham. Less fundamentalist than Graham, Peale has performed weddings for the first family and shares Graham's salesmanlike qualities. He Americanizes Jesus by claiming, "He'd be at the Super Bowl game. He wouldn't want to miss a World Series game. . . . He was a with-it person."[85]

The Reverend Granville Oral Roberts has broadcast weekly to 300 television stations reaching a total of 27 million viewers. From tent preaching and healing through the laying on of hands in the 1950s to presidency of his own Oral Roberts University, Roberts' slogan has been, "Expect a miracle." Begun in 1965, his campus occupies 500 acres of suburban Tulsa, Oklahoma, is worth more than $50 million, has some 1,500 students, and features a 200-foot blue and gold mirrored prayer tower that has become Tulsa's chief tourist attraction. Roberts also illustrates that strong tie between Christian fundamentalism and puritan Americanism. No drinking, dancing, or smoking are permitted on campus; shirts and ties for men and dresses for women are required for classes. Intramural athletics are required for all four years at ORU, and Roberts is obsessed with having a national championship basketball team. Their success, he feels, would make a Christian witness to millions of sports fans "who won't go to church or tune off the religious radio and TV programs."[86] The preacher for the dedication of Oral Roberts University was none other than Billy Graham.

The most popular West Coast religious figure began his ministry in Los Angeles preaching from the tarpaper-covered roof of the refreshment stand at the Orange Drive-In Theater in 1955. The Reverend Robert Harold Schuller parlayed that into the 7,100 member Garden Grove Community Church featuring reflecting ponds, fountains, a 252-foot Tower of Hope topped by a 15-ton neon cross, a 14-story office and sanctuary complex, and, of course, a sound-equipped drive-in area in his "22-acre shopping center for Jesus Christ." Schuller's "possibility thinking" is spread through "televangelism" to 60 stations weekly, is viewed by 2.5 million, and has the highest religious ratings in New York, Philadelphia, Chicago, and Washington, D.C. In a typical five-minute stretch in a televised sermon, Schuller praised the United States as "a great land offering you young people g-r-e-a-t opportunity!", contradicted that by condemning the cut-throat dog-eat-dog atmosphere in society, and attacked as "anti-Christian" a bill in Congress that would place a public representative on the board of each major oil company.[87]

There are, of course, also major expressions of popular religion in the United States that differ substantially from Billy Graham but are less widely followed. Popular Catholicism and Judaism have their own peculiar expressions. Black churches have maintained a more expressive, kinesthetic, and socially conscious tradition than has the neo-Calvinist fundamentalism of white churches. The preaching of Martin Luther King, Jr., paralleled Graham's mass magic in certain stylistic ways but differed sharply in political focus, ethical emphasis, and social outcome. The Reverend Ike represents the flamboyant form while the Honorable Elijah Muhammad's Nation of Islam, the Black Muslims, represents the disciplined, militant forms of black American religion.

Culturally Dominant Mass-Mediated Religion

Mass media effectively transmit certain aspects of religion as traditionally practiced but tend to vitiate other aspects. The *unidirectional* organization of mass media systems built up for marketing purposes severely limits opportunities for the audiences to provide direct feedback to the producers of media and messages. As a result, mass media contribute to a passive, internalized religion. Believers are removed from the interactive religious exchange possible in primary face-to-face interpersonal communication.

Billy Graham and the other most popular and culturally dominant expressions of mass-mediated religion can transmit religious messages to unprecedented numbers via media. However, because of the organization of media technology, they cannot provide for the spontaneous, flexible, and internally directed development of group religious feelings and convictions that traditional small-group religion offered. A live crusade partially overcomes this barrier. Crusades are mass media insofar as messages are transmitted one-way via public address systems and other electronic relays, but they are interpersonal insofar as participants can directly respond to the others gathered together and to the preacher, if only by joining in singing and coming forward at the call. The home viewer of a crusade is prevented from such direct feedback. The authoritarian structure of church buildings, which have one pulpit for transmitting and many pews for receiving is thus maintained and strengthened in mass-media transmission of religion.

The most successful expressions of mass-mediated religion in the United States share two additional characteristics:

1. Their use of a medium is highly sophisticated in *la technique* ("unrelenting efficiency," as Ellul defines that phrase; see final chapter). They maximize their outreach by using a highly polished professional style in their personal presentation and by utilizing individual media and cross-media potential.

2. Their message respects the limits of the conditioned expectations of mass audiences and the preferences of the economically and politically powerful. Voices of opposition like Father Daniel Berrigan, S.J., or the Reverend Jesse Jackson, however stylistically and charismatically effective they may be, find their outreach limited to the extent that they exceed the bounds of popular tastes and vested interests.

The result is that popular mass-mediated religion in the United States, like institutionalized religion in general, favors cultural stability and continuity over cultural innovation and adaptation. Together with mass-mediated sports, politics, health, and education, mass-mediated religion reflects the political economy and maintains the sociocultural system.

More specifically, Graham and his counterparts represent what Robert N. Bellah considers the dominant American traditions of *biblical religion* and *utilitarian indivdualism,* which were corrupted into a purely *private pietism* in the nineteenth century. Its voluntarism and positivism paralleled developments in science, technology, and bureaucratic organization. In the twentieth century these trends came into conflict with political dissent, ecological movements, drug experiences, Asian spirituality, and a new religious consciousness that valued bodily awareness, inner experience, harmony with nature, nonmanipulative relationships, a sense of the unity of all being, and a resistance to dogmatism.[88] While Graham generally resisted such developments, mass-mediated religion as a whole seemed to absorb aspects of the new religious consciousness in their more innocuous forms.

Billy Graham's Cultural Role

This investigation of Billy Graham and contemporary mass-mediated religion has been constructed somewhat like a mandala, the centered, spherical design popular in Asian mysticism; that is, (a) at the center of the mandala is the ethnographic description and identification of Graham's text (both medium and message) especially as that text appears in the videotaped televised crusades; (b) broadening outward from that center, exegesis of the text in historical and cultural context attempts to define the text's meaning, especially in ideological and ethical terms; (c) expanding still further from the center, analysis of other popular religious figures extends the study to parallels of Graham's mass-mediated role and message; and finally, (d) at the edges of the outer circle lie critical comments on the text, its meaning, and its parallels.

Complex strategic problems arise in assessing any social phenomenon, including the Reverend William Franklin Graham, Jr. A priori choices must be made of investigative methodology and explanatory theory. For methodology, this study of Graham has drawn on ethnography and exegesis in order to develop primary empirical evidence. For theory, it has drawn eclecticly from historical, theological, anthropological, journalistic, and psychological sources. Our final theoretical considerations are taken from the continental sociologists Durkheim, Weber, and Marx. Since Graham has been so hard on them, especially Marx, it seems in keeping with the fairness doctrine and the provision for equal time to inquire how they would evaluate the mass medium, Billy Graham.

The mass appeal and success of Graham's crusades come not from supernatural causes but rather from the human need to find simple overriding explanations to account for actions, objects, emotions, and experiences that stem from complex collective life in society, as Durkheim explained them. The functions and experiences of religion, including especially mass evangelism, are quite real but are the causes and effects of natural social experience, not divine activity. Barnhart's book on Graham takes this position, stating, "There is no need to resort to the hypothesis of supernatural variables to explain Graham's success."[89]

On a more specific level, the variety of religion that Graham represents is a blend of Reformation Protestantism and economic capitalism. Graham's evangelism fits the dominant political economy in the United States and its allies, providing a combination of individual righteousness and social authoritarianism. One ethical result is that strange Watergate morality of private machiavellianism overlaid with public puritanism.

Marxism takes these critiques a step further. Not only does religion misleadingly explain collective and personal experiences, and not only do Protestantism and capitalism feed on each other, but Marxism holds that religion and Protestantism are *wrong* to do so. They provide fantastic realizations of identity insofar as the individual or group lacks genuine identity. Religion provides a "false consciousness" that masks the real causes of human alienation, which lie in the maldistribution of priorities and power and in the negative, exploitative structural and motivational base of private-enterprise capitalism. In a Marxist perspective, Billy Graham's mass mediation obscures rather than resolves the contradictions and injustices of nationalism, imperialism, internal colonialism, racism, poverty, sexism, militarism, malnutrition, and the other material realities of the world that cry for solutions. Graham, by emphasizing individualism, distracts attention from institutions and systemic problems. He fails to speak out against an alienating system that exploits workers and even managers; in fact, Graham serves as one of the system's principle supports. To a Marxist, Graham obstructs social progress and prevents needed revolution (a) by representing as ultimate what is produced by man in society, and (b) by providing an ultimate principled sanction of a specific political-economic arrangement. Metaphysically, Graham does not offer God as an internal overriding principle of the totality of the universe, but as an external anthropomorphic *deus ex machina* preoccupied with trivial private anxieties and tasks. This constricts both the human symbolic (spiritual) potential for necessary utopian planning and the capacity for critical analysis of the concrete conditions of material life. Moreover, Graham's ethics force the individual, under the threat of divine retribution, to suppress and sublimate legitimate natural tendencies in order to accept and adjust to exploitative work environments, mechanical school processing, and fragmented nuclear family roles. To Marx, his critic Billy Graham represents the ultimate manifestation of the opiate of the masses.

In his defense, Graham might point out that he did not create the system and that, from his position, the American capitalist system looks more benign than malevolent. In fact, he seems to believe that strongly. He is a professional and a perfectionist in what he does, and he does it well. He is sensitive to his target audience, he is an excellent organizer, and he seems sincerely to believe in his vocation as medium for the masses. Drawing on a loving, caring, altruistic, if dogmatic, cultural tradition, Christianity, Graham appeals to the perceived personal and private wants of average people, helping them symbolically to construct their universe as Graham believes it has been revealed to be. In a cold, mechanical universe, he tries to stand for the personal and for love. If Graham's conclusions are different from Marx's, it is because their premises are different. Graham is clearly not a materialist, not a socialist, and not overwhelmingly concerned with replacing the current arrangements of power with possibly better ones. To the extent that Graham's *Weltanschauung* can be proven to be destructive—as perhaps in the unqualified anti-communism that leads to red-baiting, McCarthyism, and Vietnams, or the anti-intellectual totalitarianism that contributes to Watergates—Graham's position warrants opposition. In Mao's term, he may require reeducation. But on the ultimate questions, the discussion would have to exceed the bounds of the present study and might recall the opening of Francis Bacon's essay on truth: " 'What is truth?' said jesting Pilate; and would not stay for an answer."

Notes

1. *Pittsburgh Press,* September 25, 1952; quoted in William G. McLoughlin, Jr., *Billy Graham: Revivalist in a Secular Age* (New York: Ronald Press, 1960), p. 5.

2. Constant H. Jacquet, ed., *Yearbook of American Churches 1971* (New York: Council Press, 1971), p. 186.

3. Emile Durkheim, *The Elementary Forms of the Religious Life* (Glencoe, N.Y.: Free Press, 1947), p. 419.

4. Ibid., p. 427.

5. The six telecasts were videotaped off the air from KTLA–TV, Channel 5, in Los Angeles, California. The telecasts on June 4, 5, and 6, 1974 were from the Billy Graham Arizona Crusade in Tempe, Arizona, and those telecast on June 5, 6, and 7, 1975, were from the Billy Graham New Mexico Crusade in Albuquerque, New Mexico.

6. My designation of *exegesis* is a combination outlining the general method as developed in German exegesis since the time of Rudolph Bultmann and now prevalent among prominent scripture scholars throughout much of Western Europe and North America. C. H. Dodd, Joachim Jeremias, and Barnabas Ahern are typical. I am especially indebted in my understanding of the methodology to the Rev. Raphael Quinn, professor of Sacred Scripture, St. Paul Seminary, St. Paul, Minnesota.

7. John Pollock, *Billy Graham—The Authorized Biography* (Minneapolis: World Wide Publications, 1969), pp. 19–20.

2. Ibid., p. 20.

9. This summary of the revivalism of the four "great awakenings" in United States history relies heavily on McLoughlin, *Revivalist,* pp. 5–24.

10. McLoughlin, *Revivalist,* p. 17.

11. Ibid., p. 19.

12. Ibid.

13. Ibid.

14. Most of the biographical information and crusade data are based on Pollock, *Billy Graham,* on McLoughlin, *Revivalist,* and on Joe E. Barnhart, *The Billy Graham Religion* (Philadelphia: United Church Press, 1972).

15. Pollock, *Graham,* pp. 67–68.

16. McLoughlin, *Revivalist,* p. 47.

17. Ibid., p. 49.

18. Ibid., p. 56. See also Pollock, *Graham,* p. 77.

19. Pollock, *Graham,* p. 112.

20. McLoughlin, *Revivalist,* pp. 98–99.

21. Pollock, *Graham,* p. 109.

22. Ibid., p. 245.

23. Ibid., pp. 210–11.

24. See Val Adams's column in the *New York Times,* May 26, 1957, sec. X, p. 13.

25. Ibid.

26. Anthony F. C. Wallace, "Culture and Cognition," *Science* 135, no. 3501 (February 2, 1962); available in a Bobbs-Merrill reprint, no. A-358.

27. Claude Lévi-Strauss, *Structural Anthropology*, trans. Claire Jacobson and Brooke Grundfest Schoepf (New York: Basic Books, 1963), p. 2.

28. Wallace, "Culture," p. 1.

29. The origin of the six one-hour videotapes is described in note 5 above.

30. McLoughlin, *Revivalist*, p. 182.

31. Ibid.

32. Pitirm A. Sorokin, "The Power of Creative Unselfish Love," in Abraham M. Maslow, ed., *New Knowledge in Human Values* (New York: Harper, 1959), pp. 4–5.

33. Alan Watts, *This Is It and Other Essays on Zen and Spiritual Experience* (New York: Random House, 1960).

34. Yves Congar, *Lay People in the Church* (New York: Herder and Herder, 1963).

35. William F. Lynch, S.J., *Christ and Apollo* (New York; Sheed & Ward, 1962).

36. Barnhart, *Graham Religion*, p. 162.

37. Ibid.

38. Billy Graham and others, *Is God "Dead"?* (Grand Rapids, Mich.: Zondervan Publishing House, 1966), p. 76.

39. Barnhart, *Graham Religion*, p. 82.

40. McLoughlin, *Revivalist*, p. 77.

41. Ibid., p. 76.

42. Ibid., p. 70.

43. Ibid., p. 90.

44. Ibid., p. 136.

45. Ibid., p. 88.

46. Barnhart, *Graham Religion*, p. 20.

47. Graham, *Is God "Dead"?*, p. 76.

48. Pollock, *Graham*, p. 280.

49. Billy Graham, *Peace with God* (New York: Pocket Books, 1953), pp. 181–82.

50. Pollock, *Graham*, p. 280.

51. Ibid., p. 201.

52. McLoughlin, *Revivalist*, p. 215.

53. Graham, *Peace with God*, pp. 39–40.

54. Graham, *Is God "Dead"?*, p. 72.

55. McLoughlin, *Revivalist*, p. 221.

56. Ibid., p. 90.

57. Barnhart, *Graham Religion*, p. 182.

58. McLoughlin, *Revivalist*, p. 128.

59. Graham, *Peace with God*, pp. 182–83.

60. McLoughlin, *Revivalist*, p. 17.

61. Ibid., p. 202.

62. Barnhart, *Graham Religion*, p. 39.

63. Pollock, *Graham*, p. 288.

64. Ibid., p. 287.

65. Barnhart, *Graham Religion*, p. 40.

66. Max Weber, *The Protestant Ethic and the Spirit of Capitalism* (New York: Scribner's, 1958).

67. Billy Graham, *The Jesus Generation* (Grand Rapids, Mich.: Zondervan Publishing House, 1971), pp. 123, 125.

68. Quoted in McLoughlin, *Revivalist*, pp. 90, 99.

69. McLoughlin, *Revivalist,* p. 130.

70. Ibid., p. 111.

71. McLoughlin, *Revivalist,* pp. 97–98.

72. Graham, *Is God "Dead"?,* p. 81.

73. Barnhart, *Graham Religion,* p. 14.

74. McLoughlin, *Revivalist,* pp. 97–98.

75. Barnhart, *Graham Religion,* pp. 229–30.

76. Ibid., p. 34.

77. McLoughlin, *Revivalist.* p. 211.

78. Ibid., p. 213.

79. Reinhold Niebuhr, "Literalism, Individualism, and Billy Graham," *Christian Century,* May 23, 1956, pp. 641–42.

80. Bronislaw Malinowski, *Magic, Science and Religion and Other Essays* (Garden City, N.Y.: Doubleday, 1948), p. 17.

81. Ibid., p. 89. For modern studies of popular religion, see David Burner, Robert D. Marcus, and Jorj Tilson, eds., *America Through the Looking Glass: A Historical Reader in Popular Culture,* two volumes (Englewood Cliffs, N.J.: Prentice-Hall, 1974); W. J. McCutcheon, "Subway Salvation, An Essay in 'Communication Theology,'" *Journal of Popular Culture* 5, no. 1 (Summer 1971), pp. 79–101; Ronny E. Turner and Charles K. Edgley, "'The Devil Made Me Do It!' Popular Culture and Religious Vocabularies of Motive," *Journal of Popular Culture* 8, no. 1 (Summer 1974), pp. 28–34; Robert Galbreath, ed., "The Occult: Studies and Evaluations," *Journal of Popular Culture* 5, no. 3 (Winter 1971), pp. 627–754.

82. Martin E. Marty, "M.E.M.O.," *Christian Century* 91, October 16, 1974, pp. 963–64.

83. William C. Martin, "The God-Hucksters of Radio," in George H. Lewis, ed., *Side-Saddle on the Golden Calf: Social Structure and Popular Culture in America* (Pacific Palisades, Calif.: Goodyear Publishing Company, 1972), pp. 49–55. Martin presented sound-tape samples of these preachers at the annual convention of the Popular Culture Association, St. Louis, Missouri, March 21, 1975.

84. Michael R. Real, "Trends in Structure and Policy in the American Catholic Press," *Journalism Quarterly* 52, no. 2 (Summer 1975), pp. 265–71; Michael R. Real, "Communications and Social Change: A Case History of the *National Catholic Reporter,*" unpublished doctoral dissertation, Urbana, Ill., 1972; available from University Microfilms, East Lansing, Michigan.

85. Quoted by Charles McCabe, "Religion, American-Style," *San Francisco Chronicle,* April 15, 1975. For a historical review of trends, see Douglas T. Miller, "Popular Religion of the 1950s: Norman Vincent Peale and Billy Graham," *Journal of Popular Culture* 9, no. 1 (Summer 1975), pp. 66–76.

86. Dennis Eckert, "Faith-Healing Preacher Builds Top Cage Team," *Los Angeles Times,* December 12, 1971, sec. D, p. 13; see also "Miracle U," *Time,* February 7, 1972, p. 53.

87. Russell Chandler, "A Bold Experiment in Modern Religion Arrives at a Milestone," *Los Angeles Times,* March 17, 1975; the telecast referred to was on KGTV, Channel 10, San Diego, on June 15, 1975.

88. Robert N. Bellah, "New Religious Consciousness," *New Republic,* November 23, 1974, pp. 33–41; see also Robert N. Bellah, *The Broken Covenant* (Berkeley: University of California Press, 1974).

89. Barnhart, *Graham Religion,* p. 239.

Cross-Cultural

The "Lost City of the Incas" and the chewer of coca leaves (opposite) reflect the past and present of the Indians of the Andes. Their wisdom and achievements typify Third World aural cultures, which contrast with and are often threatened by the ethnocentric West and its mass-mediated culture.

7

An Indian Fiesta in the Andes: Non-Western Culture

How can popular culture (and mass-mediated culture) be studied in a comparative, cross-cultural framework?

How do the Indians of the Andes celebrate their popular culture?

Why does a Peruvian Aymara fiesta structure the open-air market, party, school commemorations, religious observances, and healing rituals as it does?

What cosmology, worldview, perceptions, and values lie behind the fiesta?

What are the dominant communication forms and value structures of modernized "CWAWMP" societies as opposed to traditional societies?

High in the Andes, more than two miles above sea level, lies the dusty village of Ilave, Peru. Once part of the proud and prosperous Inca empire, the people of Ilave still have roots in the ancient cultures of Peru and the traditions of the Indians of the Americas. Each July 16, the peasant farmers, llama herders, and families of the Ilave region celebrate a typical festival, the feast of Our Lady of Carmen, in much the same way that, before their conquest by the Spanish, they honored the "Earth Mother." Having suffered through domination by the Conquistadores, the people of Ilave now face the onslaught of mass-mediated culture.

Cross-Cultural Study of Popular Arts and Media

Margaret King has described the need for scholars to overcome their restrictive definitions of popular culture and their ethnocentric biases in order to "broaden popular culture study to include a global range of cultures and life-styles, both old and new." She notes that elitist and Western-centered bias has unnecessarily prevented mining the rich lodes of popular culture from other countries and has narrowed the diggings in the emerging "International Style" of popular culture.[1] Floyd Matson has similarly argued that popular culture be defined as all the "informal interactions and noninstitutional pursuits of everyday life," rather than as merely the transmissions of mass communication in industrialized societies.[2] The choice of the phrase "mass-mediated culture" in these pages frees the phrase "popular culture" to be defined as an umbrella label for popular expressions of culture in any region of the world and during any historical period. The broader definition of popular culture allows the inclusion of cross-cultural studies by folklorists, anthropologists, historians, and others investigating nontechnological societies.

The fruits of the broader, cross-cultural approach to popular culture are evident in the Comparative Popular Culture Research Seminars conducted by the East-West Communication Institute at the University of Hawaii. The studies reported there on traditional media and popular gathering places provide revealing counterpoints to the study of mass media and popular culture in Western industrialized countries. They include Abbasi on Bangladesh folk festivals; HjAman on gathering centers in peasant fishing communities in Malaysia; Motamed-Nejad on story telling in Iran; Mulia on the leaves of the Sirih plant as a medium in Indonesia; Opubor on theatrical forms in Black Africa; Rakesh on community gathering places for young people in Nepal; and Virulak on folk media of central Thailand.[3]

In addition to expanding awareness of other cultures, a cross-cultural approach offers a comparative context for understanding one's own culture. As an example, this chapter on a popular cultural expression *not* mediated by mass communication offers a contrast that brings together various threads of the previous chapters. When contrasted with a thoroughly different cultural milieu, the similarities among Disney, the Super Bowl, Welby, Nixon, and Graham become more apparent.

Contrasting Human Ecosystems

The first chapter summarized metadisciplinary theories of culture in institutions, communication, and consciousness (see Figure 7–1, page 210).

As the preceding case studies illustrate, mass-mediated cultural content tends to reflect the material structure of industrialized, capitalist mass democracies, to communicate that structure, and to structure internal consciousness accordingly. In contrast, traditional non-Western, Third World cultural systems tend to reflect and structure the material organization of agrarian or hunt-and-gather priorities. The contrast is summaried in Figure 7–2 (see page 210).

The two contrasting systems resemble opposite sides of the same coin, modernized *Gesellschaft* and traditional *Gemeinschaft*, although there are variations and gradations in actual systems that would require additional diagrams and would fit between these two extremes. In all systems, popular cultural expressions provide the *mythic* structures that regulate ecological processes. Communication in each "fixes" the socially dominant definition of reality and, therefore, guides responses of the individual organism to the environment.

The "modernized" system, in which mass-mediated culture occurs, finds its most extreme form when managed by Capitalist, Western, Adult, White, Male, Print oriented persons. The acronym, *CWAWMP*, identifies that grouping as an updated, internationalized version of the familiar

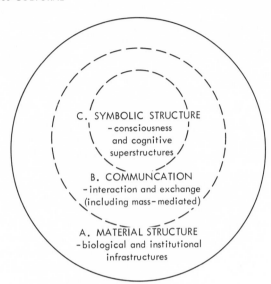

FIGURE 7–1   Metadisciplinary Approach to Culture

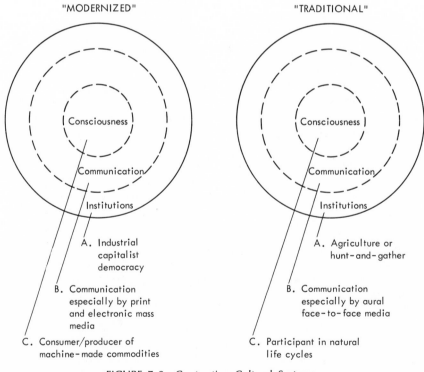

FIGURE 7–2   Contrasting Cultural Systems

WASP racial and religious designation. Despite their self-image as culturally inclusive and unbiased, CWAWMPs like Graham, Welby, Disney, and Nixon value certain cultural priorities and reject others. Edward C. Stewart's thorough examination, *American Cultural Patterns: A Cross-Cultural Perspective*, describes American assumptions and values by their orientation to action, measurable achievement, materialism, property, progress, optimism, competition, and individualism. These assumptions and values recur frequently in Disney, Graham, and other dominant expressions emanating from CWAWMP origins. Table 7–1 contrasts pre-

TABLE 7–1. Dominant Communication Forms and Values in Contrasting Cultures

MODERNIZED "CWAWMP"	TRADITIONAL "SEEYFA"
A. Institutional forms	
Industrial	Agrarian
Mechanical	Animistic
Technological	Aesthetic
Quantitative	Qualitative
Elite/Mass	Folk/Popular
Consumption	Preservation
Progress	Tradition
History	Nature
Modernization	Liberation
B. Interactional forms	
Competition	Cooperation
Aggression	Acceptance
Argumentation	Experience
Detachment	Involvement
Objectivity	Subjectivity
Cerebral	Physical
Rational	Sensual
Intellective thinking	Intuitive feeling
C. Internal forms	
Visual	Aural
Digital	Analogic
Linear	Mosaic
Straight	Stoned
Analytic	Gestalt
Explicit	Tacit
Sequential	Simultaneous
Literal	Figurative
Dissociative	Unitive
Left hemisphere of brain	Right hemisphere of brain

dominantly CWAWMP characteristics with their contraries, which tend to be found more often among Socialist, Eastern, Ethnic nonwhite, Youth or elderly, Female, Aural oriented groupings (*SEEYFA*), from which liberation struggles have emerged to balance and resist CWAWMP dominance.[4]

The popularity of the search for non-CWAWMP alternatives is evident in a wide range of popular culture. Rock music reintroduced the West to powerful collective beats, rhythms, and dances. The Beatles brought back sitars and gurus from India. The physical fitness culture of Charles Atlas and the dance studios of Arthur Murray are joined by classes in yoga, meditation, karate, kung fu, and tai chi. Arica, Silva mind control, EST, and zen compete with Billy Graham. Martin Luther King transplanted Mahatma Gandhis' philosophy and practice of nonviolent resistance. In psychic phenomenon, consciousness expansion, psychoactive drugs, biofeedback, psychocybernetics, astrology, and communicators from space, the West seeks less mechanical, commercial experiences. A number of figures have become popular by translating Asian insights into Western modes: Alan Watts, John Lilly, Gary Snyder, Baba Ram Dass, Oscar Ichazo, Herman Hesse, Timothy Leary, L. Ron Hubbard, Maharishi Mahesh Yogi, Maharaj Ji, A. D. Bhaktivedanta Swami Prabhupada (founder of Hare Krishna), J. Krishnamurti, Paramahansa Yogananda, Swami Muktananda, and D. T. Suzuki, among others.

The field study of Ilave, Peru, was undertaken as a single, in-depth case study of an expression of popular culture thoroughly variant from the contemporary CWAWMP mass-mediated form. For the most part, the Aymaras are nonliterate, nonwhite, noncapitalist, and non-Western. They are a Third World people of color. The ethnographic description focuses on a popular cultural event, the July 16 feast of Our Lady of Carmen as celebrated by the Aymaras in and around Ilave, Peru. In that one event are contained typical elements of the day-to-day popular recreation, art, trade, and religion as practiced in parts of the world not yet dominated by CWAWMP mass-mediated culture.

Ilave, Peru—July 16

Ilave, Peru, has 7,000 residents and is located about half-way between Puno and the Bolivian border on the Pan-American Highway, which is at that point a narrow dirt and gravel country road. Its elevation is slightly greater than the 12,506 foot altitude of Lake Titicaca several miles to the east. The town was characterized by a resident as more dirty than average

Through these rites a three-fold peace was established.
The first peace, which is the most important,
is that which comes within the souls of men
when they realize their relationship, their oneness,
with the universe and all its Powers,
and when they realize that at the center of the universe
dwells Wakan-Tanka, and that this center is really everywhere;
it is within each of us.
This is the real peace,
and the others are but reflections of this.
The second peace is that which is made between two individuals,
and the third is that which is made between two nations.
But above all you should understand
there can never be peace between nations
until there is first known that true peace
which, as I have often said,
is within the souls of men.

From *The Sacred Pipe: Black Elk's Account of the Seven Rites of the Oglala Sioux,* by Joseph Epes Brown. Copyright © 1953 by the University of Oklahoma Press.

---

as he quoted a tired *gringo*: "Brown hills, brown roads, brown buildings, brown complexions—everything the color of dried shit." Multicolored clothing and frequent festivals balance the drabness.

Virtually everyone in the Ilave region is Aymara (pronounced ī–mä–rä). The 1 million Aymaras constitute the second largest linguistic group in South America.[5] They were among the first Americans who crossed the Bering Straits in several migrations from 30,000 to 10,000 years ago. Physically the Aymaras resemble the Alaskan Eskimoes. They are quite short, with tanned and ruddy complexions, and have exceptionally large lung capacities due to the two-mile elevation. For clothing, the women wear picturesque rock-hard bowler derbies over braided black hair, go barefoot, and, no matter how poor, wear several brightly colored skirts (*polleras*) with knitted sweaters and shawls over their shoulders. The men generally wear Western-style shoes, pants, and shirts, but in colder weather add a poncho (*ruana*) and a characteristic stocking cap (*chullo*), which has ear tabs and ties under the chin.

Unlike many North American Indians, the Aymaras have managed to preserve their language, much of their land, and substantial parts of their culture despite 400 years of oppression by the Spanish and other

Westerners. Their cultural substratum, including their language, remains more Asian than European. The Aymaras widely use shamans as folk-healers, share an animistic sense of the energy-charged vitality of their environment, and utilize organic drugs, especially coca leaves.

The Market

When an Aymara farmer first emerges from his adobe home at the end of a cold night in the chilling altitude, he may stand silently for a time in front of a light-colored wall facing the sun. Gradually the sun, which seems closer in the thin air at such an altitude, seeps through his body with warmth to last the day.

Activity on the day of July 16 begins with Aymara rural peasants (*campesinos*) carrying bundles of goods into the central square in Ilave and spreading them for sale. As on other festivals and Sunday market days, by midday the square fills with stalls and spread-out goods as perhaps a hundred people sit or stand quietly vending items that range from cheap cigarette lighters and nail clippers to hand-made shawls and alpaca rugs. Aymaras are primarily subsistence farmers who only occasionally work in cities or mines. They sell potatoes, barley, cereals, beans, skins, hand-made fabrics, coca leaves, amulets, and a variety of traditional and modern clothing. The Ilave festival market is personal and provides direct

FIGURE 7–3   An Aymara Marketplace

distribution by which farmers and townspeople exchange products of their efforts among friends in the populace.

Surrounding the temporary market in the square are permanent adobe shops, which through the week offer more modern products and services such as auto repairs and mass-produced clothes. Capital is concentrated in the hands of mixed-blood (*mestizo*) urban merchants, military personnel, professionals, large landowners, and outsiders. Merchants with capital buy cheaply and live comfortably, while rural Aymara families earn an average of $125 per year.

The Party

Along with the market, Aymaras and the urban mestizos spend a substantial part of July 16 at a large party hosted by an *alferado*. Reflecting ancient customs, an alferado volunteers to host a fiesta to gain honor and to advance to greater responsibilities in the social structure. For the feast he hosts he must provide free potatoes, meat, music, dancers, costumes, fireworks, beer, alcohol, and coca leaves. The expenses frequently exceed the host alferado's annual income, but refusal to be an alferado brings great shame. The system reflects a preconquest sense of community and shared responsibility; it redistributes wealth and prevents the successful Aymara or *mestizo* from becoming disproportionately richer than his neighbors. An Aymara accepts community leadership by organizing a dance group, sponsoring a minor fiesta or an outdoor shrine, protecting the common fields, and finally hosting a major fiesta.[6] Ilave's highest official is the elected mayor, who also happens to be the community's only medical doctor.

The School Celebration

On the afternon of July 16, Ilave's secondary school for women, Nuestra Senora del Carmen, celebrates its feast day with parades and speeches. Some 300 students from Ilave schools line up in rows wearing dark shoes, gray sweaters over white shirts, and gray slacks or skirts. Each school marches behind its small brass band and the girls' school features a female drum and bugle corps with majorettes in white, miniskirted uniforms and dark sunglasses. The school's queen, usually very anglo in appearance, is presented to the mayor, military commandant, and other officials. The school's directories delivers an extensive address about the school, women, and Aymara culture on a public address system to the standing rows of students and area residents. Despite that liberation rhetoric, the school component of the July 16 celebration, in its modern clothing, linear organization, Western music, literary speech making, and promlike honors reflects a Western assimilationist model of culture. It recalls a North American high school homecoming celebration.

The Religious Rituals

The most non-Western component of the July 16 fiesta is its religious celebrations. The rituals aim at healing—religiously, medicinally, and psychologically.

Between the town square and the Ilave Catholic church is a tree-shaded courtyard about 100 feet in length. All day long on July 16 on each side of the walk local folk-healers of various ranks sit listening to individual problems, suggesting remedies, reading coca leaves, and blessing articles. These shamans by the church door symbolize the juxtaposition of 400 years of externally imposed Catholicism and millenia of Aymara folk beliefs and practices.

Aymara religion, art, and medicine are blends of native and foreign elements. The Conquistadores and their missionaries attempted to stamp out indigenous religious beliefs as pagan heresies and as alien forces that separated the Indians from complete Spanish domination and control. Aymara beliefs survived "underground," and many center around coca, "the divine plant of the Incas."[7]

In the harsh *altiplano*, the sedative effect of coca, the source of the extract cocaine, is a welcome relief from cold, hunger, and exhaustive labor. Men, women, and children may be seen at any time of the night or day chewing coca leaves combined with a lime that liberates the alkaloid in the leaves. In addition, coca is brewed as a tea for many illnesses, is used to ward off evil spirits or defend against enemies, is "read" to decipher the future, is preserved for religious and social occasions, is an item of trade, is carried or given as a symbol, and is utilized for a multitude of similar purposes. Feast days in this atmosphere become a confused juxtaposition of cultures. They combine Inca observances of the natural agrarian cycle of coca and other crops with the theological cycle of the Christian liturgical year.

The official religious observances begin in the Ilave parish church at 9 A.M. North American priests concelebrate mass before some 500 local parishioners who represent less than 1 percent of the nominally Catholic population of the parish. The traditional but slightly personalized liturgy lasts more than an hour. Following it comes an event that photographers travel around half the world to witness, a procession through town with a statue of Mary, a brass band, and the incredibly colorful, strangely costumed dancers.

After mass, the brilliant procession emerges from the church and proceeds slowly around the square. It is led by six dancers moving in a slow, swaying shuffle in time with the dirgelike music. The costumes of the dancers are called "slave" costumes; they parody the ostentatious metallic garb of the Conquistadores. The three-foot plumes on the silvery helmets are highly visible from any vantage point as the dancers proceed in two parallel lines ahead of the band and statue. Blue, white, and red swirls of beads dominate the stiff cardboardlike body coverings that extend from the shins up to the heavily decorated shoulders. Slightly reminiscent of a matador's costume, the outfits are large and cumbersome with a complete ring of white string fringe at the bottom of the jacket and the dresslike lower half, as well as on the shoulder decorations and the helmet. Each dancer wears white boots. They maintain impassive expressions on their faces and carry with both hands a ten-inch doll decorated in like manner. The overall effect of the costume on a Westerner might bring to mind a large suit of armor completely redecorated with psychedelic extravagance. They rent for $30 to $40 per festival.

The small band blares out ponderous, somber melodies as the procession moves in time to slow drum beats between the crowds around the square. The six trumpets, two tubas, three bass horns, one snare drum, and one bass drum manage a mildly shrill, dissonant unity that was undoubtedly born on the flutes of Andes llama herders.

Rising behind and above the rest of the procession is the statue of Mary, the mother of Jesus. The statue possesses a doll-like quality, similar

FIGURE 7–4　An Aymara Procession

to the popular Eastern European figure of the Infant of Prague. It rises to a height of some seven feet above its platform, which is carried on the shoulders of ten men. The statue is made up of two parts. The bottom half consists of a round, pink, puffy base with strings of roses attached. Resting on this, a representation four feet tall of the Blessed Virgin Mary stands in a stiff wide black robe covered over with a full-length white cape. Both garments are decorated with gold brocade. On her left arm rests a regally dressed baby Jesus and on her head sits a golden crown emanating silver rays. The shape and color are those of pink cotton candy on a white, cone-shaped holder, all turned upside down.

The procession of dancers, musicians, platform carriers, and others continues several times around the perimeter of the market square. It then files slowly into the church and mounts the statue of Mary on a stand for veneration. The marchers continue through the streets of Ilave throughout the day.

While the nominal liturgical ritual for observing the feast of Our Lady of Carmen is Roman, the roots of Ilave's July 16 celebration are substantially preconquest Indian. Mary represents a visible reincarnation of the ancient *Pacha Mama*, or Earth Mother, nourisher of humans and all living things. The statue recalls an Inca princess or the Virgin of the Sun. The platform carried in procession once brought the Inca emperor to celebrations of the sun god Inti-Raymi and conveyed the mummified remains of emperors through the Inca capital, Cuzco. Food, drink, and music celebrated ancient Peruvian harvests, venerating the powers in nature, *wacas* (*huacas, guacas*), and ancestral powers, *pacarisca* (*pacarina*).[8]

The very choice of July 16 as a major feast stems from the Aymara worldview of ecological processes. Since the central Christian feast of "new life" at Easter occurs problematically in early winter rather than in spring in the southern hemisphere, Aymaras have established their own emphasis in liturgical cycles to match their agricultural year. The resulting list of major feasts, with their Inca festival origins in parentheses, appears on page 219 in Table 7–2.[9] Each major feast, despite its European liturgical origins, becomes a convenient indicator specifying tasks necessary for material survival. Only the feasts of All Saints and All Souls do not serve as practical agricultural markers.

The religious rituals of July 16 and throughout the Aymara year illustrate the principle of *homology*. A homology exists maintaining consistent parallels between the *technical* or causal-functional system and the *symbolic* or logico-meaningful system in a given society.[10]

To Aymaras, nature is immediate and powerful. Rural Aymara life is dominated by the organic cycles of nature itself, not the urbanized rhythms of school calendars, sports seasons, fiscal years, or political regimes. Aymara cosmology is *animistic*, holding that internal life-forces

TABLE 7–2. Aymara Feasts

DATE	FEAST	ACTIVITY
July 16	Our Lady of Carmen (Earthly Purification)	Very early plowing
July 25	St. James, Apostle (God of Thunder)	Protection from lightning and thunder (early planting in Santiago)
October 7	Rosary (Festival of the Water)	Beginning of planting
November 1–2	All Saints-All Souls (Procession of the Dead)	Commemorate the dead
December 8	Immaculate Conception (The Principal Festival)	End of planting (check Santiago potatoes)
Late February	Mardi Gras (The Great Ripening)	Crops in bloom; initial dig to check harvest
May 3	Santa Cruz (Song of the Harvest)	Bless harvested potatoes
Late May	Pentecost (Festival of the Sun)	Celebrate completion of harvest

("spirits") create and activate reality, while industrialized cosmology is more "mechanical," seeing laws of leverage and principles of motion uniformly accounting for all phenomena in the universe. Not mass-mediated cultural patterns but the sun and the seasons organize Aymara life. The destructive terror of a lightning storm makes important the feast of Santiago (St. James), who has succeeded Illapa, the Inca good of thunder and lightning, as the patron saint protecting against such storms.

The most important crop, potatoes, makes up 68 percent of the Aymara diet[11] and therefore decorates statues of Mary carried in a procession on December 8, foretelling harvest success each spring in Ilave. Sorcery and folk healing, the Aymara traditions least influenced by CWAWMP ways, further illustrate their animistic, epistemological conception of the structure of the world.

The Healers

Aymara folk-healers, not burdened by Western dichotomies between mind and body or spirit and matter, combine the functions of medical doctor, psychiatrist, and religious minister. Their labels vary from region to region, but around Ilave there are four ranks of folk-healers. Given the expense and inaccessability of modernized medical practices, for most rural Aymaras, folk-healers are the only recourse for physical, psychological, or spiritual ailments. The *yatiri* or *sabio* is the most broadly competent, performing many rituals and referring persons to the other, more specialized healers. The *curandero* is considered especially competent for coping with disorders of a primarily physical nature. The *paqo* specializes in more spiritual matters and may be a *bueno*, a good paqo, or a *laiqa*, a specialist in evil spirits. The *resiri* specialize in praying and were numerous outside the Ilave church on July 16. Before Pizarro destroyed the unity of Peruvian culture by executing ʒhe Inca emperor Atahualppa and shipping $100 million worth of gold back to Spain,[12] Aymara and neighboring Quechua folk-healers were respected priests handing down traditions of learning and leadership.

"Padre Jaime" Madden is a Catholic missionary who has worked in Peru for over fifteen years. From 1971 to 1977 he was not engaged in formal church activities but was conducting an experimental project in which he attempted to live the life-style of poor, rural Aymara peasants. From his one-room mud hut, Madden worked closely with Aymara folk-healers and sorcerers. Reversing previous missionary exclusiveness, Madden concelebrated mass with them and would not perform religious services for the sick or for groups unless a local folk-healer participated. Despite their skepticism of outsiders, folk-healers are so numerous—perhaps every tenth adult is some rank of healer and nearly every family clan has its own—that Madden has worked closely with many of them.

Following the July 16 procession in Ilave, the tall, blond, blue-eyed native of Illinois, Father Jim Madden, joined a short, dark, brown-eyed curandero, Ricardo Ramos, for a prayer service that completed a series of curing rites the curandero had performed over a period of weeks. The encounter is worth looking at in detail as a mingling of cultural traditions outside the technological mass-mediated world of Billy Graham and Marcus Welby.

Near midday, Jim Madden set out from his simple one-room home where a poster of Che Gueverra, who died among the Bolivian Aymaras, adorns one wall. Madden wore his usual hiking books, jeans, sweat shirt, worn peacoat, and Aymara-style ear-tabbed stocking cap. He carried a cloth bag in one hand.

Jim walked the several miles over slight hills to Ricardo's house, greeting neighbors in their yards and fields along the way. He stopped a quarter of a mile away in front of Ricardo's and watched for a few moments to see if Ricardo was outside, then let out a single short yell. Shortly, Ricardo appeared, waved his arm, went back inside, and then hustled down toward Madden. Madden's not approaching the front door directly was partly an observance of Aymara courtesy and partly a precaution against being attacked by one of the vicious dogs that each family keeps in its yard for protection. Trust and open doors are in short supply among the oppressed Aymaras.

Ricardo Ramos is a minor curandero who, like most around Lake Titicaca, treats primarily relatives and close friends. He is in his middle fifties, about five feet four inches, and not overweight. His face has the classical Aymara-Quechua features that were highly prized during the Inca period. The face and nose are long, the forehead recedes, and the complexion is ruddy and deeply tanned from the sun. That day he was wearing Western-style clothes—a worn, loosely fitting dark suit over a white turtleneck sweater and old black shoes split up the back and front. He carried in his hand a ball of gray yarn with two knitting needles.

They started the several-mile walk up the hill away from the lake. Ricardo informed Jim of his preparations for a meeting the two of them were convening the next week for healers to translate certain ancient Aymara rites and line up appropriate Biblical passages for use by local folk-healers.

They walked parallel with the crest of the hill for a while and Ricardo explained that the hacienda just below, whose owner lived off in Puno, thanks to government land reform, would soon belong to the nearby community of twenty homes called "Little Bomba." Ricardo added, "I do not think we can get the owner's tractor with the land. We should rent one since a tractor can work three times the land that oxen can."

As they continued up a dry creek bed, Ricardo stooped, picked a small, green, dry plant, and explained to Jim, "This plant is good medicine for a fever." A few feet further he pointed to another: "Boiled as a tea that relieves stomach pains." He picked others, had Madden smell them, and explained which were good for colds, for headaches, for soreness, and similar ailments. Later, Ricardo stopped, turned his back to the steep hill, swept his arm slowly out over the countryside, and explained in Aymaran, "This is our drug store, our pharmacy."

As they continued on, he added that Aymaras have a form of x-ray. A guinea pig is placed on top of the sick person for a night. In the morning the guinea pig is cut open to find what is wrong with it, with the assumption that the ailment transfers from the person to the pig during the night. As Western science reevaluates its own naive rejection of traditional folk medicines, perhaps even this "superstitious" practice will be empirically validated by way of energy fields and kirlian auras. Ricardo simply commented, "You use rays. We use guinea pigs."

They were now on a dusty path winding gradually across and up the even mountainside through the sparse vegetation. They walked steadily, conversing all the while, even though the oxygen level at this two-and-a-half-mile altitude is less than half of sea level. Far below, Madden could barely make out two speck-size figures moving along the road. Ricardo identified two women neighbors and observed, "They are on their way to Chucuito to visit their relatives." Madden looked again and still could see only dots that seemed a sixteenth of an inch high. Aymara eyesight is highly developed, and across the bare land through the clear air Ricardo could tell by the gait, pace, and shape of the figures who they were and could estimate why they were walking in that direction at that time.

Finally they approached a cluster of six homes some 1,000 feet up the gradual slope of the mountain above the lake and valley floor. From the nearest house, a long-haired German shepherd charged barking and snarling viciously. The two men held up the large rocks they carried in their hands for such occasions. The dog stopped at the wall by the lane and a woman emerged from the house to call it back. She was the wife of the head of this small community. They chatted for a few moments. She was chewing a cheekful of coca leaves.

Ricardo and Jim walked another fifteen feet and entered the yard of another home in the cluster and immediately a woman emerged greeting them. She was Victoria, the woman who had been ill. She was, in fact, Ricardo's second wife. His first wife had died after they had raised six children.

Victoria was about four feet ten inches with a broad face, strong, even features, wise-looking crinkles in the corners of her eyes and mouth, and a calm, serious expression. Overall she exuded mature, sturdy attractiveness. She wore an orange skirt of burlap material. The outer layer was wearing through, but there were many other layers underneath. Several dark sweaters kept her warm and on her head was a gray bowler hat with three tassles dangling from the brim. She wore no shoes and her feet had the rhino-hide quality of toughness common in the area; they enabled her to walk unnoticing over rocks as if she wore sturdy boots. The three-year-old daughter of Victoria and Ricardo advanced shyly behind her, dressed similarly. Soon their four-year-old son also appeared, attired in worn gray slacks, a new gray sweater over a white shirt, shoes split off in the back like open sandles, and one sock. His stockinged foot was sore, a fact that quickly became the subject of conversation.

Victoria went back inside and emerged with a folded blanket that she placed on top of the low rock wall for Jim to sit on. She placed a skin next to it for Ricardo. Such seating is an Aymara social rule. A man stepped through the low gateway from next door with some twigs and seeds for Jim.

Ricardo, Jim, and Victoria conversed seriously as she lowered herself slowly onto a folded blanket on the ground. She described her illness and gradual recovery under Ricardo's herbal brews. Weeks ago she had fallen and hurt her hip, subsequently experiencing pain and some emissions of blood. She was now basically recovered but had been made extremely anxious last week by the sight of a large ball of fire coming over a nearby hill. It had brought a bad spirit on her. To a Westerner the account might have sounded absurd, but at exactly this time back in the United States, millions were listening unquestioningly to John Denver singing high in the Rockies, "I've seen it raining fire in the sky." In any case, the group discussed the experience seriously for some time.

Eventually, they decided the ceremony should begin. Jim pulled from his plain cloth bag an Aymara New Testament, a small cross, and some holy water which he then gave to Ricardo, and a mimeographed page in Aymara with short ceremonies and prayers on it.

An actual curing ceremony requires many details not necessary for this simple concluding prayer service. As the film *The Healer*[13] indicates, a serious curing ceremony requires that the folk-healer/sorcerer fast from the noon preceding to the noon following. The ceremony takes place at night. The healer prepares himself by gathering personal power with concentration, rites, and ingestion of coca or other allies. The sick person and his or her family sit in a circle inside their small, one-room home. Several candles burning in the center of the room provide light and focus. The healer may provide herbal brews for the patient or may apply organically based substances to affected parts of the body. (Archeological remains of skulls reveal that simple brain surgery was even practiced in ancient Peru.) The healer carefully arranges his altar and recites prayers and incantations in a low voice, mingling ancient Aymara customs with Latin and Spanish phrases. As Claude Lévi-Strauss has shown in his study of shamanistic curing among the Cuna Indians of Panama, these symbolic incantations may be effective for precisely the same reasons that psychotherapy and other modern rituals are effective.[14] Besides providing external remedies, these rites generate internal power that biofeedback and other modern techniques verify are genuinely therapeutic.

Since Ricardo had already completed such a series of curing ceremonies, on this occasion Jim sat quietly and began by reciting a brief prayer. Ricardo followed with a prayer. After a pause, Jim read a selection from the New Testament.

At this point everyone, including the neighbor, stood and placed his hands on Victoria's head as she sat quietly. The two children had wandered off, so they were retrieved and asked to place their hands, too, on their mother's head. Aymaras consider the prayers of children especially effective. For a moment everyone stood quietly with hands interlocked over Victoria's black hair. There was no sound but the quiet rustle of the wind in the leaves. The air was neither hot nor cold. The afternoon sky was clear. In Aymaran, Jim offered a quiet prayer. Ricardo followed, praying, "Lord, join your hands with ours on her head and keep her well."

Everyone, including the children, who were a bit puzzled and uncertain, held there silently for a moment.

The participants then moved back to their original seats. Another prayer was read as Jim opened the container of holy water and sprinkled Victoria and the area around her. He continued, sprinkling everyone present. Ricardo quietly reminded Jim of Victoria's recent anxiety. They formed everyone into a procession and walked fifty feet through the brush to the spot from which Victoria had seen the ball of fire. They sprinkled water there and returned. Each one then embraced in the formalized "kiss of peace" and wished each other well, again including the children. Jim and Ricardo recited another prayer and the ceremony concluded. No weird chanting, no drums, no "natives" dancing in breechcloth, no coca leaves and datura, no ecstacies. Just personal concern and a simple rite.

Afterward, everyone exchanged a "buenos tardes." Ricardo stayed at his wife's house with her and the children and began his knitting. Victoria gave Jim five fresh eggs as a gift. Jim started down the path where a neighbor was herding three llamas. His last visit to the States flashed to mind and he reflected how far a curandero "house call" was from mass-mediated "Marcus Welbys," "Ben Caseys," and "General Hospitals." He walked briskly down the long mountainside toward the level areas nearer the lake, toward the highway where cattle trucks packed with thirty or forty Aymaras spewed out "modern" noise, speed, danger, and dust.

Cross-Cultural Comparisons and Interaction

The simple rite described above illustrates cultural content seldom conveyed by mass-mediated culture. Aymara beliefs, agricultural rituals, and folk-healing—like a great deal of the cultural preferences of Third World peoples—receive little exposure in mass-mediated culture. Only perhaps 1 percent of international mass-mediated culture originates from and is under the control of the two-thirds of the human race who live in the Third World.[15] The remainder originates in the advanced industrial states of the developed world. The following example illustrates the cultural content transmitted by mass media into the Third World.

On that same July 16 evening, *El Triturador*, a mafiosa movie starring Charles Bronson, was showing in Puno, Peru, a few miles north of the location of the Ilave festival and Ricardo's curing ceremony. The theater was large, seating between 500 and 1,000, and the film played to full houses—teens, children, the elderly, people in modern dress, and traditionally clad Aymaras.

When the audience was seated and attention concentrated, 20 minutes of commercials were shown in the form of still slides and short film spots. All the commercials advertised modern consumer goods and services, items such as radios, modern clothes, cars, cafes, and beauty parlors. There were, of course, no references to the durable traditional goods sold in the public markets. Similar commercials precede film showings throughout much of the Third World.

The film starred Charles Bronson, perhaps the most popular actor in the Third World.* His forte is the shoot-'em-up, action-adventure saga. He has starred innumerable times as a private detective, a city policeman, a spy, a cowboy, a criminal, in low- or medium-budget features loaded with technological gimmickry, tough-guy heroics, macho exploitation, vigilante law and order, and quantities of killings, blood, and beatings. Significantly, his appeal may be related to that of mythological gods and heroes.

El Triturador played in English-speaking countries as *The Stone Killer* and was based on a novel titled *A Complete State of Death*. The story features Martin Balsam as an elderly mafia don who is secretly training Vietnam veterans in a desert training camp to pull a bloody coup against other mafia leaders in revenge for a massacre four decades earlier. Bronson plays a New York police detective, Lieutenant Lou Torrey, who has been deported to Los Angeles for the quick-trigger killing of a young Puerto Rican suspect trapped on a fire escape. Without overtly judging the incident, the film implies that a decisive, heroic cop has got to work that way despite the predictable protests of ethnic and civil rights pressure groups.

The plot develops as Bronson's curiosity is piqued by the murder of several small-time criminals in Los Angeles. Bronson had previously beaten one around in the interrogation room and learned that each had information about preparations for a large-scale criminal activity. After a series of wild chases and a few more killings, Bronson discovers the desert training site. There, following a bloody shootout during which several dozen persons are killed on screen, Bronson learns that a large team of assassins has already headed out for their job. He flies back to

---

*During visits to some thirty countries in recent years, this author has viewed Charles Bronson films on four continents. Third World theaters specialize in low-budget imports of action-adventure films, comedies, sexy romps, and musicals, while television features "Bonanza" and cartoons. Hence, Bronson is not atypical of the cultural level of Western media exports to the Third World.

New York where he and a number of machine gun–wielding New York City policemen corner the execution team just after it has gunned down —on screen, of course—half a dozen of the top mafia dons from across the country. In a multilevel underground parking garage in a wild flurry of shooting, racing cars, explosions, fires, and bloody deaths, Bronson puts an end to the team, the mafia plot, and, it seems, anything else that moves.

Like most films popular in American drive-ins and Third World theaters, *El Triturador* glorifies *individualistic* heroics and *violence* while it teaches only the surface skills of physical and mental agility; it does not portray compassion, personal feelings, or constructive social aware-ness, nor does it present analyses of the institutions it portrays.

One scene in *El Triturador* brought an audible gasp from the audience. It was an aerial view of Manhattan at night, seen from Bron-son's airplane as it flew over the bright lights, the skyscrapers, the spar-kling contrasts of soft darkness and electrical glitter, the tiny autos, and the vast bridges and buildings—a vision of Shrangri-La. Of course, the audience could not sense from the screen the difficult-to-breathe air, the grit of dirty skin, and the inconveniences that are a part of being physi-cally present in New York and other cities. Even the crime, fear, conges-tion, speed, and noise that come through in films almost become attrac-tive themselves when projected on a wide screen in full color with stereophonic sound.

What role does a Bronson film and the remainder of mass-mediated culture play among the Aymaras and throughout the Third World?

Generally, they are the major part of a one-way flow of cultural prod-ucts from developed to less-developed countries, supported by a flow of profits in the opposite direction. The unidirectional imbalance occurs in films,[16] television,[17] and other technological media. The incidental learning of values and ideology in Billy Graham, Disney, "Welby," "Bonanza," Bronson, and throughout mass-mediated culture from the United States and Western Europe implants *c*apitalist, *W*estern, *a*dult, *w*hite, *m*ale, *p*rint priorities. These inevitably compete with traditional Aymara cultural patterns from the *s*ocialist monarchy of the Incas, *E*ast-ern Asian origins, *e*thnic rather than Caucasian racial identification, *y*outhful and aged *f*reedom of perception, *f*eminine as well as masculine awareness, and *a*ural rather than print origins. In this one-sided CWAWMP versus SEEYFA struggle, the West rationalizes its hegemony by depicting itself as an iconic endpoint of human "modernization" and "develop-ment" to be sought by all peoples.

Table 7–3 indicates the country of origin of films viewed in South and Central America. The figures show the answers by young people, considered

TABLE 7–3. Foreign Film Reception in Middle and South America

SOURCE	MIDDLE AMERICANS (n = 119)	SOUTH AMERICANS (n = 190)
United States	96	82
France	41	57
Italy	35	51
West Germany	26	12
Mexico	25	4
Great Britain	17	15
Eastern Europe	3	6
Spain	5	3
Argentina	4	3
Sweden	0	5
Japan	0.8	3
India	0	0.5

to be potential agents of change in South and Central America, to the question, "From what country or countries are the films you see most?"[18] A sampling of films showing in Latin American capitals in the middle 1970s found these titles: *Battle for the Planet of the Apes, Trouble Man, Secrets of the Cosa Nostra (The Valachi Papers,* with Charles Bronson), *The Great Gatsby, When Legends Die, The Fantastic Voyage of Sinbad, Robin Hood, Valdez's Horses, Rosemary's Baby, The Sting, The Barefoot Executive, The Dirty Dozen, Kamasutra, The Infallible Gun, The Texan and the Women, Baby Love—the Temptress, Passion for Danger, Rifles of Revenge, Operation San Antonio, The Treasure of Tarzan,* and numerous lesser-known titles.[19]

Harold Osborn, in *The Indians of the Andes,* states what many have observed: "The Indian . . . has never accepted that the benefits offered him by European civilization are worth the change in his traditional habits which their enjoyment demands."[20] But how long can Aymara culture hold out against modern means of mass communication and persuasion?

Ultimately, despite altruistic rhetoric, mass media convert cultures to a Western, capitalist life-style in order (a) to increase the number of consumers ꞌseeking manufactured goods, and (b) to make local natural resources and cheap labor available for the production of goods for richer markets elsewhere. Increase in corporate profits in the parent country is the explicit motive, according to official reports to stockholders, for multinational penetration into the Third World. Such global expansion increases consumer goods and energy available in the West but may only maintain or increase economic and cultural dependency and underdevelopment in the Third World.

The imposition of Western commercial communications is defended as part of the "free flow of information." However, as Herbert Schiller has emphasized, freedom—or, more accurately, lack of regulation—in an exchange presupposes equality of power between parties.[21] Given present imbalances of power, the "free flow" between Western and Third World countries recalls Emmanuel Cellar's summary of ITT's antitrust defense: " 'Every man for himself,' said the elephant as he danced among the chickens."[22]

At stake among the Aymaras and throughout the Third World is preservation of even part of an indigenous cultural system. Conversion from a folk-healer to Charles Bronson represents a much larger transition from a traditional non-Western cultural system to a modern capitalist political economy.

Table 7–1, page 211, helps explain the Aymara experience, one that is common in the Third World and that illustrates an ethnocentric and ahistorical bias in orthodox theories of development. The high civilization of the Indians of the Andes regressed under European domination, yet the legitimacy of their culture is now to be measured by its approximation to "the characteristics of West European and North American society as goal-states from which calibrated indices of underdevelopment can be constructed."[23] Traditional non-Western cultural values and communication forms from the righthand column of the table are replaced by mass-mediated messages from the lefthand column that dangle a Western, middle-class life-style before the Aymaras like a carrot. Not only are the past and the nature of Aymara life ignored; the mass media imply a future standard of living for Aymaras and other Third World peoples that is impossible within the normal limits on distribution of wealth and sources of energy. In short, replacing traditional *brujos* with mass-mediated Bronsons and following the Western "modernization" model of development to the end would benefit Western economies and the multinational corporations, but such cultural imperialism violates the principle of self-determination and promises incalculable loss to the variety of human culture.

An Indian fiesta in the Andes offers a unique vantage point from which to raise cross-cultural and international questions about mass-mediated culture. Only half the challenge is the obvious task of understanding non-Western peoples, their communication genres, the possibilities for human culture they express, and their plight in the face of mass-mediated culture. The other half, perhaps more difficult, but not unrelated, is for the modern capitalist, industrialized West to see *itself* and its mass-mediated culture in critical perspective.

Notes

Note: The field research for this chapter was conducted throughout July and August of 1974 and was funded in part by a grant from the Committee on Reseaich of the Academic Senate of the University of California at San Diego.

1. Margaret J. King, "Problems of Cross-Cultural Popular Culture Study," Communication Institute, East-West Center, Honolulu, Hawaii, March 1975.

2. Floyd W. Matson, "Where It's At: Popular Culture Revisited," Communication Institute, East-West Center, Honolulu, Hawaii, July, 1975.

3. All of the studies cited were presented to the Comparative Popular Culture Research Seminar on "Traditional Media" at the East-West Communication Institute, Honolulu, Hawaii, July 7 to August 1, 1975.

4. Stewart's study is number three in the series, "Dimensions of International Education," published by the Regional Council for International Education, University of Pittsburgh, 1971.

The table of contrasts is based on distinctions developed by C. P. Snow, Susan Sontag, William Foxwell Albright, Paul Tillich, Eldridge Cleaver, Imamu Amiri Baraka (Leroi Jones), Eric Gill, Martin Buber, Marshall McLuhan, Edmund Carpenter, Alan Watts, Dorothy Lee, D. T. Suzuki, Robert Orstein, Andrew Wiel, Karl Marx, Benjamin Lee Whorf, and others.

5. William E. Carter, *Aymara Communities and the Bolivian Agrarian Reform* (Gainesville: University of Florida Press, 1964), p. 1. The Reverend James Madden, M.M., who is affiliated with the Aymara Institute in Chucuito, Peru, and whose work is described later in this chapter, states there are 1 million Aymaras in traditional communities in Peru and Bolivia but perhaps a half million more who have migrated elsewhere. Their numbers are said to have remained relatively constant since preconquest times. Madden and his confreres provided lodging, introductions, translations, and a great deal of information for this study.

6. Carter, *Aymara.*

7. W. Golden Mortimer, *Coca, The Divine Plant of the Incas* (New York: 1901).

8. Pierre Verger, *Indians of Peru* (New York: Pocahontas Press, 1950).

9. The popularity of Aymara feasts is from members of the Maryknoll mission in Ilava, Peru. Inca feasts are from Luis E. Valcarcel, "The Andean Calendar," *Handbook of South American Indians,* vol. 2 (Washington: J. H. Vail, 1946), pp. 471–76.

10. James L. Peacock, *Consciousness and Change: Symbolic Anthropology in Evolutionary Perspective* (New York: John Wiley, 1975), especially pp. 62–63.

11. Ibid., p. 24.

12. J. Alden Mason, *The Ancient Civilizations of Peru* (Baltimore: Penguin, 1968), p. 137. See also the classic history, William H. Prescott, *The Conquest of Peru* (New York: New American Library, 1961). Douglas Sharon has studied folk healing in northern Peru, unpublished Masters thesis, University of California, Los Angeles, 1972.

13. *The Healer,* a film made and distributed by Maryknoll Communications, Maryknoll, New York, features Rev. Innocente Salazar narrating scenes of Aymara life, especially rites involving his friend, a blind Aymara folk-healer, Marcellino Davin.

14. Claude Lévi-Strauss, "The Effectiveness of Symbols" in *Structural Anthropology,* trans. Claire Jacobson and Brooke Grundfest Schoepf (New York: Basic Books, 1963), pp. 187–205.

15. Kaarle Nordenstreng, "Mass Media and Developing Nations," *The Democratic Journalist,* no. 1 (1975), pp. 6–7.

16. Thomas Guback, "Cultural Identity and Film in the European Economic Community," February, 1974; quoted in Herbert I. Schiller, "The Appearance of National-Communications Policies," *Gazette* 21, no. 2 (1975), p. 86.

17. K. Nordenstreng and T. Varis, "Television Traffic—a One-Way Street?" UNESCO, Paris, 1974.

18. P. Deutschmann, H. Ellingsworth, and J. McNelly, *Communication and Social Change in Latin America* (New York: Praeger, 1968), p. 79.

19. These films were advertised at movie theaters or in newspapers in 1974 in various cities of South America, including Lima, Peru; LaPaz, Bolivia; Buenos Aires, Argentina; Rio de Janeiro, Brazil; Bogota, Columbia; and Caracas, Venezuela.

20. Harold Osborne, *Indians of the Andes: Aymaras and Quechuas*, (London: Routledge and Kegan Paul, 1952), p. 18.

21. See, for example, Herbert I. Schiller, "Freedom from the 'Free Flow'," *Journal of Communication* 24, no. 1 (Winter 1974), pp. 110–17.

22. Anthony Sampson, *The Sovereign State of ITT* (Greenwich, Conn.: Fawcett Publications, 1974), p. 160.

23. Peter Golding, "Media Role in National Development: Critique of a Theoretical Orthodoxy," *Journal of Communication* 24, no. 3 (Summer 1974), pp. 39–53.

8

Conclusions
and
a Critique

What precisely is contemporary mass-mediated culture?

How are cultural studies, policy research, and textual-contextual analysis useful?

What are common misrepresentations and general characteristics ("principles") of mass-mediated culture?

In what sense are popular arts and media a "consciousness industry" exercising cultural hegemony by technological manipulation?

How can the experience of alienation be alleviated through the liberating potential of media?

The concern of these studies has been the nature, organization, and quality of contemporary cultural life, as widely disseminated through characteristic expressions in the mass media. The opening chapter looked at the size, influence, evaluations, systemic character, and significance of mass-mediated culture. The intervening chapters comprised a series of in-depth ethnographic, exegetical, and critical case studies of specific dominant expressions of culture as they are transmitted by mass means of communication and as they represent specific sets of cultural values and ideology from among the variety of choices available to the human species. This final chapter draws out the generalizations and patterns common to those case studies in particular and suggests a radical critique of contemporary mass-mediated culture in general.

Vantage Point: Cultural Studies and Policy Research

Definitions

The precise meaning of the phrase *contemporary mass-mediated culture* indicates dimensions of the system of which the case studies are representative parts and indicates what is included and what excluded from the focus of this book.

Culture is the generic term in the phrase. Claude Lévi-Strauss offers an operational definition of culture:

> What is called a "culture" is a fragment of humanity which, from the point of view of the research at hand and of the scale on which the latter is carried out, presents significant discontinuities in relation to the rest of humanity.... The same set of individuals may be considered to be parts of many different contexts: universal, continental, national, regional, local,

etc., as well as familial, occupational, religious, political, etc. This is true as a limit; however, anthropologists usually reserve the term "culture" to designate a *group* of discontinuities which is significant on several of these levels at the same time.[1]

The interpretation of culture calls for a theory of symbols and symbolic processes in their relationship to social order.[2]

Mass-mediated specifies the particular species within the genus culture. Culture disseminated by mass means of communication by definition reflects an authoritarian, hierarchical organization of message transmission. The communication flows from a single individual or institutional source to an audience that is relatively large, heterogeneous, and anonymous. Feedback is indirect—for example, through the purchase of goods advertised within the course of the transmission. Speaking of "mass-mediated" rather than "mass" culture avoids the complex debate on whether modern society is or is not mass while focusing on a set of instruments of modern society, namely the media, which are indisputably mass. "Mass-mediated culture" includes widely disseminated expressions of "popular culture" but not the variety of unmediated forms of popular culture that precede and surround the mass-mediated forms. In this sense, mediated culture is a category within popular culture. Mass-mediated culture also includes expressions of elite and folk culture, although, again, the categories of "elite" and "folk," like "popular" culture, include expressions not transmitted by mass media.

Defining the subject as **contemporary** mass-mediated culture specifies a temporal focus and implies a geographical limit. Unlike the term "modern," which implies a specific period and style, "contemporary" means in-the-present and suggests a current, continuing phenomenon. "Contemporary" is preferable to "American" mass-mediated culture for the purposes of the studies included because Billy Graham, the Disney universe, and other prevalent forms of mass-mediated culture are not confined to a single country or continent. They may emanate from the United States, from Great Britain, from France, and even from less central points in current multinational societies. Because of the ownership and organization of the media of communication—such as satellites, wire services, the music industry, film and television production and distribution, periodical and book publishing—the technologically advanced countries of North America and Western Europe, as well as Japan, provide the point of origin for the transmission of the vast majority of mass-mediated culture. But reception is scattered throughout the world. Only the limited technology of Third World countries and the politically motivated resistance of the Soviets and Chinese prevent a complete global immersion in one coordinated system of mass-mediated culture.

Thorough investigation of contemporary mass-mediated culture draws from a variety of disciplines: sociology, psychology, history, literature, art, drama, and any number of other pursuits. To provide a focus for such scholarship, the Popular Culture Association was founded in 1967 for thorough and serious study of those productions, both artistic and commercial, designed for mass consumption. The founders were convinced, as first president Russell B. Nye stated, that this vast body of material encompassed in print, film, television, comics, advertising, graphics, and other media "reflects the values, convictions, and patterns of thought and feeling generally dispersed through and approved by American society."[3] Scientific and scholarly organizations concerned with communication and media extend that investigation beyond the borders of the United States.

Communications Policy Research

Mass-mediated culture warrants investigation by applied research aimed at policy considerations as well as by pure research aimed at accurate understanding. As communications technology and the geographical spread of its popular cultural content have increased exponentially, the permissible distance between research investigations and policy decisions has been reduced. Research and education share in the responsibility for informed decision making by governments, corporations, and individuals.

Policy research accepts the reality of normative questions about structures, effects, and alternatives in popular arts, media, and communication systems. The accumulation of empirical data and the application of sustained critical inquiry offer indispensable guidance for understanding, projecting, and directing the impact of developments in cable television, international satellites, political use of media, communication and national development, economic support systems, public access, and other complex areas of media and culture. Ithiel de Sola Pool emphasizes the value of such inherently multidisciplinary research. Previous media research informed middle-level decisions about which programs to offer and how to persuade audiences; it seldom entered into fundamental decisions about what the communication system should be. "More enlightenment in the making of such decisions can only help," according to Pool.[4]

Douglass Cater has also argued the need for communications policy research on an expanded scale. He warns that George Orwell's *1984* approaches rapidly with its all-pervasive communication environment controlled by an exploitative elite. He cites five reasons for the inadequate attention to the use of communications for the public good:

1. Our commercial enterprises spend vast funds to develop the hardware of the new technologies while software enterprise languishes, incapable even of exploiting the potential of the old technology.
2. Universities with few exceptions treat communications as a second-class discipline unworthy of the best scholarship.
3. Research institutes for communications are usually dominated by experts of the harder sciences, not recognizing that humanistic disciplines—law, philosophy, political science—have a vital role to perform in this area.
4. Foundations have been reluctant to invest in communications research on a scale commensurate with their activities in other critical social problem areas, such as schooling, health, and ecology.
5. Government has made a belated start to coordinate telecommunications policy, a development that in the absence of countervailing institutions could compound our Orwellian dilemma.[5]

The problem affects not only public policy but also individual lives. Private citizens, especially in the absence of clear leadership from corporate, governmental, and educational bodies, constantly face complex "policy decisions" in their own use of mass-mediated culture. Communications policy research can improve the "micro" personal level of the consumer as well as the "macro" public level of institutions.

Cultural Studies

"Cultural studies" at first blush appears an awkward and nebulous label for human activity. The power of this label, however, is that it offers a bridge between the confines of social science on the one hand and the arts and humanities on the other. It also lifts communication study above the contrasting limitations that have been placed on it in the United States and Europe. James Carey and Raymond Williams have outlined the nature of cultural studies.

Carey notes the gap between European and North American approaches to communication. His observations recall James Halloran's remark that Continental studies of communication are 90 percent philosophical introduction and 10 percent data, while Anglo-American studies are proportioned oppositely.[6]

American studies are grounded in a transmission or transportation view of communication. They see communication, therefore, as a process of transmitting messages at a distance for the purpose of control. The archetypal case of communication then is persuasion, attitude change, behavior modification, socialization through the transmission of information, influence, or conditioning.

By contrast, the preponderant view of communication in European studies is a ritual view of communication: communication is viewed as a process through which a shared culture is created, modified, and transformed. The archetypal case of communication is ritual and mythology, for those who come at the problem from anthropology; art and literature, for those who come at the problem from literary criticism and history. A ritual view of communication is not directed toward the extension of messages in space, but the maintenance of society in time . . . : not the act of imparting information or influence, but the creation, representation, and celebration of shared beliefs.[7]

Carey proposes cultural studies as a means to move beyond the American emphasis on studying the precise psychological and sociological conditions under which persuasion occurs. The behavioral and attitudinal focus thus widens to an investigation of specific expressive forms of culture—art, ritual, journalism, etc. Cultural studies also consider "the relation of these forms to social order, the historical transformation of these forms, their entrance into a subjective world of meaning and significance, the interrelations among them, and their role in creating a general culture—a way of life and a pattern of significance. . . ."[8] To deal with these matters, Carey prescribes neither a behavioral science aimed at the elucidation of laws nor a formal science aimed at the elucidation of structures. He prefers a cultural science whose objective is the elucidation of meaning. Thus, cultural studies have modest objectives:

It does not seek to explain human behavior, but to understand it. It does not seek to reduce human action to underlying causes and structures, but to interpret its significance. It does not attempt to predict human behavior, but to diagnose human meanings. It is, more positively, an attempt to bypass the rather abstracted empiricism of behavioral studies and the ethereal apparatus of formal theories and to descend deeper into the empirical world . . . attempting to be truer to human nature and experience as it ordinarily is encountered.[9]

The approach to mass-mediated culture in this book is that of "cultural studies." Neither the approach of American social science research on the transmission of messages nor the European humanities analysis of ritual is, in isolation, adequate to the subject of mass-mediated culture.

Problems in Scientific Perspectives. Some years back Jay W. Jensen diagnosed a malady in communications research that remains uncured. Assessing a sense of atrophy among communications researchers, Jensen pointed to an inordinate, uncritical attachment to scientism and positivism as the cause of the illness. Jensen's diagnosis explains why immense amounts of data and statistical analyses concerning mass media have revealed so little scientific understanding of contemporary mass-mediated culture.

The limited perspectives of scientism and positivism have restricted both the investigative methodology and the theoretical conclusions of communications research, as well as much of social science in general. By *scientism* Jensen means

> ... the parochial view according to which the primary, if not the sole, aim of science is prediction and control by means of experimental techniques, and according to which scientific method is restricted to operations whereby phenomena, including the social and the cultural, are reduced to observable, measurable and quantifiable physical entities. Thus, in the social sciences (and in communications research) I associate this perspective with experimentalism, mechanism, atomism, physicalism and behaviorism.[10]

Compounding that reductionist mistake, *positivism* is defined by Jensen as

> ... the radically restrictive conception of reality as simply the product of the knowing subjects, and the concomitant theory of knowledge which admits to investigation only what may be immediately apprehended in sense experience.... Thus, in the social sciences (and in communication research) I associate this perspective with psychologism, subjectivism, sensationalism, operationalism and relativism (among others).[11]

One debilitating result of scientism and positivism is that sociocultural reality is presumed to be atomistically structured and is approached with "value-free," quantitative procedures that in avoiding normative judgments also eliminate logical deduction. As a corrective measure, Jensen prescribes that symbols, sets of symbols, and sociocultural reality must be accepted as objective data, freeing them from their *scientistic* enslavement to individual perceptions and atomistic behavioral effects. More generally, the concept of science and research must be rectified: "No number of statistical correlations, however many and precise, can ever constitute a body of genuine knowledge."[12] Jensen's conclusion calls for a radical shift in perspective for American approaches to mass media in society:

> What seems reasonable, therefore, to prescribe for the malady afflicting communications research is a heavy dose of the doctrine which defines science as a theoretical body of knowledge grounded in system, order and generality, and of the conception of reality which postulates an objective existence for socio-cultural phenomena, in some sense independent of the sensory experience of knowing subjects.[13]

Only such a step can open up the kinds of problems that may legitimately be investigated, the range of conceptualization, and the significance of results concerning the subject of mass-mediated culture.

Limitations on Approaches from the Arts. Raymond Williams has argued the same case as Carey, the need for "cultural studies." The approach to culture from communications must include a concern not only with processes and technologies but also with an aesthetic analysis of artifacts and practices as well as social analysis of institutions. In developing this position, Williams specified inadequacies in approaches to contemporary cultural practice on the part of aesthetic analysis from the arts and humanities.

Williams notes that many disciplines are well developed for dealing with expressions from the past in the form of "poems, paintings, buildings, songs, novels, films, symphonies, newspapers, advertisements, political speeches; styles of dress; a whole range of cultural practice which may be separated as artifacts for more specific study."[14] But the emphasis on artifacts from the past does not absolve disciplines from investigating comparable practices in their own time. In the study of literature at Oxford, there was for many years a classical time-stop at 1830. Such cultural studies are confined by the principle, "[A] practice has to become an artifact, and moreover an artifact of the kind that is conventionally found in libraries and museums, to deserve much attention."[15] For example, literary study, from an original concern with discourse in writing and speech since the time of the Renaissance gradually "had been specialized and even restricted to printed imaginative compositions of a certain quality . . . written in the past."[16] In addition to these historicist and elitist assumptions, the arts and humanities lacked the social methodology to undertake communication impact studies and the study of social institutions: "The great or at least large institutions of modern communications need intensive and continuous study."[17]

Cultural studies, then, for Williams, constitute an area of overlap utilizing both the specifically aesthetic and the specifically social methods of study while filling in inadequacies in each. He notes, "What the practice of aesthetic analysis contributed was a capacity for sustained and detailed analysis of actual cultural works." For matters beyond that of cultural and social generalization, other disciplines act as a check and an incentive: "The study of cultural institutions or of cultural effects could not properly be pursued by projected aesthetic analysis."[18]

Text and Context. The study of communication, especially communications research, has generally been approached as a social science. Widening attention from communication to cultural studies shifts the balance toward the humanities. Carey defines this concept of cultural studies:

> A cultural science of communication then views human behavior, or more accurately human action, as a text. Our task is to construct a "reading" of the text. The text itself is a sequence of symbols—speech, writing, gesture—that contain interpretations. Our task, like that of a literary critic, is to interpret the interpretations.[19]

The metaphor of a text brings cultural science closer to literary criticism and scriptural scholarship than to behavioral science.

Cultural studies are freer than behavioral studies to place a high priority on the symbolic and creative capacity of humans: "The achievement of the human mind and its extension in culture—though it is as much an abject necessity as an achievement—is the creation of a wide variety of cultural forms through which reality can be created."[20] Carey's final remarks contain important methodological and theoretical implications. The "old model" of human thought was overly dominated by a simplistic, even imperialist, notion of the role and power of science. Carey writes

> Human thought does not consist in the production of irrefragable maps of the objective world [science] and error-filled sketches of a mystic reality. Human thought, on the new model, is seen more as interpretations men apply to experience, constructions of widely varying systems of meanings, whose verification cannot be exhausted by the methods of science. What men create is not just one reality, but multiple realities. Reality cannot be exhausted by any one symbolic form be it scientific, religious, or aesthetic. . . .
>
>   The task remains the same: to sieze upon the interpretations people place on existence and to systematize them so they are more readily available to us. This is a process of making large claims from small matters: studying particular rituals, poems, plays, conversations, songs, dances, theories, and myths and gingerly reaching out to the full relations within a culture or a total way of life.[21]

Carey sees the question raised by popular culture as a simple but profound one:

> What is the significance of living in the world of meanings conveyed by popular art? what is the relationship between the meanings found in popular art and in forms such as science, religion, and ordinary speech? how in modern times, is experience cast up, interpreted, and congealed into knowledge and understanding?
>
>   The remarkable work of Clifford Geertz . . . [and] Europeans working in phenomenology, hermeneutics, and literary criticism, has served to clarify the objectives of a cultural science of communications and has

defined the dimensions of an interpretive science of soicety. The task now for students of communications or mass communications or, as the British prefer, contemporary culture, is to turn these advances in the science of culture toward the characteristic products of contemporary life: news stories, bureaucratic language, love songs, political rhetoric, daytime serials, scientific reports, television drama, talk shows, and the wider world of contemporary leisure, ritual, and information.[22]

The purpose of identifying "cultural studies" is to locate, academically and humanly, the place of study of mass-mediated culture. In addition, designating the scope and role of cultural studies helps to legitimize the serious significance of a converging set of fields: communications, popular culture, ethnic studies, American studies, contemporary culture, and similar stepchildren and orphans of traditional academic disciplines. Cultural studies provide a conceptual framework that links these fields together and creates a generic home for them. As traditional specializations encounter difficulty in achieving the multidisciplinary scope necessary for dealing with numerous real-world problems, even the administratively convenient separation of the social and behavioral sciences from the humanities and arts must be transcended both methodologically and theoretically.

Lessons of the Case Studies

The text of cultural studies is human action and symbols broadly conceived; the context is the set of historical and institutional arrangements that structure action and symbols in a particular way in a given society. The result of studying the texts and contexts of cultural expression may incline toward the European emphasis on *significant* research more than toward the Anglo-American emphasis on *precision* in research. It is difficult to have it both ways: Dealing with important questions in their full complexity requires substantially different intellectual operations than does narrowing research questions down to precise, manageable subdivisions that may in themselves be of little significance.

In the case studies in this book the *text* has been conceived as the full communication process of sender, message, code, medium, receiver, and feedback or effect. The *context*, except for the Aymara non-Western point of contrast, has been the historical and cultural tradition of the West and the political economy of the advanced industrial states. The remainder of this final chapter concerns generalizations that have emerged from these analyses.

Methodological procedures and theoretical explanations varied in the case studies according to the subject matter of each.

Data on the Disney universe was gathered through a *consumer survey* and was interpreted through an analogy with morality plays. The study approached Disney typologically, assuming that the utopian and multimedia dimensions of Disneyland would provide a prototype of the internal landscape and semiotic significance of the Disney universe of semantic meaning. The study identified, among other evidence, virtues approved by Disney productions as means to "happiness." Further indications of Disney values and ideology suggested an ethnocentric insensitivity especially toward Third World peoples, an ahistorical selectivity in idealizing the American past and the technological future, and more subtle presentation and reinforcement of a North American, capitalistic worldview and motivational structure. Despite these aesthetic and ideological limitations, sixty years of Disney "imagineering" has opened the potential of imagination, fun, nature, and optimism to hundreds of millions throughout the world.

The study of the annual Super Bowl assessed the textual data of the telecast in the light of theories of traditional *mythic rituals and symbols*. Using the spectacle as a cultural indicator, the study found evidence of an American cultural preference for complex, technological, violent competition for property and monetary rewards. For some 80 million viewers, the telecast offered an opportunity for personal identification with a live drama, a projection of heroic archetypes, an occasion for coming together with increased social cohesion, a set of markings for self-identification and activity in space and time, and a coordinated series of mechanisms regulating aspects of the larger ecological system.

The method of *genre and formula analysis* was applied to "Marcus Welby, M.D.," and the overall televised picture of health and health care. From the dramatic conventions emerged a view of health care in which fatherly concern and personal attention abound, bureaucracies and mechanical depersonalization do not exist, and every patient receives the best that money can buy. The medical genre tends to compensate for medical reality at least as much as it reflects it. Generally, research indicates that explicit information on health care is not often available on television and is more than offset by unhealthy practices promoted by advertising.

Concepts from *propaganda theory* explained how Nixon's generously financed and professionally engineered CRP campaign in 1972 persuaded American voters. The persuasion campaign drew on concentrations of economic and political power to capitalize on prepropaganda, control the agenda, orchestrate media coverage, convey negative images and subvert opponents, protect covert sources, separate image from substance, manipulate artificially created wants, and pollute accurate information necessary for the self-determination of peoples. In the name of preserving the republic and the free-enterprise system, the campaign exemplified the cynical manipulation of consciousness possible within the context of a mass-mediated culture.

Ethnographic description and exegetical analysis identified Billy Graham's combination of religion and media. His professional use of media gave evidence of spreading a message of Calvinist puritanism and capitalist individualism. In the absence of critical self-consciousness, especially in political and economic matters, Graham's gospel tends to be ethnocentric and nationalistic as well as Christocentric and scriptural. He and his counterparts in popular mass-mediated religion salve the alienation of millions and preserve the established social hierarchy.

Fiesta rituals among the Aymara Indians of the Peruvian Andes occasioned the use of *cross-cultural comparative method and theory* in popular culture. The ancient Aymara cultural heritage contrasts with Western, capitalist, caucasian, technological, industrial culture. Market-day festivals are marked by aural, personal communication, without the assistance or intrusion of modern media and institutions. The value structure of this agricultural society and its folk-healers contrasts with the "CWAWMP" values of Charles Bronson's and others' movies and mass marketing, reflecting larger international power struggles.

The communication emphasis in the study of each case is classified in Figure 8–1.

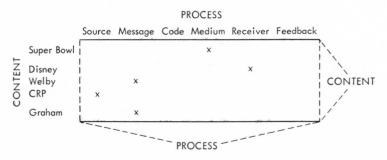

FIGURE 8–1 Communication Emphasis in Case Studies

Each X designates the area of primary focus in each case study. A number of small x's could be inserted in virtually every location on the grid to indicate at least a secondary interest in each stage of the process throughout every case study. The differing primary emphasis (X) was chosen to ensure a feeling for the major steps in the entire process, rather than to focus on only one stage such as "message" in all the case studies.

The *systemic* dimension of mass-mediated culture begins to appear in the areas of overlap between individual case studies. For example, teams in the Super Bowl have religious chaplains and include many members of the Fellowship of Christian Athletes, reflecting a Billy Graham type of popular religious orientation.[23] Presidents Nixon and Ford followed the Super Bowl avidly, and the 1972 CRP campaign included appearances by Nixon with Billy Graham. Graham's southern California crusades are held near Disneyland, and his youth committees canvas the park, although Graham's personal visits to the park have been frustrated by crowd recognition.[24] Nixon is prominent in the Disneyland film and displays of the Walt Disney Story on Main Street, U.S.A. Indirect connections between the case studies are almost infinite. For example, in 1969 Governor Ronald Reagan of California delivered a welcoming address at Graham's southern California crusade[25] and lobbied for Disney's Mineral King ski resort to repay Walt Disney's past support for Reagan, Murphy, Goldwater, and other conservative Republicans.[26]

Other generalized patterns emerge from the parallels in the case studies. On the positive side, Disney, Graham, Nixon, and Super Bowl coaches reveal certain common characteristics. First, each is generally a *perfectionist*, maintaining close quality control over diverse aspects of their far-flung operations; they ensure that *their* goals dominate even when they personally have little to do with most of the enterprises associated with their name. Second, each is a master at estimating the *average preferences* of the vast middle range of the population; Disney and Graham in fact seem to achieve a maximum personal identification with that average intelligence, imagination, and taste. Third, each accepts and perhaps needs the *feeling of importance* and power that comes from knowing he is providing a point of personal identity and social cohesion for many millions of persons. On the less impressive flip side of the case studies have emerged the recurring examples of (a) authoritarianism, (b) ethnocentrism, and (c) ahistorical nationalism.

The recurring generalized features of the case studies move the analysis of mass-mediated culture a step closer to inclusive theoretical, scientific formulations. Guided by the empirical data but not confined to them, the inductive process moves from concrete facts to generalized principles. As the problems become more abstract, deductive solutions become possible. What can be said of mass-mediated culture that will apply not only to a few cases but to the central features of the varied expressions of contemporary culture transmitted by mass communications?

Characteristics of Contemporary Mass-Mediated Culture

There is difficulty and danger in attempting a brief summary of characteristics of contemporary mass-mediated culture. Characteristics found in some media like television or certain genres like science fiction may not be present in other media like specialized periodicals or other genres like news reporting. Marketing systems such as United States commercial television may differ substantially from noncommercial systems such as those in Eastern Europe or partially commercial arrangements such as the Public Broadcasting System. The variety of media involved and the plethora of genres prevent many generalizations. Very few of today's observed arrangements are *necessary* outcomes of either modern media or contemporary culture.

Nevertheless, by a kind of averaging process, an investigation of expressions and underlying structures makes possible specific generalizations that apply to mass-mediated culture especially in the United States, generally in Western Europe and Japan, in certain respects in Eastern Europe and the Soviet Union, increasingly in areas of the Third World where American and European influence is felt, and generally everywhere in the world except where modern technology is totally absent or where liberation movements have taken culture and media technology in a different direction.

A first set of generalizations clears away widespread misconceptions about contemporary mass-mediated culture—myths and misrepresentations that have sometimes been fostered by the media industries themselves.

Misrepresentations

It is inexpensive, even "free."

In both economic and social cost, contemporary mass-mediated culture is anything but free. Movie theater owners' efforts to suppress *direct* pay television by plastering theater lobbies with posters declaring "Save Free Television" illustrate the double talk. Television is paid for by advertising that may constitute anywhere from 5 to 50 percent of the price of goods and services. A consumer may pay more to support television and radio programs that he or she never follows and newspapers and periodicals he or she never reads through the indirect support system of advertising than he or she pays in taxes for schools, highways, police, and other services. The United States television industry requires $50 to $60 billion in consumer outlay,[27] a generally hidden price tag that indicates a part of the economic cost of mass-mediated culture to the consuming culture. The social cost to the overall sociocultural system is perhaps even greater by virtue of the vast resources devoted to and the tremendous effects resulting from contemporary mass-mediated culture.

It has no effect.

The media industries have variously attempted to spread the myth that their offerings, especially entertainment, have no tangible influence over individuals or society. The Surgeon General's three-year, multimillion-dollar study of the effects of televised violence on children's social behavior became in the early 1970s a microcosmic battleground for this issue. By censoring out certain researchers, dominating the editing of the findings, and arguing against any public action, the television industry, through network representatives, greatly watered down but could not quite kill the conclusion that television does indeed influence human behavior.[28] It was the same struggle against accountability that broadcasting has waged since the airwaves were first defined as *public* not private property in 1927 and the "hypodermic needle" image of direct automatic media influence received serious consideration. Clare Booth Luce once summarized the scientifically defensible charges against the media. While her late husband Henry Luce had been one of the most powerful print media barons and hardly an angel, she fastened her scorn on television:

> TV has done the most disgraceful cop-out in our history. Television is a school for criminals, an academy of murder, rape and violence. The greatest educational medium known to man has taken the absurd position that books, plays, movies and drama have no power to educate for evil, but only for good. They fall back on the most disgraceful excuse of all: this is what the people want. Such hypocrisy! How dare they be so high and mighty on the one hand, acting as if they were responsible for the moral authority in the White House, and yet say they have no responsibility for what they put on the air![29]

The pervasiveness of media is so great in everyday life that the burden of proof has shifted in the opposite direction: Can it be proved that media do *not* influence society and behavior? Beyond the micro studies of experimental behaviorism, macro cultural studies point out the long-range and large-scale effects of establishing the dominant symbolic configurations in the minds and imaginations of entire societies, providing either constructive or destructive understandings of and approaches to violence, sexuality, personal identity, the family, work, the public agenda, and every other personal and/or public issue. Even the home and the school system have been partially replaced as socializing agents by mass media. Yet media managers decry public and governmental "interference" with their freedom from accountability even as a generation is reared by Walt Disney, Billy Graham, Howard Cosell, Marcus Welby, Patrick Buchanan, Benjamin Spock, Jacqueline Suzanne, Walter Cronkite, comic books, fashion and auto magazines, disc jockeys, rock groups, used-car salesmen, and the thousand and one other sensible and sensational media creations that populate their every waking minute. Precise media effects may be complex or subtle, but to deny media influence in general is to bury one's head in the sand.

It is strictly democratic.

Contemporary mass-mediated culture has a democratic, egalitarian aspect in that individuals have certain choices and that widely popular presentations are offered and survive. However, as has often been pointed out, the range of offerings is limited by precedent and finance, audiences are conditioned by what they have been exposed to, and the underlying structure of commercial media ensures that no interests alien to or deviant from their own will long survive no matter how much the public may naturally be attracted.

Mass-mediated culture could be democratic only if the political-economic infrastructure were democratic. Because media decisions are based on the ability to pay rather than on direct voting, considerations other than what the entire public might democratically prefer are prominent. The media marketing system is heavily authoritarian, as the concentration of ownership in newspapers[30] and other media baronies[31] indicates. The controlling interests in media, which limit production and publication in a variety of ways, reflect the pyramidal structure of the American political economy with a small controlling elite perched on top. Media are owned and controlled by executives responsible to stockholders; less than 15 percent of Americans own stock of any kind.[32] Roughly two hundred corporations own two-thirds of all manufacturing assets in the United States. Less than 2 percent of the American people own stock in these corporations.[33] According to the Lampman report, less than 1 percent of the population owns almost half the corporate stock in the country.[34] Income is equally maldistributed. Some top corporate executives earn over $800,000 per year in salary alone while 79 percent of American family incomes, almost four out of five, are under $15,000.[35] This oligarchic economic pyramid is protected and strengthened by mass-mediated culture.

It is balanced, objective, multicultural, and open.

The recurrence of ethnocentrism and nationalism in the case studies of Disney, Graham, the Super Bowl, and the others brings into question any inclusive, egalitarian claims that mass-mediated culture might make. Generally, contemporary media offerings are managed by and represent the cultural orientations of capitalist, Western, adult, white, male, print-oriented persons. The method which Ellul calls *la technique* represents the single skill of multinational corporate leadership and management techniques. Both the organization and content of mass-mediated culture reflect that orientation away from humanism, creativity, spontaneity, and pluralism, and toward efficiently designed and measured ledger-book results.

Embarrassing examples abound: the treatment of Native Americans in westerns; the stereotyping of American blacks in radio, film, and television entertainment; the portrayal of Japanese and other Asians in war movies; the images of traditional societies of Africa and other Third World countries in all media including novels; the pictures of Russians and other Communists in Cold War propaganda; the stereotypes of women in movies and commercials; and the idolatry of youth and the trivialization of old age in marketing campaigns.

The point is not that mass-mediated culture is narrower or worse than other systems of culture but merely that it represents, as do all others, one particular extreme of culture, as noted in the previous chapter. This would pose no problem were mass-mediated culture merely one expression among many. But it is becoming omnipresent and victorious over alternatives—more through aggressive power than intrinsic merit. The choice for minority groups and less-developed countries becomes assimilation or ostracism. Roughly 16 of the more than 400 black-oriented radio stations in the United States are black owned.[36] Thus, the black population in the United States, perhaps 15 percent of the total, owns only about 4 percent of the *black*-oriented stations and perhaps .2 percent of all radio stations. Yet, when blacks and other under-represented groups petition the Federal Communications Commission and others for *access* to communications, they are rebuffed and told that normal procedures are adequate correctives. Bill Moyers, former press secretary to Lyndon Johnson, has remarked that of all the myths of American news journalism, "objectivity" is the greatest. Mass-mediated culture as a whole is no less partial.

Through individual manipulation it regresses from previous higher culture.

Although a few critics have tried, they have failed to substantiate the argument that contemporary mass-mediated culture is the first, only, or worst expression of low culture. As David Manning White insists, previous cultures, including the most classical, have had their bear-baiting and other cruelties, their bacchanalia and other debaucheries, their coliseums and other spectacles.[37] The media may succumb to sensationalism in pandering to profit, but only conservative literary elitism and neo-primitivism look for a less spoiled past as a model.

While individual manipulators may express and implement the exploitative potential of the system, the causal source of most contradictions and exploitation lies in the structure—the narrow economic priorities dictated by the political economy of capitalism or the bureaucratic centralism of state socialism. Attacks on individuals and their decisions miss the infrastructural roots of the problems.

It is unimprovable.

Two opposite positions tend toward a static, immobile stance in regard to contemporary mass-mediated culture. The proponent of the current system may elevate present achievements into an iconic endpoint of human accomplishment that can be improved only quantitatively. At the contrary extreme, the cynical opponent of the status quo may conclude that the evil and manipulation of the system are so great that nothing can be done. Neither has penetrated the possibilities.

In a yin-and-yang manner, there are overlapping negative and positive aspects to every example of mass-mediated culture. Within the current context of mass-mediated culture, increased *critical consciousness* of the nature and effects of trends in politics, advertising, and other areas can remove persons from the treadmill, increase productive potential, and diminish destructive tendencies. For the system as a whole, optimism becomes *historical* not *individual*; that is, even if one may not reap the full rewards of major changes immediately and personally, those historical improvements are possible and virtually inevitable over a long enough period of time. A few of these possibilities are suggested later in this chapter.

Principles

Beyond the common misrepresentations described above, mass-mediated culture does exhibit certain universal characteristics. These can be called "principles"—not necessarily in the sense of generative causal sources but in a more descriptive sense. These principles are essential constituents that are always present and operative as axioms or rules in any expression of contemporary mass-mediated culture. They may be summarized as the principles of *symmetry, choice,* and *utility.*

Symmetry. The Disney and other studies confirmed hypotheses that media reflect the political economy, channel popular tastes, and cause individual and social effects. Mass media and popular culture tend to "typify" the dominant ideology. In a general systems perspective, these hypotheses mean that there is symmetry or homology between mass-mediated culture and the larger social whole of which it is a part. The dominant, peculiar contours and tendencies of either one will be found in the other. The concept of symmetry implies that neither exclusively causes the other but that causality runs in both directions. The social

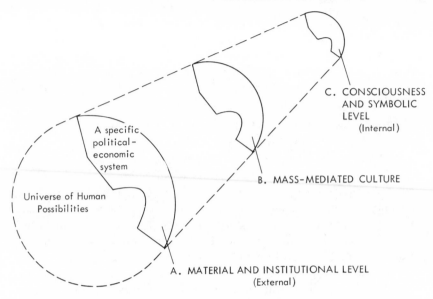

C. CONSCIOUSNESS
AND SYMBOLIC
LEVEL
(Internal)

A specific
political –
economic
system

B. MASS–MEDIATED CULTURE

Universe of Human
Possibilities

A. MATERIAL AND INSTITUTIONAL LEVEL
(External)

FIGURE 8–2   Principle of Symmetry

system facilitates the expression of certain forms of mass-mediated culture that in turn strengthen and reinforce the system.

The principle of symmetry includes the notion that media exercise hegemony and social control over members. There is a diversity of expressions of culture, but a *limited* diversity. The dominant characteristics of the social system act as a choice-restricting mechanism for individuals and society. On the other hand, new infusions into mass-mediated culture such as counter-cultures and alternative life-styles may gradually modify aspects of the overall system.

Identifiable societies, by definition, have a "central zone," and membership in society consists of relationships with the central zone. The central zone is the center of the order of symbols, values, and beliefs that govern the society. The center is ultimate and irreducible. It is to that central zone, structured in a political economy and reified in an ideology, that the principle of symmetry points us. The common elements running through Disney, Graham, the Super Bowl, and the rest reveal the central zone of contemporary mass-mediated culture. Malinowski speaks of the "principle of totality" in a culture: "It is a tenet of belief embodied in institutions or traditional texts, and formulated by the unanimous opinion of all competent informants."[38] A symmetry also exists between the central zone of the social system and the totality of its mass-mediated culture. *Achievement,* from Billy Graham's individualism to the Super Bowl's organization men; *optimism,* from Disney's Pollyanna and wishing upon a star to Welby's medical and emotional cures; *ethnocentrism*, in Disney, Graham, Hollywood, and prime-time portrayals of nonwhite and/or remote peoples; *economic profit* from Nixon's protection of corporate interests to Graham's promises of earthly rewards; and many other characteristics selected out of democratic and capitalist traditions reveal the central zone of contemporary mass-mediated character.

Choice. From the limited diversity available in any system of mass-mediated culture, every consumer makes personal choices. By making goal-seeking, personal choices—not, of course, free from social influence—individuals selectively expose themselves to specific expressions of mass-mediated culture. Given a choice of various keys, rhythms, and melodies, they play their own tunes. The exact relationship between the macro transmissions and the micro receptions is complex, but it would be misleading not to emphasize that individuals and groups create their own unique combination out of the range of offerings of mass-mediated culture.

The principle of choice does not contradict the principle of symmetry. The larger system limits the choices, and only within those choices does the individual exercise liberty. For example, it is difficult in many parts of the country to receive good black jazz on the radio, even though that tradition has historically been perhaps the most fertile creative source in American music. Ironically jazz, both black and white, is easier to hear overseas where the Voice of America and Armed Forces broadcasts transmit it for propaganda purposes as America's unique contribution to world music. At home it is not economically profitable enough to be widely aired.

Each choice is made from at least two categories. A choice of media can be made from among television, radio, film, newspapers, magazines, books, comics, and others means of audio, visual, or combined delivery systems. A choice of genre may draw from westerns, comedy, science, history, politics or news-documentary, detective-fiction, love and romance,

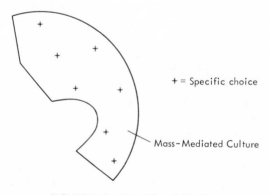

FIGURE 8–3 Principle of Choice

religion, sports, or other conventional formats. The principle of choice means simply that the individual selects his or her preferences from among the real but limited variety of offerings presented by mass-mediated cultural systems.

Utility. For both the individual and the social system, the selection of specific expressions of mass-mediated culture is made for utilitarian purposes. The usefulness of culture to its producers tends to be calculated in monetary terms. Consumer motives vary.

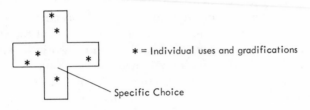

FIGURE 8–4   Principle of Utility

This principle of utility can be observed in traditional considerations about *leisure*. While normative discussions of leisure tend to reflect elite-class biases and the Western tradition of rational individualism and self-improvement (the Greek word for leisure was *scholé*, from which we get "school"), the activities with which people actually fill their leisure time and the uses those activities serve do not generally fulfill the goals of classical philosophies of leisure from the Greeks to the present. Leisure is undertaken not as work for a deferred reward, but *in se pro me*. The uses of leisure exemplified in selections of mass-mediated culture range from learning to escaping, from insight to conformity, from enjoyment for its own sake to searching for instruments with which to cope with daily problems. The usefulness of mass-mediated culture might be described as *educational*, not in the tedious manner of school systems, but in the imaginative, rhythmic manner of the lessons of myths and rituals among nonliterate peoples.

The utilitarian purposes that mass-mediated culture serves could be categorized in a variety of ways. Below is a discussion of a somewhat random list of what it provides as uses or purposes.

Purposes of Mass-Mediated Culture

Consumership. Individuals use mass-mediated culture to learn to buy in general and to direct their selection. Pepsi jingles and McDonald arches are among the thousands of messages that contemporary consumers instantly recognize. Directly through advertising, and indirectly through the consuming life-styles proposed as models throughout the media, *consumers* learn to internalize socially desirable "virtues" of possessive individualism and conspicuous consumption.

Escape and Relaxation. The overt intent of many persons utilizing mass-mediated culture may be "to take a break," "to loaf and kill time," "to recuperate," and similar negative-sounding definitions. Viewing and participating in sports—mediated like the Super Bowl or unmediated like camping, hiking, skiing, and other recreational activities—often have no conscious ulterior motive. Individuals driven by the Calvinist or capitalist achievement ethic and the frenetic consumer ethic require opportunities and assistance to *do nothing.* That is one of the attractions of Transcendental Meditation and similar "anti-activities." The usefulness, then, of much irrelevant entertainment is that it allows the individual to laugh, fear, get angry, feel affections, or be bored without a feeling of any responsibility or an awareness of any consequences. Predictable entertainment tends to be attacked for its failure to challenge. However, it is precisely that quality that most appeals to large numbers of people. Perhaps they know, in ways yet unverified by science, what is best for them.

Identity. An individual's personal identity both grows from and finds reinforcement in expressions of mass-mediated culture. He or she may find identity in conforming to group norms proposed by the Mickey Mouse Club or Lawrence Welk or may be compensating for personal inadequacies by projecting his or her identity into an established star such as Robert Young or Roberta Flack. In each of the case studies, the element of personal identification between the receiver and the mass message was fundamental. Remove mass-mediated culture and you remove basic points of reference for the personal identity of billions.

Security. The examples of Disney, Graham, Welby, and Nixon have encouraged a feeling of security within individuals that life is not chaotic and someone is tending the shop. Similarly fascinating is the way television and movie crime fighting in "Kojak," "Hawaii Five-O," and Clint Eastwood and Charles Bronson movies compensate for the feelings of insecurity persons in urban centers experience in the face of rising crime rates and social disorder. Would faith in police, courts, justice, and other public institutions survive sufficiently to prevent social disintegration if fact rather than law-and-order fiction filled the public imagination?

Tradition. People also use mass-mediated culture to share in the tradition, literally the handing on, of their cultural heritage. For example, the song "City of New Orleans" has a tradition of its own and shares the larger tradition of railroad songs. Written by Steve Goodman, it tells of a ride from Chicago to New Orleans on the Illinois Central Railroad. Arlo Guthrie recorded the hit version that implanted the refrain in the repeating film loops of the human biocomputers of millions:

> Good morning, America, how are ya?
> Don't ya know me, I'm your native son.
> I'm the train they call the City of New Orleans.
> And I'll be gone 500 miles when the day is done.[39]

This song is a relatively miniscule example of the presence and power of tradition in mass-mediated culture. Multiply it by ten thousand and you have the anchoring in mass-mediated tradition of perhaps one person.

Formulas. Horace Newcomb identified numerous predictable patterns in *TV: The Most Popular Art.*[40] Formulas appear in situation and domestic comedies, westerns, romances, mysteries, doctor and lawyer programs, adventures, soap operas, sports, news, and documentaries. These formulas develop patterns of perceptions in the minds of viewers, which can be used for a variety of practical and fantasy purposes in daily life.

Frame. Erving Goffman's concept of *frame analysis*[41] is one of the many academic theories that can be converted to explain uses of media and popular culture. Mass media and the popular arts offer frames of reference, a grounding for experience, and a horizon or lens for viewing and interpreting everyday life.

A shift in "frame" distinguished *The Godfather* Parts I and II from earlier and subsequent mafia films by picturing organized crime as connected with businessmen, politicians, and policy makers, rather than as a criminal fringe. Disney and Graham, in different ways but with similar results, provide frames for interpretation and appreciation of experiences in everyday life. Not only in specific cases but in general, mass-mediated culture provides a frame of interpretation for world events, social conflict, and even private encounters.

Compensation. Individuals constantly use contemporary mass-mediated culture as *compensation* for loneliness, lost love, immobility, poverty, and similar frustrations. When *Earthquake, The Towering Inferno, Jaws,* and other disaster films became popular during the depression in the middle 1970s, Joyce Brothers stated the obvious:

> One of the main reasons that the shake and bake and devour movies are such a hit on the screen is that we all face so many major problems off the screen. By watching others suffer we drain off some of our own fears. The concern over food shortages, energy conservation, inflation and the pos-

sibility of being jobless all seem less threatening when compared with an earthquake that wipes out thousands or a shark that tears bodies to shreds.[42]

Cohesion. The Super Bowl illustrates how a mass-mediated event acts as a social focus bringing people together. Television programs, movies, popular songs, and other widespread media phenomena allow persons to converse and to share what on the surface appears trivial. The content is relatively secondary whether teenagers debate pop music or businessmen argue about sports. The purpose is the coming together, and without the shared culture—shared across many thousands of miles—there might be no icebreakers save those described by Ogden Nash: "Candy's dandy, but liquor's quicker."

Deviation and Innovation. Individuals use mass-mediated culture for learning about innovations such as new dance steps on television or new political movements through the mail. They also can find blessings of deviations from social norms. Mass-media recognition of phenomena such as massage parlors and pornographic books and films tends to institutionalize deviations from norms. By depicting deviations from the law and the public morality, mass-mediated culture becomes a testing ground for various innovative individual and social developments.

Physiology. It is possible that many expressions of popular culture condemned for their mindlessness may serve significant *biological purposes.* Western culture has been separated by millenia of Manicheanism, Calvinism, Jansenism, angelism, and puritanism from the direct experience and consciousness of one's own body. For persons lacking an appreciation of the physical, sensual, and material, the "below the waistline" quality of popular culture may be a positive breakthrough. For example, even when popular music ranges from insipid to idiotic in lyric content, its physiological dimensions may provide redeeming social value. Music can increase basic body rhythms by 25 percent, increase strength in controlled grip tests, and so move people that the Washington, D.C., police department outlawed group singing during the 1968 riots. Tom Turrichi has developed a method of physiologically monitoring responses to popular songs that has proved 92 percent accurate in predicting hits.[43] If Carlos Castaneda is correct in suggesting that people should "listen to their bodies" to understand and make decisions, perhaps the "mindlessness" of mass-mediated culture is one of its stronger assets.

Meaning and Coping. In mass-mediated culture, readers, listeners, and viewers find meanings behind experience and discover methods of coping with problems. Among the more obvious examples in music, raspy shouting or soaring violins can recall the focal possibility in life of human romance and love. Blues music carries people through tragedies and allows them to express their sadness and cope with daily life. On a more mundane level, advertisements aid in coping with dirty toilet bowls, sludge in the gas line, and smelly feet.

Dreams and Fantasy. The study of Disney illustrates how Disney encouraged respondents to develop their imaginations and, at the same time, channeled those imaginations along specific lines. Mass-mediated culture frees people to experience vicariously what they seldom or never approach personally.

The daytime television serials, the "soap opera" heirs of Ma Perkins, Just Plain Bill, and Our Gal Sunday, offer an amazing blend of fantasy and reality. They are standardized in setting, characters, and plots, almost addictive after a few exposures, and readily available everywhere. As a whole they provide an emotional catharsis, a vicarious experience of wealth, romance, and tragedy, and a fantasy life enough similar to and yet removed from the viewer's life to be both exciting and safe.[44]

Insight. Besides the practical moralizing in soap operas and elsewhere, mass-mediated culture does offer genuine moments of profound insight into the human experience. Ingmar Bergman films, for example, play on television as well as in theaters. Mass-mediated culture is by no means confined to cheap, superficial junk. Its offerings of symbols, images, rhythms, rituals, myths, and ideas can make widely available the best, the most subtle, and the most sophisticated of human perception and insights. In a technical world, the mass-media emphasis on basic experiences of love, morality, drama, and personal immediacy provide welcome and necessary relief from mechanical, depersonalized daily routines.

In summary, the expressions of mass-mediated culture are constrained by and reflect the priorities of the political-economic system (the principle of symmetry), they impinge on the receiver in a limited but bewildering variety of options (the principle of choice), and the individual, whether he or she could articulate the goals and purposes, selects out and enters into expressions that are useful to the individual in some way (the principle of utility).

Toward a Critical Theory

As Chapter 1 spelled out, mass-mediated culture can be evaluated from many perspectives. It can be viewed as healthy popular art expressive of the people or as a sorry bastardization of the achievements of elite art. However, only with great difficulty can standard liberal and conservative positions narrowly conceived account for both the heights and depths of popular mass-mediated culture. The principles of symmetry, choice, and utility partially explain the seeming contradictions by distinguishing between collective and individual levels of significance. Further penetration into the inadequacies and potential of media and culture is suggested by the tradition of critical theory.

At root, critical theory is skeptical of Platonic or atomistic conceptualizations of the role and source of art and media. It stresses instead the dialectic interaction between the internal symbolic level and the external material and institutional level of culture and expression. Critical theory insists that the outer circle in our diagram of human ecosystems from Chapter 1 (Figure 8–5) can never be omitted in assessing a work of art or exchange *in toto*.

What are the structural determinants of success and influence in mass-mediated culture? Internal creative genius is, of course, necessary for noteworthy productivity in any system. Beyond that, what separates

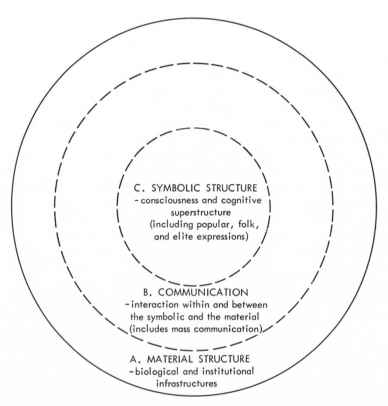

C. SYMBOLIC STRUCTURE
– consciousness and cognitive
superstructure
(including popular, folk,
and elite expressions)

B. COMMUNICATION
– interaction within and between
the symbolic and the material
(includes mass communication)

A. MATERIAL STRUCTURE
– biological and institutional
infrastructures

FIGURE 8–5 Human Ecosystems

successful from unsuccessful genius in contemporary mass-mediated culture? Why are Graham, Disney, Nixon, Welby, and the Super Bowl dominant expressions of popular culture? What is the nature of the political economy that causes these to be the most popular expressions of religion, education, politics, health, sports, and recreation throughout much of the Western world and elsewhere?

Certain details of each case study suggest a critical theory grounded in Marxist political economy. Why did media barons like Hearst and Luce, as well as other *nonreligious* political and economic leaders, place their blessings on Billy Graham thereby ensuring, if not that he would have continued international multimedia success, at least that he would encounter no powerful opposition to achieving that success? Was Disney's retreat from the innovations and occasionally unfettered creativity of the 1920s and 1930s to the cautious ethnocentrism, consumerism, and ahistorical xenophobia of the 1960s and 1970s the result of increased economic "realism" in a corporate economy that is more concerned with profit margins than creativity, spontaneity, or genuine happiness? Why did a law-and-order administration allegedly representing the silent majority of middle Americans indulge in well-financed, manipulative media practices and illegal activities? Why is the most popular annual spectacle in the United States a passive consumption of violent competition for property and payoffs?

There are, of course, positive aspects besides the above problems in each case study. There are also more thoroughly positive subjects that could be selected for examination as case studies. But, given those qualifications, the problem remains: Authoritarian, one-way representations of ethnocentrism, racism, nationalism, sexism, violence, exploitation, and manipulation consistently rise to the top in the current Western system of mass-mediated culture. Why? Is the cause intrinsic to human nature, or do the failings arise from less universal and changeless human arrangements? An answer requires an extended look at evolution, media, and industrial organization.

The Origins of Social Organization

As Aristotle noted, humans are social animals. Human social organization at once reflects and transcends its parallels in other animal species. Human social organization far surpasses that of other species in its complexity and subtlety, just as symbols surpass signs. "Signs" bear a one-to-one *physical* relation to the signified, as smoke is a sign of fire. "Symbols" are *arbitrarily* related to the signified, as the printed marks shaped to make "fire" are symbols of the physical event-object fire. Humans are immensely more sophisticated in their symbol-making and symbol-using abilities than are even the other high primates. Symbolic expression makes possible large, complex social organization and the achievements of human culture.

Social systems, as Darwin indicated, are adaptive mechanisms that facilitate basic life processes and that provide communication networks proscribing interaction and regulating relations between and within the biological and symbolic subsystems. Studies in ethology describe primate species as *centripetal*; When under stress their members flee toward rather than away from others of their species. In centripetal systems submissive gestures can transform stress situations into stable cohesion, thus creating rank ordering within the group. High rank is marked less by successful fighting than by the individual's ability to bind attention in the group. Certain groups, such as baboons and macaques, are dominated by the *antagonistic* interaction of fighting, while others, such as chimpanzees, achieve a *hedonistic* interaction in which auto-arousal can replace stimulation from the external environment and individuals can enjoy and seek contact with other members of the species. Primate societies thus evolve centripetal, hierachical, and cohesive social organizations that can sustain members through self-contained activity as well as interaction with the environment.[45]

With the development of speech among humans, a new level of communication, and therefore social interaction and organization, became possible. The human range of symbolic achievements gradually set humans off from the relative simplicity and limitations of primate social organization and behavior. Humankind's development of tools, agriculture, shelters, weaving, pottery, graphics, music, dance, and other "media" made its culture intriguingly complex and creative.

Media and History

Innis, McLuhan, Carpenter, and others sometimes labelled "technological determinists" have argued that changes in the dominant means of communication have caused the major shifts in the history of human culture from its beginnings. Five axioms summarize what is far more than a faddish "McLuhanacey" of "Mediolotry." The axioms are:

1. "Media" are any extensions of the human sensory apparatus including the range of tools, technology, and means of production as well as more narrowly defined communications media.

2. Media are more important than their content and messages, and changes in the dominant forms of media are the causal sources of all other major historical and cultural transformations.

3. Because media are extensions of the senses, changes in media alter the internal sensory balance between eye, ear, and the other organs.

4. Because media changes cause other changes, the dominant forms of media will dictate aesthetic preferences and forms of social, political, and economic structuring in society.

5. Intensive ("hot") media of high definition of a single sense call forth only low participation from the receiver; inclusive ("cool") media of low sensory definition invite a high degree of participation from the receiver, who must in a gestalt manner fill in gaps in the transmission.

Application of the axioms distinguishes three major historical epochs in the development of human communication—aural, print, and electronic. In the first era, nonliterate, aural peoples lived (and many still live) in collective mythic interaction with tribe and natural environment. The second era, print, began slowly with the development of pictographic, ideographic, and hieroglyphic notation. Phonetic writing, based not on visual images but on human vocalizations, facilitated a sequential, linear order in communications proceeding from the beginning of the line, page, and scroll or book and proceeding point by point to the end. The development of moveable type by Gutenberg created the first modern mass production of communications and greatly accelerated the historical changes initiated by ideographic and phonetic writing. Intellectual processes and social organization shifted from aural inclusive modes to sequential, linear, individualized forms. In the third era, electronic communication beginning with the telegraph and telephone reversed print's exclusive focus on the eye, lineality, and individualism. The now-emerging electronic era maintains elements of print culture but partially recovers aural, inclusive, in-depth modes from nonprint cultures. The eras can be roughly schematized as follows:

Era	Approximate Beginning Date
1. Aural nonliterate	4,000,000–400,000 B.C.
2. Print	
a. ideographic	3,300 B.C.
b. phonetic	900 B.C.
c. printing press	A.D. 1456
3. Electronic	A.D. 1844

A variety of intriguing speculation has emerged from this schema of media and history. The schema rejects the common model of unidirectional human development through primitive, archaic, historic, and modern periods in strict sequence. Its partially circular pattern parallels Marxist divisions of history into (a) neolithic precapitalist subsistence and barter, (b) capitalist development from mercantilism through global imperialism, and (c) revolutionary socialist and eventually communist society. However, McLuhan's media approach bypasses the Marxist emphasis on the organization and control (ownership) of the means of production (media), and it eliminates the needs for struggle in moving beyond the capitalist/print era. Despite these irreconcilable disagreements between Marxists and McLuhanists, there may well be a connection between *print* and *capitalism* in initiating private property, class structures, nation-states, European-based global empires, and separations between the West and the Third World.

Mass Technical Society

The resulting contemporary societies in which mass-mediated culture predominates reflect the structures of the print and capitalist eras. Jacques Ellul, as a social historian and philosopher, characterizes these societies and their media by their technical reasoning and bureaucratic organization.[46]

Ellul's organizing idea is *la technique*, the modern pursuit of unrelenting efficiency. Ellul describes the dominant spirit and method of society today as a technological bureaucratic style that has infused imaginations until all values are conceived in administrative terms. Through this lens Ellul views common understandings of authority, nationalism, community, information, entertainment, manipulation, propaganda, mass communications, and popular culture.

Mass societies held together by *la technique* and propaganda provide perfect conditions for the success of a Billy Graham, Walt Disney, "Marcus Welby," Richard Nixon, or the Super Bowl. In contrast to traditional societies, Ellul sees modern society as composed of isolated individuals who have been cast out of their traditional groupings and stranded as atoms and nuclear units. They are then processed into mass education, mass media, an average level of culture, and an average standard of living. The society is thus at the same time individual and mass. Individuals and organs of the state are interconnected by what Ellul calls "propaganda," a concept similar to what has here been labelled "mass-mediated culture."

Propaganda usually refers to means of altering or maintaining power ratios in a group by modifying or strengthening attitudes through the manipulation of symbols. Ellul prefers to go beyond such exclusively psychological definitions, however, by emphasizing in addition that propaganda is employed by an organized group to bring about the active or passive participation in its actions of a mass of individuals. Mass advertising, marketing, public relations, personality cults, and political persuasion create a thoroughly propagandized mass-mediated culture.

Ellul greatly expands the notion of propaganda beyond the stereotype of the political leader irrationally agitating for change. Beside obvious political propaganda, pervasive *sociological* propaganda such as entertainment presents group norms that establish a life-style. Beside agitation for change, *integration* propaganda molds individuals into the patterns of twentieth-century modernized culture. Beside a leader's vertical propaganda down to a crowd, *horizontal* propaganda from inside the group establishes norms through peer pressure. Beside the emotional appeals of irrational propaganda, *rational* propaganda overwhelms individuals and groups with selected knowledge, information, statistics, and figures.

Ellul's notion of propaganda is much more inclusive than the usual discussions of such techniques as stereotyping, labelling, selection, assertion, bandwagon, and use of authority. Ellul identifies modern propaganda systems in the United States, China, and the Soviet Union, as well as in Hitler's Germany. All are characterized by being *total*, involving the varieties of mass and interpersonal media; *continuing*, leaving no gaps and having no end; *organized*, orchestrated to bring individuals under physical influence by organizations; and aimed at *orthopraxy*, bringing conformity in action (praxis) not just ideas (doxis). The psychological effects of propaganda include providing heroes for the impotent, friends for the alienated, and simplified attitudes for the uncertain. The sociopolitical effects include the partitioning off of traditional groups from one another and the modification of individualistic self-determination.

Propaganda is not necessarily pernicious and, as a concept, is virtually interchangeable with mass-mediated culture. Human social organization, especially in the West, has evolved into a system held together by mass-mediated propaganda.

Critical theory probes beneath the mass technical society described by Ellul and identifies a consciousness industry that produces mass-mediated culture.

The Consciousness Industry

Industry. Whatever other talents may be employed within the media, decision making, and therefore ultimate priorities, rest in the hands of economic managers of the system that conveys the contemporary expressions of culture. In this sense, Disney, Graham, and other figures prominent in mass-mediated culture are visible in the superstructure, the tip of the iceberg, while the infrastructure remains largely unperceived. Running the show from off-stage, the media managers have one absolute criterion in decision making: corporate profit. Their assignment, stated baldly, is to maximize corporate profits by appealing to and, whenever necessary, manipulating the consciousness of what can only be called in this context the masses.

They manage the infrastructural base where capital is invested, programs or copy are produced, ratings and audiences are attracted, advertising and/or sales are increased, and profit is returned to the original sources of advertiser and media capital. Further, because mass-mediated culture is organized as an industry, it must be understood in *institutional* rather than personal terms.

Contemporary mass-mediated culture, especially in the United States, is at root an industry. Western commercial media systems are not primarily "political" as are media in, for example, the Soviet Union. They are also not primarily "aesthetic," despite important considerations of media as "art forms." Media managers and much of the other "talent" in the industry exhibit their preference for the economic over the political or aesthetic by reading periodicals and attending meetings that concern the technical business core of the industry rather than ideological, aesthetic, humanistic, or cultural matters.

The industrial organization of mass-mediated culture is frequently played down by referring to the consumer of culture as the "king" in the exchange. But there are no fixed points of reference for the consumer as there are in the case of material goods and tangible services. The industry trades in a slippery reality sometimes called consciousness.

Consciousness. The most obvious connection between industry and consciousness in mass-mediated culture is found in advertising. Images, associations, slogans, hopes, and occasionally even information are implanted in viewer, listener, or reader consciousness in such a way that future product selection will be influenced.

Critical theory emphasizes the primacy of material conditions but recognizes the importance of consciousness in accurately or falsely reflecting conditions and thereby providing for maintenance or change of material conditions. C. Wright Mills described this role:

> Between consciousness and existence stand communications, which influence such consciousness as men have of their existence. . . . The mass communication system of the United States is not autonomous: it reflects society, but selectively; it reinforces certain features by generalizing them, and out of its selections and reinforcements creates a world. Insofar as people live beyond their immediate range of contacts, it is in this world they must live.[47]

Hans Magnus Enzensberger describes the consciousness industry as "the mind-making industry":

> The mind industry's main business and concern is not to sell its product; it is to "sell" the existing order, to perpetuate the prevailing pattern of

man's domination by man, no matter who runs the society, and by what means. Its main task is to expand and train our consciousness—in order to exploit it.[48]

Enzensberger sees the individual effect as "the industrialization of the human mind," a concept similar to Jurgen Habermas's "scientization," a practice that in the name of avoiding ideology reifies science and technology into the ultimate ideology. Such manipulation creates a confused consciousness of political and economic conditions among "the depoliticized mass" and legitimizes current institutionalized power.

The cultural hegemony exercised by the consciousness industry results in what Dallas Smythe calls the homogenization of culture and standardization of tastes. The culture industry displaced "part or all of the various ethnic distinguishing characteristics from the culture of the peoples who went through the melting pot." Traditions that satisfied human needs for goods and services through heterogeneity, flexibility, and personalization were replaced by mass-produced "standardized, commercial services and products." All levels of culture were influenced. According to Smythe

... the effect of cultural industry is to standardize taste and to give it a commodity orientation. This standardization affects not only the taste of the moderate-income family which is the prototype consumer of the product of cultural industry; it also affects the taste for high culture by pre-empting artistic talent from that area, or by driving "high culture" into nihilistic and cynical alternatives to mass culture. And, inevitably, the standardization of cultural industry picks up and homogenizes such remnants or innovations of folk culture as are available to it. . . .[49]

In brief, mass-mediated culture provides cultural symbols from the consciousness industry, which symbols perform as a choice-restricting filter or screen in individual and group understandings of the concrete conditions of material life. The problem of *manipulation* remains paramount. A generation ago the father of cybernetics, Norbert Wiener, wrote

It is only in the large community, where the Lords of Things as They Are protect themselves from hunger by wealth, from public opinion by privacy and anonymity, from private criticism by the laws of libel and the possession of the means of communication, that ruthlessness can reach its most sublime levels. Of all the anti-homeostatic factors in society, the control of the means of communication is the most effective and the most important.[50]

Alienation in Daily Life

In currently organized systems of mass-mediated culture, motivation is maximized and threats to the system minimized by maintaining a consistently high but not chaotic level of "alienation" within and between individuals and groups. Overt repression becomes unnecessary.

Alienation and estrangement are the personal existential result of manipulative media and an exploitative political economic system. Camus's *The Stranger* provides a classic example of the existential experience. A wide variety of modern literary works, plays, films, and even popular music convey a similar empty, frustrated, or rebellious feeling, from Paul Simon's "Sounds of Silence" to Bob Dylan's "Ain't Gonna Work on Maggie's Farm No More," to Elton Johns's "Good-bye Yellow Brick Road." As dictated by institutional structures and priorities, daily life at work, school, and home expresses the subjective experience of alienation: individuals finding their interests in conflict and being left with loneliness and anxiety, a sense of normless anomie, vague or obvious desires to escape and flee, jealousy over the success or privileges or even aimlessness of others, helplessness over the impossibility of improving the quality of political or private life, and on and on and on.

Marxist critical theory places alienation within the grasp of humans to understand and resolve. Exclusively religious, psychological, philosophical, or positivist explanations generally end in pessimistic resignation to "man's unfortunate condition" by ascribing alienation to universal human nature and experience. Instead Marxism holds that, in the words of George Novack

> Alienation is the outgrowth of specific historical conditions which have been brought into existence by man's unwitting activity and which can be changed at a higher stage of economic and social development by man's conscious collective action.[51]

In Marxist theory, alienation is bred by capitalist organization of the means of production and the consequent alienation of wage labor in which the worker is separated from control over, and the product of, his own labor. The capitalist system then reproduces this condition of alienation on all levels of social existence. "Labor becomes alienated when the producer works, not directly for himself or a collective united by common interests, but for another with interests and aims opposed to his own."[52] Through progressive loss of the power of self-determination, workers become estranged from body, nature, individuality, and from fellow human beings. Schools, then, as feeders for industry, recreate these conditions and experiences. Homes and private life also feel the effect because they are expected to provide compensating personal satisfaction for job and school alienation.

Mass-mediated culture has come to play a curious dual role under the conditions of alienation. First, in its role of training consumers for nonrational consumption—the necessary corollary of nonrational production policies—the life-style and advertising conveyed by mass-mediated culture contribute to the condition of alienation. Second, in its role as a diversion and false resolver of the effects of alienation—the sedative functions of the vast wastelands of commercial entertainment and leisure —mass-mediated culture is expected to compensate for and mask the experience of alienation.

The effect of alienated culture on the human ability to enjoy and communicate is disastrous. The emphasis on nonrational consumption and then disposal of consumer goods, proposed by advertising as an end in itself and a means to everything, creates what Marx called a "commodity fetishism." The personal identity of the consumer shifts from what David Reisman labelled "inner-directed" to an other-directedness aimed not at personal relations but at commodities which then take on the qualities of a fetish. Besides creating ecological chaos, such consumerism threatens what previously was considered mental health. This and related alienating experiences lead to what Marx called *reification*, the tendency to transform relations between human beings into relations between things. Other persons become mere signs of achievement convenient for status and name dropping or objects to be consumed, as in the case of depersonalized sex partners. The ability to communicate openly and spontaneously is inhibited. The above trends are reinforced by the competitive individualism of the capitalist ethic, which defines one's individual and group self-interest as in conflict with those of everyone else. Not only business competitors but students, potentially allied minority groups, even members of the same family, become more alienated and lose the ability to communicate productively and to see the commonality of their interests by buying a definition of success that is inherently antagonistic and elitist. Mass-mediated culture not only uncritically distributes these dysfunctional social perceptions and tendencies; it vividly portrays and reinforces the results in televised violence, kinky pornography, addiction to alcohol and other drugs, family break-ups, and numerous other surface signs of the deeper pattern of alienation and social disorder.

Viewed in this perspective, more substantial explanations of the motives of consumers of mass-mediated culture become possible. The follower of Billy Graham and popular religion experiences daily alienation and seeks relief wherever it is offered. The follower of Richard Nixon and popular politics sees the disruption of social order all around and, in lieu of genuine explanations and alternatives, falls prey to the "false consciousness" of reactionary rhetoric. Disney fans need a utopia to relieve the oppressive chaos of "normal" fantasy and social life and to provide reassurance that life can be just, meaningful, and happy at least in the imagination. Viewers of "Marcus Welby," missing the experiences in their own lives, want to believe that someone can take an intense

Radio would be the most wonderful means of communication imaginable in public life . . . if it were capable not only of transmitting but of receiving, of allowing the listener not only to hear but to speak, and did not isolate him but brought him into contact. Unrealizable in this social system, realizable in another, these proposals help toward the propagation and shaping of that *other* system.

Bertold Brecht, "Theory of Radio" (1932), Gesammelte Weke, Band VIII, p. 129, seq. 154. Quoted in Enzenberger, "Theory of Media."

interest in them, diagnose all their ills, and make them feel better. In general, the passive consumption of mass-mediated entertainment that displaces expressive and learning activities in leisure time can be criticized as an escape from and a compensation for the "lives of quiet desperation" led by members of mass society.

Progressive Disalienation and the Liberating Potential of Media

A complete reversal of alienating causes and experiences grows from a revolution in political-economic organization (infrastructure) and a revolution in cultural expression (superstructure). However, even in the present arrangements, concrete social reality tends to break through the manipulation. Women, minority groups, students, unemployed, and others outside the power elite express dissatisfaction with what is fed them through socializing institutions, including education and mass communication. The "Counter-Culture," as Theodore Roszak defined it, as well as sexual, racial, national, and other liberation groups, are organized results of the distance between possibility and actuality. Herbert Marcuse, both hero and critic of movements of the late 1960s and early 1970s, summarized one movement's radical expression tending toward a total transformation of values:

> This is the political heritage of the counter-culture: You can live without spending a lifetime at unnecessary, inhuman, and stupid work; there is such a thing as creative work that may not be only a hobby; the male aggressiveness and competitive virility of patriarchial civilization may have become a fetter to human progress; a beautiful environment is not merely a whim, but may well turn out to be a vital need.[53]

While the accidental periphery of capitalist culture may place a premium on human, social, beneficial qualities, the essential core remains private corporate economic profit. Social costs and benefits may *occasionally* be weighed; economic ones *always* are. There is nothing in the technology of media or the nature of popular culture that dictates this; it

266

rises from the political-economic infrastructure. Media, in fact, can have a quite different organization and effect.

Enzensberger's summary of his critical theory of media is given in the following list:[54]

Repressive Use of Media	Emancipatory Use of Media
Centrally controlled programme	Decentralized programme
One transmitter, many receivers	Each receiver a potential transmitter
Immobilization of isolated individuals	Mobilization of the masses
Passive consumer behaviour	Interaction of those involved; feedback
Depoliticization	A political learning process
Production by specialists	Collective production
Control by property owners or bureaucracy	Social control by self-organization

Enzensberger emphasizes first the obvious mobilizing power of media. He claims, "For the first time in history, the media are making possible mass participation in a social and socialized productive process, the practical means of which are in the hands of the masses themselves." By mobilizing, he means not pushing around passive objects in marches but making more *mobile*, "as free as dancers, as aware as football [soccer] players, as surprising as guerilla." It is not only the *control* of media that constitutes power; it is the *organization* of media that distinguishes repression from emancipation.

Neither capitalist nor socialist countries have yet fully utilized "the mass self-regulating learning process which is made possible by the electronic media," according to Enzensberger. The electronic, newer media are egalitarian in structure. They do away with educational privilege. Anyone can be sender as well as receiver by a simple switching process. Programs are not material objects and can be reproduced at will, reducing ownership oligopolies. They are instantaneous, complicating censorship efforts. Thus, they extend persons beyond what preliterate cultures could achieve, but they are subject to fewer restrictions than books, painting, art objects, and other older mass media.

Crucial to the potential of the newer media is their *collective structure*. As opposed to the individualism of writing and reading, the newer media call forth collective efforts and social organization. This less individualistic, less competitive, less elitist quality is obvious, but the full structural potential is realized only if "those concerned organize themselves" and break down the debilitating contradictions between producer and consumer; the individual and the collective; the active and the passive; artistic creativity and documented life; male and female; black and white; static objects and dynamic processes; the artist and the masses.

Both the technology and the need are present to develop utopian possibilities beyond the limits of contemporary mass-mediated cultural systems. Mass-mediated culture can be rendered more understandable and humanistic by increasing cultural studies and policy research, by continuing consumer activism and reform efforts, by reducing the role of private capital and profit, by reversing authoritarian one-way transmission, by decentralizing, and by developing in the wake of structural revolution a cultural revolution that returns to top priority the full, collective humanity of persons, the value of life, and the appreciation and balanced development of the environment.

An alert consumer of mass-mediated culture at times may feel like a member of the religious order in *The Last Western*, the Silent Servants of the Used, Abused, and Utterly Screwed Up.[55] Of course, even for the individual within the present system there remains a potential for nutritious bread; but how separate the wheat from the chaff?

A few directives may summarize most simply the lessons of these studies for the individual consumer.

- Learn principles of art and leisure that contribute to positive, developmental growth.

- See contemporary mass-mediated culture within the range of the full historical and multi-ethnic possibilities of human culture.

- Think through cultural expressions to sense critically their ideological and aesthetic roots and implications.

- Activate responses of the body, the feelings, of collective consciousness, as well as the individual intellect in responding to cultural expressions.

- In light of the above, select and pursue the most fully human cultural expressions.

- Act as well as think, organize as well as analyze, contribute as well as criticize, produce as well as consume.

Cultural Futures and Freedom

What will future books on mass-mediated culture write of as the expressions dominant in the United States, English-speaking countries, Western Europe, and throughout the world?

The future depends on policy choices made now, in the present. The self-conscious human organism possesses unique communicative abilities, an *animal symbolicum*, as Ernst Cassirer summarized it. Evolution moves from biological development to the evolution of cognition and consciousness, from "biosphere" to "noosphere" in Teilhard de Chardin's terminology,[56] making the collective internal life of humans and, as a consequence, mass-mediated culture, ever more important. With instantaneous global communications and self-monitoring, humans possess the ability to program the emotions, thoughts, and ecology of entire cultures. McLuhan rhapsodizes about a future with "the promise of a technologically engendered state of universal understanding and unity, a state of absorption in the logos that could knit mankind into one family and create a perpetuity of collective harmony and peace. . . ."[57]

Previous cultures may have been born of necessity. With the growth in human ability to understand and control symbols and, through them, the environment, present and future cultures become matters of conscious choice. Policy choices in the present, made consciously or by default, determine whether the future will hold the terrifying uniformity of a "brave new animal farm of 1984" or the utopian satisfaction of a liberated, diverse, and humanized global village encompassing spaceship earth.

All of us, impotent consumers or omnipotent administrators of mass-mediated culture, face the burden of freedom described nowhere more powerfully than by Ivan in his story of "The Grand Inquisitor" in Dostoyevsky's *The Brothers Karamazov*.[58]

> Ivan sets his parable in Spain in the most terrible time of the Inquisition, when fires were lighted every day to the glory of God and "in the splendid *auto da fé* the wicked heretics were burnt." A man comes quietly among the suffering masses of the people. He moves silently in their midst with a gentle smile of infinite compassion. He offers them His hands and healing virtue comes from contact with Him. A blind man is given sight, a dead child raised to life.
>
> At that moment the Grand Inquisitor passes and sees. He is an old man, almost ninety, tall and erect, with a withered face and sunken eyes, in which there is still a gleam of light. He is not wearing his gleaming red cardinal robes but a coarse monk's cassock. The "holy guard" follows him. He holds out his finger and bids the guards arrest the man.
>
> In his dungeon cell that evening, alone the Grand Inquisitor visits him. The Grand Inquisitor speaks.
>
> "For fifteen centuries we have been wrestling with your freedom, but now it is ended and over for good. Do you not believe that it's over for good? You look meekly at me and refuse to be angry with me. But let me tell you that now, today, people are more persuaded than ever that they have perfect freedom, yet they have brought their freedom to us and laid it humbly at our feet. That has been our doing. Was this what you did? Was this your freedom?
>
> "Instead of taking men's freedom from them, you made it greater than ever! Did you forget that man prefers peace, and even death, to

freedom of choice in the knowledge of good and evil? Nothing is more seductive for man than his freedom of conscience, but nothing is a greater cause of suffering. And behold, instead of giving a firm foundation for setting the conscience of man at rest forever, you chose all that is exceptional, vague and enigmatic; you chose what was utterly beyond the strength of men, acting as though you did not love them at all—you who come to give your life for them! Instead of taking possession of men's freedom, you increased it, and burdened the spiritual kingdom of mankind with its sufferings for ever.

"We too have a right to preach a mystery, and to teach them that it's not the free judgment of their hearts, not love that matters, but a mystery which they must follow blindly, even against their conscience. So we have done. We have corrected your work and have founded it upon *miracle, mystery* and *authority*. And men rejoiced that they were again led like sheep, and that the terrible gift that had brought them such suffering, was, at last, lifted from their hearts. Were we right teaching them this? Speak!"

The prisoner never speaks. The old man repeats that tomorrow the obedient flock will heap up the pile on which the prisoner will burn. Still the man does not speak. The inquisitor waits, weighed down with the silence. Suddenly the prisoner approaches the old man and softly kisses him on his bloodless aged lips. The old man shudders. He goes to the door, opens it, and orders Him: "Go, and come no more . . . Come not at all, never, never!" He let him out into the dark alleys and the prisoner went away.

Humans are radically free, or, as Ivan states it, "Everything is lawful." We are free, not from consequences, not from consciousness, but from external domination by subhuman doctrines and false gods perpetuating poverty, hunger, violence, sexism, racism, exploitation, and alienation—*if we choose to be*. Humankind has the freedom, on the one hand, to appreciate what is freeing and, on the other hand, to change what is not. Contemporary mass-mediated culture calls for the exercise of both capacities.

Notes

1. Claude Lévi-Strauss, *Structural Anthropology*, trans. Claire Jacobsen and Brooke Grundfest Schoepf (New York: Basic Books, 1963), p. 295.

2. Clifford Geertz, *The Interpretation of Cultures* (New York: Basic Books, 1973).

3. PCA mailing, February, 1976.

4. Ithiel de Sola Pool, "The Rise of Communications Policy Research," *Journal of Communication* 24, no. 2 (Spring 1974), p. 31.

5. Douglass Cater, "Communications Policy Research: the Need for New Definitions," An Occasional Paper (Palo Alto, Calif.: Aspen Institute Program on Communications and Society, 1974), p. 1.

6. James D. Halloran, interview, Leicester England, April, 1973.

7. James W. Carey, "Communication and Culture," *Communication Research* 2, no. 2 (April 1975), p. 177.

8. Ibid., p. 179.

9. Ibid., p. 184.

10. Jay W. Jensen, "Perspectives in Communications Research: A Critique," paper delivered to the Association for Education in Journalism, Pennsylvania State University, August 31, 1960, p. 4.

11. Ibid.

12. Ibid., p. 10.

13. Ibid.

14. Raymond Williams, "Communications as Cultural Science," *Journal of Communication* 24, no. 3 (Summer 1974), p. 19.

15. Ibid.

16. Ibid., p. 21.

17. Ibid., p. 23.

18. Ibid.

19. Carey, "Communication and Culture," p. 187.

20. Ibid., p. 189.

21. Ibid., pp. 189–90.

22. Ibid., p. 191.

23. "Super Bowl Rivals Emphasize Spiritual Values; Prayer Is Given Much Credit for Their Success," *New York Times*, January 5, 1973.

24. John Pollock, *Billy Graham—The Authorized Biography* (Minneapolis: World Wide Publications, 1969), pp. 219, 271, and 305.

25. Ibid., p. 308.

26. Richard Schickel, *The Disney Version*, p. 8.

27. Nicholas Johnson, "Media Barons: Mass Control," lecture at the University of California, San Diego, May 20, 1975.

28. See Douglass Cater and Stephen Strickland, *TV Violence and the Child: The Evolution and Fate of the Surgeon General's Report* (New York: Russell Sage Foundation, 1975); the government report is *Television and Growing Up: The Impact of Televised Violence.*

29. Shana Alexander, "Listening to Clare Booth Luce," *Newsweek*, November 26, 1973, p. 38.

30. See Raymond B. Nixon, "Trends in U.S. Newspaper Ownership: Concentration with Competition," *Gazette* 14, no. 3 (1968), pp. 181–93.

31. See "The American Media Baronies," *Atlantic* (July, 1969), pp. 83–86, 90–94; see also Johnson, *How To Talk Back*, and Alan Wells, ed., *Mass Media and Society* (Palo Alto, Calif.: National Press Books, 1975).

32. Nicholas Johnson, "Media Barons," lecture; see also the statement by James D. Smith and colleagues that, although 30 million Americans own corporate stock, only 1.3 percent of the United States adult population owns 53 percent of the value of all privately held corporate stock, "Wealth, Thickly Spread," *Psychology Today*, December 1973, p. 70.

33. *Fortune*, May, 1971, pp. 172–78.

34. Robert Lampman, *The Share of Top Wealth-Holders in Personal Wealth, 1922–1956* (Princeton, N.J.: Princeton University Press, 1960), pp. 75–80, 97, 208. A well-documented study of "Capitalism: Myths and Facts" by Eugene Toland, Thomas Fenton, and Lawrence McCulloch appeared in *Channel* 10, no. 3 (Spring 1972), pp. 3–14, available from Maryknoll, New York.

35. In 1973 Harold Geneen, head of ITT, received $814,299 in salary and bonus; R. C. Gerstenberg, chairman and chief executive of General Motors, received $923,000; and Edward N. Cole, president of General Motors, received $833,000, according to John Kenneth Galbraith, "Perfecting the Corporation—What Comes After General Motors," *New Republic*, November 2, 1974, p. 15. In 1974 5 percent of United States families earned over $30,000, and 21 percent over $15,000 in pretax annual income, according to "Can Capitalism Survive?" *Time*, July 14, 1975, p. 61.

36. Fred Ferretti, "The White Captivity of Black Radio," *Columbia Journalism Review*, Summer 1970, pp. 35–39.

37. See David Manning White in his anthologies, *Mass Culture, Mass Culture Revisited*, and *Pop Culture in America* (Chicago: Quadrangle Books, Inc., 1970).

38. Bronislaw Malinowski, *Magic, Science and Religion* (Garden City, N.Y.: Doubleday, 1948), p. 245.

39. "City of New Orleans," words and music by Steve Goodman. Copyright © 1970, Buddha Music Inc./Turnpike Tom Music (ASCAP). All rights administered by United Artists Music Co., Inc.

40. Horace Newcomb, *TV: The Most Popular Art* (Garden City, N.Y.: Anchor Books, 1974).

41. Erving Goffman, *Frame Analysis* (New York: Harper Colophon Books, 1974).

42. Joyce Brothers in "The Jaws of the Super Shark," *Time*, July 14, 1975, p. 6.

43. Michael Gross, "The Hits Just Keep on Coming," *New Times*, January 1975, pp. 41–45.

44. See Nora Scott Kinzer, "Soapy Sin in the Afternoon," *Psychology Today*, August 1973, pp. 46–48; and Marjorie Perloff, "Soap Bubbles," *New Republic*, May 10, 1975, pp. 27–30.

45. This paragraph is a summary of various studies and positions and is based on a review by Raymond R. Larsen, "Charisma: A Reinterpretation," unpublished mimeographed paper, parts of which were presented under a different title at the Southern Political Science Association Annual Meeting, November, 1973.

46. Jacques Ellul, *Propaganda*, trans. Konrad Kellen (New York: Alfred A. Knopf, 1965); Jacques Ellul, *The Technological Society*, trans. John Wilkinson (New York: Vintage, 1967); Clifford G. Christians, "Jacques Ellul and Democracy's 'Vital Information' Premise," paper contributed at International Communication Association annual meeting, April 26, 1975; Clifford G. Christians, *Jacques Ellul's "La Technique" in a Communications Context*, unpublished doctoral dissertation, University of Illinois, Urbana, 1974.

47. C. Wright Mills, *White Collar* (New York: Oxford University Press, 1951), pp. 332–33, 334.

48. Hans Magnus Enzensberger, *The Consciousness Industry* (New York: Seabury Press, 1974), p. 10; see also Hans Magnus Enzensberger, "Constituents of a Theory of Media," *New Left Review*, no. 64 (November/December 1970), p. 17.

49. Dallas W. Smythe, "Time, Market and Space Factors in Communication Economics," *Journalism Quarterly*, Winter 1962, pp. 5–6.

50. Norbert Wiener, *Cybernetics or Control and Communication in the Animal and the Machine* (New York: John Wiley, 1948).

51. Ernest Mandel and George Novack, *The Marxist Theory of Alienation* (New York: Pathfinder Press, 1970), p. 6.

52. Ibid., p. 62.

53. Herbert Marcuse, "Capitalism in Crisis," lecture at University of California, San Diego, February 24, 1975.

54. Enzensberger, "Theory of Media," p. 27.

55. Thomas S. Klise, *The Last Western* (Niles, Ill.: Argus Communications, 1974).

56. Teilhard de Chardin, *The Phenomenon of Man* (New York: Harper Torchbooks, 1962).

57. Morshall McLuhan, "Interview," *Playboy,* September 1969, p. 74.

58. This excerpt greatly condenses the passage from book five, chapter two of Fyodor Dostoyevsky, *The Brothers Karamazov,* trans. Constance Garnett, abridg. Edmund Fuller (New York: Dell, 1956), pp. 181–201.

Selected Bibliography
of Cited Books

Popular Culture

BURNER, DAVID, ROBERT D. MARCUS, and JORJ TILSON, eds. *America Through the Looking Glass: A Historical Reader in Popular Culture.* Englewood Cliffs, N.J.: Prentice-Hall, 1974.

BROWNE, RAY B., et al. *Frontiers of American Culture.* Lafayette, Indiana: Purdue University Press, 1968.

BROWNE, RAY B., MARSHALL FISHWICK, and MICHAEL MARSDEN, eds. *Heroes of Popular Culture.* Bowling Green, Ohio: Bowling Green University Popular Press, 1972.

BROWNE, RAY B., and RONALD J. AMBROSETTI, eds. *Popular Culture and Curriculum.* Bowling Green, Ohio: Bowling Green University Popular Press, 1970.

CAWELTI, JOHN G. *The Six-Gun Mystique.* Bowling Green, Ohio: Bowling Green University Popular Press, 1973.

DORFMAN, ARIEL, and ARMAND MATTELART. *Para Leer al pato Donald: Comunicacion de masa y colonialismo.* Buenos Aires: Siglo Veintuno Argentian Editores, 1972.

FINCH, CHRISTOPHER. *The Art of Walt Disney: From Mickey Mouse to the Magic Kingdom.* New York: Harry N. Abrams, 1973.

GANS, HERBERT J. *Popular Culture and High Culture: An Analysis and Evaluation of Taste.* New York: Basic Books, 1974.

HALL, STUART, and PADDY WHANNEL. *The Popular Arts.* New York: Pantheon, 1965.

JACOB, NORMAN, ed. *Culture for the Millions.* New York: Van Nostrand, 1961.

LEWIS, GEORGE H. *Side-Saddle on the Golden Calf: Social Structure and Popular Culture in America.* Pacific Palisades, Calif.: Goodyear, 1972.

NEWCOMB, HORACE. *TV: The Most Popular Art.* Garden City, N.Y.: Anchor Books, 1974.

NYE, RUSSELL. *The Unembarrassed Muse: The Popular Arts in America.* New York: Dial Press, 1970.

REGUSH, NICHOLAS M. *Open Reality.* New York: G. P. Putnam's Sons, 1974.

ROSENBERG, BERNARD, and DAVID MANNING WHITE, eds. *Mass Culture Revisited.* New York: Van Nostrand Reinhold, 1971.

ROSENBERG, BERNARD, and DAVID MANNING WHITE, eds. *Mass Culture: The Popular Arts in America.* New York: Free Press, 1957.

SCHICKEL, RICHARD. *The Disney Version: The Life, Times, Art and Commerce of Walt Disney.* New York: Simon & Schuster, 1968.

WILKINSON, ENDYMION. *The People's Comic Book: Red Women's Detachment, Hot on the Trail and Other Chinese Comics.* Garden City, N.Y.: Doubleday, 1973.

WRIGHT, WILL. *Sixguns and Society: A Structural Study of the Western.* Berkeley: University of California Press, 1975.

Media

ACKERMAN, PAUL, ed. *This Business of Music.* New York: Billboard Publications, 1971.

BLUMLER, JAY G., and ELIHU KATZ. *The Uses of Mass Communications: Current Perspectives on Gratifications Research.* Beverly Hills, Calif.: Sage Publications, 1974.

CARPENTER, EDMUND, and MARSHALL McLUHAN, eds. *Explorations in Communication.* Boston: Beacon Press, 1960.

CATER, DOUGLASS, and STEPHEN STRICKLAND. *TV Violence and the Child: The Evolution and Fate of the Surgeon General's Report.* New York: Russell Sage Foundation, 1975.

EDGAR, PATRICIA, and HILARY McPHEE. *Media She.* Melbourne: William Heinemann Australia, 1974.

ELLUL, JACQUES. *Propaganda: The Formation of Men's Attitudes.* New York: Knopf, 1966.

ENZENSBERGER, HANS MAGNUS. *The Consciousness Industry.* New York: Seabury Press, 1974.

GERBNER, GEORGE, LARRY GROSS, and WILLIAM MELODY, eds. *Communications, Technology, and Social Policy.* New York: Wiley Interscience, 1973.

JOHNSON, NICHOLAS. *How to Talk Back to Your Television Set.* New York: Bantam, 1970.

LAZARSFELD, PAUL, and FRANK STANTON, eds. *Radio Research.* New York: Duell, Sloan and Pearce, 1944.

LYNCH, WILLIAM F. *The Image Industries.* New York: Sheed & Ward, 1959.

McLUHAN, MARSHALL. *Understanding Media: The Extensions of Man.* New York: McGraw-Hill, 1964.

MAYNARD, RICHARD A. *The Celluloid Curriculum: How to Use Movies in the Classroom.* Rochelle Park, N.J.: Hayden Book Company, 1971.

SCHILLER, HERBERT I. *The Mind Managers.* Boston: Beacon Press, 1973.

SCHRAMM, WILBUR, ed. *Mass Communications.* Urbana, Ill.: University of Illinois Press, 1960.

SCHRAMM, WILBUR. *Men, Messages, and Media: A Look at Human Communication.* New York: Harper & Row, 1973.

TUCHMAN, GAYE, ed. *The TV Establishment: Programming for Power and Profit.* Englewood Cliffs, N.J.: Prentice-Hall, 1974.

WELLS, ALAN, ed. *Mass Media and Society.* Palo Alto, Calif.: National Press Books, 1975.

WRIGHT, CHARLES R. *Mass Communication: A Sociological Perspective.* New York: Random House, 1959.

General

BARAN, PAUL, and PAUL SWEEZY. *Monopoly Capital.* New York: Monthly Review Press, 1966.

CAPLAN, G. *Principles of Preventive Psychiatry.* New York: Basic Books, 1964.

CARROLL, JOHN B. *Language, Thought, and Reality, Selected Writings of Benjamin Lee Whorf.* Boston: The Technology Press of Massachusetts Institute of Technology, 1957.

CASSIRER, ERNST. *Essay on Man.* New Haven: Yale University Press, 1944.

CASSIRER, ERNST. *The Myth of the State.* New Haven: Yale University Press, 1946.

CASSIRER, ERNST. *Philosophie der Symbolischen Formen.* Darmstadt: Wissenschaftliche Buchgesellschaft, 1958.

CHARDIN, TEILHARD DE. *The Phenomenon of Man.* New York: Harper Torchbooks, 1962.

DEBORD, GUY. *Society of the Spectacle.* Detroit: Black and Red, 1970.

DEUTSCHMANN, P., H. ELLINGWORTH, and J. McNELLY. *Communication and Social Change in Latin America.* New York: Fredrick A. Praeger, 1968.

ELIADE, MIRCEA. *The Sacred and the Profane.* New York: Harper & Row, 1959.

ELLUL, JACQUES. *The Technological Society.* New York: Knopf, 1964.

EMERY, F. E. *Systems Thinking.* Baltimore: Penguin Books, 1969.

GEERTZ, CLIFFORD. *The Interpretation of Cultures.* New York: Basic Books, 1973.

GOFFMAN, ERVING. *Frame Analysis.* New York: Harper Colophon Books, 1974.

GOFFMAN, ERVING. *The Presentation of Self In Everyday Life.* Garden City, N.Y.: Doubleday, 1959.

IGNOTUS, PAUL, et al. *The Logic of Personal Knowledge: Essays Presented to Michael Polanyi.* London: Routledge & Kegan Paul, 1961.

JAMES, WILLIAM. *The Principles of Psychology.* New York: Dover, 1950.

LAMPMAN, ROBERT. *The Share of Top Wealth-Holders in Personal Wealth, 1922–1956.* Princeton, N.J.: Princeton University Press, 1960.

LÉVI-STRAUSS, CLAUDE. *The Savage Mind.* Chicago: University of Chicago Press, 1966.

LÉVI-STRAUSS, CLAUDE. *Structural Anthropology.* New York: Basic Books, 1963.

MANDEL, ERNEST, and GEORGE NOVACK. *The Marxist Theory of Alienation.* New York: Pathfinder Press, 1970.

MARX, KARL, and FREDERICK ENGELS. *The German Ideology.* New York: International Publishers, 1970.

MASLOW, ABRAHAM M., ed. *New Knowledge in Human Values.* New York: Harper, 1959.

MILLS, C. WRIGHT. *The Power Elite.* New York: Oxford University Press, 1956.

MILLS, C. WRIGHT. *White Collar.* New York: Oxford University Press, 1951.

ORNSTEIN, ROBERT. *The Psychology of Consciousness.* San Francisco: W. H. Freeman, 1972.

PEACOCK, JAMES L. *Consciousness and Change: Symbolic Anthropology in Evolutionary Perspective.* New York: John Wiley, 1975.

RAPPAPORT, ROY A. *Pigs for the Ancestors: Ritual in the Ecology of a New Guinea People.* New Haven: Yale University Press, 1968.

ROSENZWEIG, MICHAEL. *And Replenish the Earth.* New York: Harper & Row, 1975.

SAMPSON, ANTHONY. *The Sovereign State of ITT.* Greenwich, Conn.: Fawcett, 1974.

THOMPSON, C. J. S. *The Quacks of Old London.* Philadelphia: Lippincott, 1929.

THRALL, WILLIAM FLINT, and ADDISON HIBBARD. *A Handbook to Literature,* 3rd ed. Indianapolis: The Odyssey Press, 1975.

WIENER, NORBERT. *Cybernetics or Control and Communication in the Animal and the Machine.* New York: John Wiley, 1948.

Special Topics

Indians of the Americas

CARTER, WILLIAM E. *Aymara Communities and the Bolivian Agrarian Reform.* Gainesville: University of Florida Press, 1964.

CASTANEDA, CARLOS. *Journey to Ixtlan.* New York: Simon & Schuster, 1972.

CASTANEDA, CARLOS. *A Separate Reality.* New York: Simon & Schuster, 1971.

CASTANEDA, CARLOS. *The Teachings of Don Juan.* Berkeley: University of California Press, 1968.

ELK, BLACK. *Black Elk Speaks: Being the Life Story of a Holy Man of the Oglala Sioux.* Lincoln: University of Nebraska Press, 1961.

ELK, BLACK. *The Sacred Pipe.* Baltimore: Penguin Books, 1974.

McLUHAN, T. C., ed. *Touch the Earth: A Self-Portrait of Indian Existence.* New York: Pocket Books, 1972.

MASON, J. ALDEN. *The Ancient Civilizations of Peru.* Baltimore: Penguin Books, 1968.

MORTIMER, W. GOLDEN. *Coca, The Divine Plant of the Incas.* New York: 1901.

OSBORNE, HAROLD. *Indians of the Andes: Aymaras and Quechuas.* London: Routledge & Kegan Paul, 1952.

PRESCOTT, WILLIAM H. *The Conquest of Peru.* New York: New American Library, 1961.

VALCARCEL, LUIS E. *Handbook of South American Indians.* Washington: J. H. Vail, 1946.

VERGER, PIERRE. *Indians of Peru.* New York: Pocahontas Press, 1950.

Political Campaigning

ALEXANDER, HERBERT E. *Financing the 1968 Election.* Lexington, Mass.: Heath, 1971.

BARRETT, MARVIN, ed. *The Politics of Broadcasting: Alfred I. duPont–Columbia University Survey of Broadcast Journalism 1971–1972.* New York: Crowell, 1973.

BERNSTEIN, CARL, and BOB WOODWARD. *All the President's Men.* New York: Warner Paperback Library, 1975.

CHISMAN, FORREST P. *The Future of Political Communication Research.* Aspen, Colo.: Aspen Institute, 1974.

CROUSE, TIMOTHY. *The Boys on the Bus.* New York: Random House, 1972.

LANG, KURT, and GLADYS ENGLE LANG. *Politics and Television.* Chicago: Quadrangle, 1968.

McGINNISS, JOE. *The Selling of the President 1968.* New York: Trident Press, 1969.

NIMMO, DAN. *The Political Persuaders: The Techniques of Modern Election Campaigns.* Englewood Cliffs, N.J.: Prentice-Hall, 1970.

THOMPSON, HUNTER S. *Fear and Loathing on the Campaign Trail.* San Francisco: Straight Arrow Book, 1973.

WHITE, THEODORE H. *The Making of the President 1960,* and sequels in 1964, 1968. New York: Atheneum, 1961.

Race

BALDWIN, JAMES. *Another Country*. New York: Dial Press, 1964.

BALDWIN, JAMES. *The Fire Next Time*. New York: Dial Press, 1963.

BALDWIN, JAMES. *Nobody Knows My Name*. New York: Dial Press, 1960.

BALDWIN, JAMES. *No Name in the Street*. New York: Dell, 1962.

BALDWIN, JAMES. *Notes of a Native Son*. New York: Dial Press, 1958.

BOGLE, DONALD. *Toms, Coons, Mulattoes, Mammies, and Bucks*. New York: Viking, 1973.

CLEAVER, ELDRIDGE. *Soul on Ice*. New York: Dell, 1968.

MAPP, EDWARD. *Blacks in American Films: Today and Yesterday*. Metuchen, N.J.: The Scarecrow Press, 1972.

NOBLE, PETER. *The Negro in Films*. London: Knapp, Drewett and Sons, 1936.

Religion

BARNHART, JOE E. *The Billy Graham Religion*. Philadelphia: United Church Press, 1972.

BELLAH, ROBERT N. *The Broken Covenant*. Berkeley: The University of California Press, 1974.

CONGAR, YVES. *Lay People in the Church*. New York: Herder and Herder, 1963.

DURKHEIM, EMILE. *The Elementary Forms of the Religious Life*. Glencoe, N.Y.: Free Press, 1947.

GRAHAM, BILLY, and others. *Is God "Dead"?* Grand Rapids, Mich.: Zondervan Publishing House, 1966.

GRAHAM, BILLY. *The Jesus Generation*. Grand Rapids, Mich.: Zondervan Publishing House, 1971.

GRAHAM, BILLY, *Peace with God*. New York: Pocket Books, 1953.

JACQUET, CONSTANT H. ed. *Yearbook of American Churches 1971*. New York: Council Press, 1971.

LYNCH, WILLIAM F. *Christ and Apollo*. New York: Sheed & Ward, 1962.

McLOUGHLIN, WILLIAM G. *Billy Graham: Revivalist in a Secular Age*. New York: Ronald Press, 1960.

MALINOWSKI, BRONISLAW. *Magic, Science and Religion and Other Essays*. Garden City, New York: Doubleday, 1948.

POLLOCK, JOHN. *Billy Graham: The Authorized Biography*. Minneapolis: World Wide Publications, 1969.

WATTS, ALAN. *This Is It and Other Essays on Zen and Spiritual Experience*. New York: Random House, 1960.

WEBER, MAX. *The Protestant Ethic and the Spirit of Capitalism*. New York: Scribner's, 1958.

Index

283